UP THE

A 1300 mile walk from Land's End to John o' Groats

Peter Jackson

2QT Limited (Publishing)

First edition published 2012
2QT Limited (Publishing)
Burton In Kendal
Cumbria LA6 1NJ
www.2qt.co.uk

Copyright © 2012 Peter Jackson. All rights reserved.
The right of Peter Jackson to be identified as the author
of this work has been asserted by him in accordance with the
Copyright, Designs and Patents Act 1988

All rights reserved. This book is sold subject to the condition that no part of this book is to be reproduced, in any shape or form. Or by way of trade, stored in a retrieval system or transmitted in any form or by any means, electronic, mechanical, photocopying, recording, be lent, re-sold, hired out or otherwise circulated in any form of binding or cover other than that in which it is published and without a similar condition, including this condition being imposed on the subsequent purchaser, without prior permission of the copyright holder.

Cover design and Typesetting by Dale Rennard
Back cover photo by John Nicholls
All other images supplied by the author.

Printed in Great Britain by
Lightning Source

A CIP catalogue record for this book is available
from the British Library
ISBN 978-1-908098-80-1

THANKS

It's probable that the only readers who pay much attention to what is traditionally known as *Acknowledgements* are those who think they might be mentioned. This makes it a potentially dangerous business for an author when you consider the possible repercussions that might arise from the failure to name somebody he should have. Imagine the sense of loathing the spurned or ignored would feel towards the person who does the spurning or ignoring. Nevertheless, the writer enjoys being able to thank, in print, those people whose assistance have made the whole project easier or pleasanter; so, at the risk of causing great offence, here goes.

In alphabetical order, massive thanks to all of the following who offered advice about the route, lent me maps and guidebooks, walked with me, put me up, ferried me about and / or generally smoothed the path: Dave Bayliss, Adrian Birch, Phil Blamire, Chrissie Chappell, Kevin and Sheila Dawson, Phil Evans, Alison and Guy Fitzpatrick, Darryl and Madeline Francis, Clive Griffiths, John and Pat Hind, Alan and Beryl Jenkins, Maggie King, Margaret Macgregor, Dave McNamara, Elaine and John Nicholls, Goff Oldaker, Arnold Price, Bill Ridings, Joan Sanders, Julie Scattergood, Chris Smith MP, Tim Stilwell of Stilwell Publishing, Joyce Taylor, Stephen Tomlinson, and Angela and John Walmsley. What an excellent bunch of chaps.

Sincere and grateful thanks too to the following organizations that provided me with gear for the walk: Alpine Marketing of

Aspatria (Cumbria), Lowe Alpine (UK) of Kendal and the Brasher Boot Company.

Almost all the B&Bs, guesthouses, YHAs and hotels I stopped in were good and friendly but, for various reasons, some of the people I stayed with and their establishments are worthy of special mention and thanks. Unfortunately, with the passage of time since I did the walk, some of those places have closed down, or stopped doing B&B, and some have changed hands – at least one has burned down! I mention here the ones that I believe are still open and still being run by the same people: Linda and Glyn at Nanterrow Farm, Gwithian; Valerie at Buzby View, Porthtowan; and Diane at Cokerhurst Farm, Wembdon near Bridgwater. Special mention is due to the late Ken at Y Bwthyn Lon. The extra effort put in by the people at these places made my journey all the more worthwhile and enjoyable: in one or two cases, the people I stayed with might well have made the difference between my kicking the whole thing into touch and carrying on, and I'm sorry that I haven't mentioned those people who, for whatever reason, have moved on to pastures new – I wish them all the luck in the world.

I should also mention John McGuiness and Linda Pearse of the Cancer Relief Macmillan Fund for their help and encouragement. Even if you don't buy the book, go and give some money to the Macmillan Nurses. Or I'll send the boys round.

I would also like to put on record my thanks to the authors of the many books I used, not only as guides, but as sources of information and ideas for the journey.

And there is no doubt that this book would not have seen the light of day without the help and guidance of Catherine Cousins, Dale Rennard, Karen Holmes and Geraldine Keenan at 2QT Publishing.

If I've missed anybody, I'm sorry. Really I am – I didn't do it on purpose. I'll make sure you get a mention next time.

Finally, the walk – and the painfully slow creation of this book – would not have been possible without the support of Dee, Kate and Brendan, who were all brilliant – even strangely jubilant – about my prolonged absence. Thanks seem inadequate, but thanks anyway.

INTRO

HEARTBREAK HOTEL

There's a page in Wainwright's *Pennine Way Companion* where, describing the route over Redmires on the Lancashire–Yorkshire border, the author says, 'You will question your own sanity.' Hamish Brown, nearing the end of his *Groats End Walk*, just wanted to get the journey finished, and even John Hillaby, in his classic *Journey Through Britain*, felt tired and depressed by the time he'd got to Ullapool. So, if even the great and the good can have moments of doubt, it came as no surprise to me when, on a miserably wet Tuesday morning in Coatbridge, a dreary town on the eastern edge of Glasgow, I began seriously to ask myself why I had bothered setting off from Land's End at all.

With a recklessness bordering on the stupid, and born out of desperation and ineptitude, I had assumed I would have no difficulty getting accommodation in the area. In fact, after the solitude of the hills of the Southern Uplands, I'd built up a mental picture of Coatbridge as a sort of Scottish Las Vegas and was looking forward to an evening of unrestrained revelry: you know, have a few drinks, take in a show and generally paint the town red. As it turned out, I was late arriving and my ever more frantic enquiries produced the name of only one place with any vacancies for an overnight

Up the country

stay. A weary trudge through an increasingly bleak and uninspiring landscape of utilitarian housing and those sickly looking industrial units peculiar to the fringes of our big towns brought me to what turned out to be an overpriced and barely moderate B&B. My room boasted a stunning view of a busy trunk road interchange, and the roar of lorries accelerating away from the traffic lights throughout the night ensured that my sleep was, at best, fitful.

I was, though, curious to discover the secret life of this establishment. During the evening I'd been hearing some of the other guests – mostly squat, hairy types wearing tee shirts with amusing four-letter words printed on them – engaging the proprietor in very intriguing conversation.

'I need to be up for sex in the morning. Is that OK?' asked Squat Person No.1.

'Me too,' added Hairy Type.

'I've got to be up for sex as well,' chipped in Squat Person No. 2.

'No problem. Everything'll be ready for you,' the proprietor replied.

I came to the conclusion that this was why the place was so expensive, and it was only at eight o'clock the following day, when the lady who served breakfast told me that it had been raining 'since half-past sex', that the truth finally dawned.

And so, through the relentless downpour and battling against a tide of grim-faced commuters, I began to question just why I was doing what I was doing. I was struggling to find the right way out of a town which appeared to be a maze of pedestrian walkways and underpasses – gloomy, low-ceilinged places full of broken glass and other, more sinister, debris – the remnants apparently of some wild party. These concrete tunnels are certainly not for the faint-hearted, and none of them appeared inclined to take me where I wanted to go.

Eventually, after several false starts and dead ends, I did find the way and, as the morning wore on and turned into afternoon, the weather got better and my frame of mind improved. By the middle of the afternoon the sun was trying to shine, the rain had stopped, the clouds were beginning to roll back from the rim of the Campsie Fells and, as I sat and sipped my drink, I had chance to reflect on what had brought me here. 'I feel a flashback coming on', I thought and, as with all the best flashbacks, everything – the rock I was sitting on, the cows and the sheep in the fields, and my legs – all went Wibbly Wobbly Woo as I went back in time, back in time, back in time...

Ever since I'd read John Hillaby's account of his walk from Land's End to John o' Groats, *Journey Through Britain*, almost thirty years ago, I'd cherished the thought of doing something similar. As my grip on the job I'd had since leaving college became increasingly tenuous, the notion of setting off on some kind of long distance walk took a firmer hold and a chance discovery of Andrew McCloy's splendid book, *Land's End to John o' Groats* made the whole concept appear possible and within the capabilities of anybody with enough time and determination.

When the axe finally did fall my wife, Dee, thought that, before

Up the country

I went looking for another job, I ought to do something I'd always wanted to do. This was the opportunity of a lifetime and you never know what the future might bring. You might never get another chance. You might take ill, or fall under a bus. Et cetera, et cetera. Of course, because we've got bills to pay, I gave her suggestion serious and studied consideration – for about three nanoseconds – before agreeing to it. The McCloy book was still fresh in my mind and, remembering John Hillaby from all those years ago, I had very little hesitation in deciding on the Land's End to John o' Groats thing. I mean, how many of us ever get the opportunity to see our own country as intimately and thoroughly as you can when you do it leisurely, at walking speed? There was just so much of Britain I knew very little about and I felt it was about time to do something about it.

Decisions about the route had to be made and, as many walkers will tell you, much of the pleasure is in the planning. I resolved to avoid road walking wherever possible and, on the grounds that this was likely to be a one-off event, I started to prepare, in my head, a list of places I just couldn't afford to miss en route. Then, with a spectacular rush of blood to the head, I announced boldly that I would take in the three tops of Snowdon, Scafell Pike and Ben Nevis. It seemed a shame not to do them – after all, Ben Nevis is our highest mountain and lies right on the route that was beginning to take shape, and Scafell Pike isn't too far from my home in Kendal, and Snowdon ... well, Snowdon is just too good to miss.

So, now I had a few fixed points, it became only a matter of joining the dots. There was the hint of a route beginning to form, even though there were still some gaps, and nothing at all had yet been worked out for the way north of Fort William. Like Mr Micawber, I was sure something would turn up. In any case, I did not want to tempt providence by planning everything down to the last detail only to find some disaster overtaking me on Day One.

As far as training for the walk went, I'm afraid to say I was rather careless. 'You'll walk yourself fit,' people said. And I believed them, because it suited me to. I suppose, deep down, I was afraid of doing serious training walks and discovering I wasn't up to it or, worse, that I just didn't like it. Then what would I do?

Accommodation was to be an important consideration. To camp, or not to camp? Camping obviously had its attractions. It would allow me much more freedom in deciding when and where to stop and when to start each day. There would probably be no need to book ahead and it would be substantially cheaper. But... there were one or two snags. Like, I didn't have a tent. Good quality, lightweight tents are expensive – I reckoned I could get quite a few nights' B&B for the price of a decent tent. Then there's all the bits and pieces such as stoves and pans and fuel. And food. My only experience of wild camping had involved eating some revolting ready-noodle type thing, and then not being able to wash out the pan properly. And I'd have to carry a sleeping bag. And what about the entire new vocabulary of bizarre camping terms I'd have to learn? Words like geodesic, flysheet and Trangia filled me with the dread usually inspired by things to do with the internal combustion engine and were therefore, I felt, best avoided. And I like my home comforts too much. Let's face it, camping was never a serious option. So that was that then. It was to be B&Bs and Youth Hostels and accepting the kind offers of help from friends and family, many of whom were conveniently located on or near the line of the walk.

An icy January gave way to a horribly wet and windy February as I made final preparations for the trip – booking the first night's accommodation, sorting gear out and getting maps and guidebooks ready. Naturally, planning had been carried out with military precision: I would only take what was absolutely necessary, everything would be pared down to minimize the weight on my back, and complex procedures were put in place to ensure that the whole enterprise ran like a well-oiled machine. Yeah, right.

I did have one practice rucksack-packing session but became very agitated when I couldn't pick the thing up to put on my shoulders. Out went various bits of hardware and clothing and a process of trial and error did eventually bring an uneasy compromise between what I thought I needed and what I could actually lift.

In the great scheme of things, I realise that a walk from Land's End to John o' Groats is not earth-shatteringly daring. There would be no unmapped territory to venture into, no undiscovered life-forms to come across, and, apart from the Severn Bridge, no really fearsome obstacles to negotiate. But I would be visiting places I had never been to and opening myself up to a range of new experiences. So, to me at any rate, this was to be a major adventure and the sense of anticipation grew and grew as February went on.

And so, I finished work on the Wednesday and arrived at Land's End on the Friday. At last, the journey was about to begin.

Up the country

CHAPTER ONE – THE ATLANTIC COAST

STRANGER ON THE SHORE

Buccaneers, Baked Beans and Boddingtons – Land's End to Zennor

The Crowns tin mines

When I were a lad, and the world was in black and white, I used to avidly watch kids' TV when I got home from school. *The Lone Ranger*, *The Cisco Kid*, *Ivanhoe* (with Roger Moore no less), *Robin*

Hood and *William Tell*. And not forgetting *The Buccaneers*, starring Robert Shaw, who later went on to fame and fortune as one of James Bond's better adversaries, and *The Adventures of Long John Silver* which, I think, was just an excuse for some extravagant overacting by Robert Newton. In the well-mannered world of a fifties' childhood, where we had Uncle Mac and Andy Pandy and, for the really spaced out, Bill and Ben, can you imagine the effect that this eye-rolling loony had on the kids who used to watch? He would career about on his one good leg and his crutch 'haar-haaring' at everyone in sight, pausing only briefly to have a meaningless conversation with some battleaxe in a pub. I thought it was all absolutely marvellous.

Both these shows were more than likely filmed in a studio in the Home Counties, but they were really based on Sennen Cove, where my adventure began. I mean, it's obvious. The place reeks of doubloons, derring-do and piracy. Cottages cling to the hillside, mewling sea birds wheel above you, battered-looking men in woolly jumpers and bobble hats tend their nets, and the waves boom and crash as they pound the sea wall. The only thing missing was a galleon tied up at the jetty.

The journey down to Cornwall had been through the sort of weather we'd been experiencing since the end of January – rain and high winds. We couldn't remember the last time we'd seen the sun, and, if the television reports were correct, the coasts of Cornwall, Devon and Somerset had been beaten almost into submission. So, as we dropped down into Sennen Cove, the great shaft of sunlight which greeted us seemed almost miraculous. If I'd been looking for any kind of sign that the journey would be a good one, then this was it. I could not get going fast enough. We checked in at our hotel and then drove to Land's End.

Now, Land's End has its critics. They say it's over-developed, over-crowded and over-priced. Well, when we arrived at about half past four on that sunny Friday afternoon, the car park was deserted and it was FREE. With nobody about, there was an oddly forlorn feel to the place and it was an eerie walk out to the rocks beyond the hotel buildings. The famous signpost that has told thousands of visitors how far they are from their home towns had been struck dumb, its arms having been removed, presumably to protect them from a fearsome battering by the Atlantic gales, or maybe just to stop souvenir hunters nicking them.

It's here, where the concrete ends and the rocks drop into the sea, that you enter a different world. There are a couple of notices warning of dangerous rocks, then nothing but … well, dangerous rocks. And the sea. Except it's not the sea – it's the Atlantic Ocean. Fantastic. As life-defining moments go, arrival at Land's End rates high on my list. The very name of the place fires the imagination: Land's End. Descriptive, yet theatrical. If it were just called Something or Other Head, it wouldn't be anything like as dramatic. All the clichés about jagged rocks and raging seas are called to mind and they're all appropriate. But, somehow, it's the feel of the place you can't do justice to. This is the end of England, yes, but it could just as easily be the end of the world. Even by

English standards, the cliffs are not particularly high, but the sense of scale is awe-inspiring. Turn your back on Cornwall to look out to sea and there's nothing between you and America. If I hadn't needed to get cracking I'd have been quite happy standing there gazing around and clambering about on the rocks until dark.

Smartly turned out in my new jacket and trousers and brand new – and therefore ludicrously shiny – boots, I dutifully stood and had a couple of photos taken and then I set off. Strange to think that whatever direction I took, I'd eventually end up at John o' Groats, but I had to get to Sennen Cove before nightfall, so it was northwards for me. I walked past the First and Last House with its sandbagged door acting as a solemn reminder of the sort of weather they'd been having. Idly I wondered whether there were First and Last places at John o' Groats as well.

Having believed for as long as I could remember that Land's End is the westernmost point of the English mainland, it was with some surprise that I learned that Dr Syntax's Head, a pugnacious prong of rock a couple of hundred yards away is actually further west. I made a rather feeble attempt to walk out to the tip of this upstart but contented myself with getting as near as I could without losing too much height from the clifftop path I was on.

The excitement I was feeling right now was immense. I was like a child who's just opened a long-awaited and much sought-after present on Christmas morning. People had been telling me how I really should go to Cornwall. 'You really should go to Cornwall,' they'd said. But I was never interested, citing the long distance from Kendal as a reason. Well, I'd been a fool. It was gobsmacking. I took my camera out of my rucksack at Land's End and could not stop taking photos. Point, click. Point, click. Point, click. The sun setting behind me was touching the granite cliffs with golds and pinks and the strong gusty wind was whipping the sea into a flickering pattern of dark blues and whites as it attacked the base of the rocks below my feet. When I'd walked a few hundred yards I turned to look back, and the distant ocean beneath the setting sun out towards Longships Lighthouse looked like beaten copper. Yes, it really did. Poor old John Hillaby had set off at seven on a misty morning and didn't see any of this. I felt I was the luckiest man alive.

The walking itself was easy along an earthy path through the grassland, dotted here and there with pale coloured flowers, which I took to be sea-pinks. Not that I had the first idea what a sea-pink looked like – it's just that my book said there were sea- pinks here. And they were pink ... and by the sea. It was mostly level going past weather-beaten granite outcrops – some carved by the wind and rain into odd shapes, one in particular being remarkably like a rabbit's head.

Arrival on Mayon Cliff provided an uninterrupted view over Whitesand Bay to Cape Cornwall, so I was able to get a preview of the early part of the next day's walk. This was important to me because I had no idea how difficult route-finding might be. John Hillaby had struggled – admittedly thirty years previously, and before the advent of the waymarked South West Way – and my little guidebook contained enough warnings of difficulties and complications for me to take this coast walk seriously. So far, though, it had been as trouble free as I could have wished. Keep the sea on your left and you can't go wrong.

Almost reluctantly I arrived at Sennen Cove and the hotel. Who could resist setting off on a journey like this from a base called The Old Success Inn? This is a seventeenth-century fisherman's inn right on the sea front and, in the morning, I was given a tee-shirt advertising the hotel on the front and proclaiming Sennen Cove as 'the bay where the dolphins play' on the back. I didn't see any dolphins but it was a jolly fine tee-shirt nonetheless.

Time to go, tearful farewells and all that malarkey, so it was on with the boots (gleaming) and rucksack (heavy) and, after tottering twenty-five yards across the car park and the road, I thought I'd done enough for a well-earned breather against the sea-front railings. What a superb morning it was. Blue sky, thundering white waves, a keen wind scouring everything clean and views that seemed to stretch on to infinity. Hundreds of seabirds were shrieking like souls in torment. To me they were all seagulls – or, to use the correct ornithological terminology, *Shitehawks* – but I was soon to realise that there were different types of gulls, such as black-backed gulls, herring gulls and common gulls. Not only that but some of them, petrels and shearwaters and fulmars for instance, are not gulls at all. Something to do with their nostrils, for Heaven's sake. And that's not including the terns which, as any fule kno, come in nasty and funny varieties. I mean to say, how can people tell them apart? Many weeks later I was to spend a morning in the company of a proper bird-watcher and it was astonishing not just how much I didn't know but how much I didn't even notice. For the moment though, there I was with my *Boys' Book of British Birds* blissfully happy to be able to tell the difference between a gull and a wren.

Full of vigour and all that kind of stuff, I set off through the dunes of Carn Barges and very soon came across an uninhabited stone-built cottage. In amongst the tumbledown walls of what had once been the garden was a bright clump of flowers — daffodils in full bloom and blue periwinkles. There were to be many unexpected cameos like this on the trip but this was the first and the effect was so startling that I had to stop and get the camera out again. After the bright blue sea, the white surf and the golds and browns of the sand and the rocks, here was another blast of colour.

For the first hour or two, as far as Cape Cornwall, the walking was gratifyingly easy along a clear path just above the shoreline. 'It can't get any better than this,' I thought and, in some respects, it never did. I was unused to such wild and rocky coastal scenery, and there was nobody else about to share it with me. The Atlantic waves were being churned up by a combination of the tide and the strong wind, and it was oddly hypnotic watching the constant battle between ocean and rock. The other thing that surprised me about the sea when it's in this mood is the noise — a jet-like roar that would have defeated any attempts at conversation. What with the views, the technicolour scenery, the feel of the wind stinging my face and the sound of the sea, I was in danger of sensory overload as I rattled along towards the day's first objective, Cape Cornwall.

And what a great place it turned out to be. Not only is it the only Cape in the whole of England and Wales – yes, indeed – it's an impressive and dramatic spot in its own right. Uncluttered by gifte shoppes and the other trappings of commercialisation, it retains an air of isolation and mystery now lost by many other places I would later visit. So far does it jut out into the ocean that in medieval times it was believed to be further west than Land's End. It is now owned by Heinz, to be kept open to the public for ever. In an age when private land ownership is often at odds with access to the likes of you and me, this sort of public-spirited gesture does your heart good. I think we should all eat as many baked beans as possible to encourage the company to acquire more threatened places and protect them. Standing right by the disused mine chimney on this windswept and lonely place, I was able to look ahead along the coast and, for the first time, begin to get some idea of the distance involved before I would be able to say I'd completed even the first stage of the journey; the cliffs and the glittering sea just seemed to stretch away for ever.

Cape Cornwall's chimney was the first of many between here and Perranporth, relics of the tin and copper mining which had been carried on along this coast for over two thousand years. Despite valiant attempts to save it, the mining industry hereabouts is now dead, the last operating mine, Geevor, having closed in 1990. Some people find these gaunt ruins dispiriting but, to me, they were fascinating and as vital a part of the landscape as the coves and cliffs. What must have been depressing though is the daily grind of the poor buggers who had to work these hell-holes in the eighteenth century. Conditions were appalling and the workers were not protected by the law as we know it. They had to abide by the rules of their own stannary courts, and I found it hard to imagine just what life must have been like scrabbling about a thousand feet below the surface, especially after having walked miles and then climbed down a ladder to get to your mine. You have to marvel at the resourcefulness and bravery of these people, as well as that of the engineers who designed and built the places to start with. Some of the shafts run out under the sea and they say that the miners, if they were quiet, could hear the sound of the Atlantic grinding the boulders on the ocean floor above their heads.

After the grandiose scenery I'd been walking through, it made a change to pass through a scruffier area of ruined mine buildings. These are the Levant and Geevor workings where there is a museum and a preserved beam engine. Like a lot of Britain, though, it doesn't open until Easter and I soon became used to finding things closed. None the worse for that though: it meant I had a lot of places to myself, and wasn't faced with the furtive dodging about you are sometimes forced to perform in order to carry out the simplest of bodily functions.

One of the striking features about the dereliction hereabouts was the graffiti. Instead of the usual football-related stuff though, we had 'Free Cornwall' plastered in three-foot high letters on a couple of walls. I had heard that there was a Nationalist movement in the county, and had read of several people who found the Cornish people hostile and antagonistic towards strangers. D. H. Lawrence was one such but, since he and his German wife had been hounded out of the village amidst accusations of spying whilst living at Zennor during the First World War, I suppose he had reason to feel aggrieved. I'm pleased to be able to report that I had no such difficulty. It's also true that the Cornish had their own language, but the last native speaker died in 1777.

Being geographically isolated, Cornwall does suffer more acutely than a lot of places from the vagaries of the economy. Whilst I was there, it was announced that a local creamery was to close – another hammer blow to a community already ravaged by the loss of its mines and the perennial difficulties facing farming and fishing. You really can't blame people for getting what they can out of tourism when they appear to have been neglected by successive administrations. Having said all that, I wonder how much worse it suffers by reason of its geographical position than, say, West Cumbria and the Furness Peninsula. So far as I know, there are no movements in existence for a Free Workington or an Independent Barrow.

The only people around these mine workings when I was there were some blokes working on the renovation of a scaffolding-shrouded chimney, and half a dozen youths on unfeasibly noisy motor bikes. They were having a great time riding back and forth across the man-made humps and hillocks of this industrial wasteland, but make the most of it, lads. There are signs that this whole area is being done up, and I fear it will soon be packaged, heritaged and sanitized to a point where such activities as trials bike riding will be prohibited.

The lighthouse at Pendeen Watch was the next landmark but, once again, the place did not appear to be open to visitors. I stopped for lunch overlooking Portheras Cove where I had a grandstand view of a group of five or six surfers enjoying themselves every bit as much as the motorcyclists had been. I had always associated surfing with the summer, an ignorance probably born out of listening to the Beach Boys and Jan and Dean when I was a teenager – the sun always shines in California, after all. It did look great fun, but I did not envy them one bit; it must have been freezing in that cold, cold sea. Anyway, Wipe Out and Surf City and all that.

It was when I stood up again after my lunch that I realised how tired I was. The rucksack felt much heavier now and my feet were beginning to hurt. I hadn't exactly raced along since I'd left Sennen Cove but, until now, I hadn't had a rest either. The excitement and newness of it all had caused me to disregard the sensible advice about taking it steadily.

I still had plenty of daylight left to reach my destination and could afford to move a little slower, which was just as well because there was a sudden increase in the difficulty of the walk. First, there was a very steep ascent out of Portheras Cove. My South West Way guidebook had warned that the stretch from Sennen Cove to St Ives was the longest and most deserted on the whole path, and I was now getting my first real taste of what Cornish coast walking can be all about. Once out of the cove, however, there was another flatter stretch where the path moved inland a little. This provided me with yet another change of scene as the vegetation became more upland in character. The path led me through areas of bracken and heather and, more typically, gorse, some of which was already in bloom. From here to the end of the walk, I never tired of seeing the vivid yellow starbursts of this spikiest of plants.

Stone walls built out of huge irregular blocks of granite were another feature of this moorland area near Morvah and, if walls can be said to be unruly, these were. In terms of geological time, they are obviously very recent additions to the landscape and they were showing every inclination of returning to the rock they had sprung from. Rather than falling down to meet the ground, though, they appeared to be merging with it, as if by osmosis. Wild-looking vegetation was starting to colonise them. Straggling grasses and black, spidery thorns were rampant amongst the stones, and the walls, just as the ruined mines had done, told silent tales of grieving and loneliness.

By the time I reached Bosigran, the great granite rock-face which is a Mecca for rock-climbers, the weather had deteriorated. The wind had freshened even more and a squally shower rushed in from the Atlantic, which must have made life that bit more uncomfortable for the one or two brightly-clad individuals I could pick out on the slabs. The rain was short-lived though and at Porthmeor Cove the sun came out again. This is a really wild place – the terrain is such that, although the path still follows the actual cliff top, there is now to landward an area of steeply sloping scrubland and heather leading up to the unseen moorland plateau above. It was hard to believe that there was a road less than half a mile away. I'd thought from studying the map back at home that, in an emergency, I could get to it easily, but I was obviously mistaken. There wasn't a soul about and the sense of isolation was heightened by the lack of a beach. The cliffs just drop – as near vertically as makes any difference – into the sea, and the only place for a walker to go is along this slender ribbon of pathway. At one point the track sidled along the very edge of a landslip which dropped a sheer thirty feet and it was clear that sooner rather than later the path itself would follow. You could see trampled grass where previous travellers had tried to walk higher up the slope to avoid this horror. I sped across the earthy tightrope as quickly as I could, looking fearfully down and gaining comfort from imaginary handholds in the vegetation. This was the first example of what I soon called 'Oo-er Walking', and there was plenty more of it to come on the Cornish coast.

At the outstretched arm of Gurnard's Head I turned inland to find my B&B. The Head looked an exciting, rocky place to be, and a South West Way completist would no doubt walk out onto its very tip, and quite right too, but I did not feel remotely bound by such constraints. As it was, I found the short walk to Treen very hard work. It was up a modest gradient but the near gale force wind was right in my face. My rucksack now weighed several tons, my feet had been glued to the ground and it was with a great sense of relief that I finally arrived at my lodgings for the night.

One of the joys of doing this end to end walk was going to be the sampling of the local beers between Cornwall and Caithness. With the recent increase in the number of small breweries, and thanks to the unstinting efforts of CAMRA, the big breweries do not have such a stranglehold on the beer drinkers of this country any more. What would I get to drink in the Gurnard's Head Inn, I wondered? Tinminer's Scrotum? Fisherman's Old Nonsensical? Wayfarer's Jollop? Do you know what they had? Boddingtons! I mean to say: it's a good pint, Boddingtons, but it's what I drink back home. I didn't come all this way just to have some stuff that had been carted down the M6 in a lorry. Keen not to have the Boddies and resisting the landlady's advice to try the lager – I certainly hadn't come all this way to drink lager – I discovered that Flowers IPA was on offer at a bargain price.

So that was that. And very nice it was, too. The evening passed pleasantly enough as I drank my beer and listened partly to an endless tape of Elvis songs and partly to a local man telling everybody in general and nobody in particular about the trouble he had been having fighting against the wind to put a ladder up so he could re-erect his TV aerial. A triumph of hope over commonsense I'd say. Not to mention the danger. I think you'd be safer climbing at Bosigran in roller skates than being up on a roof in this weather.

On Garbage Bags, Cameras and Footprints – St Ives, Hayle and Gwithian

Exotic vegetation at St Ives

The only other people at breakfast the following morning were a couple from Lorton, a village in the Lake District, not so very far from where I live. It was good to chat and it was becoming clear that, even at this early stage of the journey, I felt I needed human contact and conversation. One of the things that used to upset me was the apparent unwillingness of some people to talk – I don't possess the gift that some travellers evidently have of being able to strike up hugely interesting conversations with total strangers. Walking alone is fine but the evenings and breakfast-times were different, and I never got over feeling slightly awkward being on my own in pubs and guesthouses. Despite all the single rooms available in B&Bs and hotels, society isn't geared up to deal with people on their tod – *Saddus Gittus Vulgaris* – and I did wonder who all this single accommodation was for, when most of the other guests appeared to be in pairs.

The morning's walking was much as it had been the previous afternoon. A strong wind, blue skies and sunshine punctuated by the odd spiteful shower, and along a switchback coastline of, literally, breathtaking grandeur. No easy, level cliff tops now. Vicious downs to lonely coves and vicious ups to rocky headlands. The area around Wicca Pool was especially dramatic, and it was near here that I met a young Canadian couple on honeymoon. They were walking part of the South West Way and had camped the previous night near St Ives. They were heading towards Land's End and were as overwhelmed by the scenery as I was. Mr Canadian showed what I thought was an almost unnatural interest in the way my rucksack was packed.

'Hey, you use the garbage bag method as well.'

'Pardon?'

'You put your stuff in garbage bags to keep it dry!'

I must admit I thought everybody did – at least they do once they realise that, if you don't, one good shower renders the entire contents of your rucksack useless. But he seemed so pleased about it I thought it best to join in the enthusiastic praise of this system. Maybe in Canada, where they tell me it's drier than here, people don't use the Garbage Bag Method so frequently. After an hour or two spent idly swapping tales about garbage bags we have known, we went our separate ways.

Just as an aside, such is the power of song that every time I listen to that other great Canadian, Laughing Leonard Cohen, singing, 'I'm stubborn as those garbage bags that time cannot decay', I'm immediately transported back to that bouldery shore in Cornwall.

The trig column above Carn Naun Point was an obvious place to halt. At 318 feet above sea level it was the highest ground I'd reached so far, the view ahead went on for ever and it marked a return to easier walking. Refreshed after a brew, and pleased with myself that I'd completed a tough bit of the coast path (my book graded it as Severe), I set off again towards St Ives. I met one Englishman who was staying with his sister at Carbis Bay and was walking along the coast to Zennor and back again, and then a German couple. Remembering the Canadians, I wasn't going to make the same mistake twice so, as I saw the German pair approaching, I quickly made sure my garbage bags were invisible to prying eyes. This time it was the Frau who latched on to me.

'Sorry to stare, but I have a camera like yours.'

I looked at her camera and it wasn't a bit like mine. She saw my glance and said, 'Oh no, this is my best camera. The one like yours is at home.'

I mentioned Geoff Hurst and Michael Owen and went about my business.

Which was to get to St Ives, the first metropolis of my journey. The patron of St Ives is St Ia, an Irish lady who decided one day to set sail for Cornwall with some mates. She must have had to dash back home to check she'd turned the gas off or something, because she missed the boat and all her friends had gone and left her. Undaunted, she said a prayer and God blew her across the sea on a leaf so that she was actually the first of her party to arrive.

Paul Theroux described St Ives as a 'grey, huddled, storm-lit town', a wonderful description but not at all appropriate to the day I was there. After the untamed scenery of the last day or so, it looked almost Mediterranean across the golden expanse of Porthmeor Beach. This was Sunday lunchtime and the north-facing bay was so sheltered from the wind that there were families out and about doing what families do – walking dogs, eating ice cream and arguing.

I was disappointed with St Ives, but then it was probably disappointed with me too, as I didn't spend any money there. Undeniably quaint and attractive, with tiny narrow streets and miniature cottages, it's easy to see why it enticed so many artists and sculptors, the most famous, I suppose, being Dame Barbara Hepworth who came to St Ives just after opening her chain of high street menswear shops. Just as I was trying to adjust to the bustle of a town and wonder which way I had to go now, I bumped into the couple I'd met at breakfast. Most days I can walk through my home town of Kendal and not see anybody I know, so you can imagine what a thrill it was to see acquaintances in a little town in Cornwall.

Artists notwithstanding, the overriding impression I had of St Ives was one of amusement arcades, burger bars and, above all, crowds. This was March the second. What must it be like in August? There were snotty notices attached to the railings along the Promenade, 'Please do not feed the seagulls – they are becoming a nuisance.' Why? What do they do? Push in at bus queues? Try to sell you double glazing? Or do they just crap on your head? 'Toilets closed due to vandalism.' This, at a Public Inconvenience in the town. Welcome back to the real world.

I never thought I'd be guilty of underestimating any part of this walk, but that's exactly what I did with the bit from St Ives to Lelant. It looks nothing on the map but there was much more up and down than I'd bargained for. The immediate surroundings had taken a turn for the worse as well. The lonely cliffs of Wicca Pool a few hours earlier had been replaced by a scrubby mess, a railway line and that flash, brash type of residential development peculiar to seaside towns. Somewhere along the duneland behind Porth Kidney Sands I got talking to a couple who had done a lot of walking in Cornwall, and they filled my head with dire warnings of the nature of the ground to come. 'Daunting' was a word Mr Walker used quite a lot. Still, we made small talk as well and the ten minutes of company was welcome. At least they didn't talk about garbage bags or make fun of my camera.

There used to be a ferry across the estuary from Lelant to Hayle but there isn't any more, and it means a long tramp on tarmac almost to St Erth to cross the river by bridge. Instead of making the detour, John Hillaby waded across the slimy river here. He must have wanted his head examining, but at least he was spared the unattractive road walk into Hayle which is a plain little town but one with a tale or two to tell. The name comes from Hayl, the Cornish word for estuary and there used to be a coal-fired power station here, right on the coast. Can you imagine such a thing?

Well, yes actually. Cluttering up the coast with power stations is one of our national pastimes. Hinkley Point, and Heysham, and Dungeness, and Dounreay. It's the plentiful supply of water for cooling, you understand, that makes the coast so attractive to the planners, nothing to do with the fact that if they go wrong and explode, only a few country folk will be blown to kingdom come. Another thing that used to be at Hayle is Harvey's Foundry where they made steam pumping engines, the biggest of which was used to pump out the Haarlem Meer in the Netherlands and is still a national monument over there. There's also what's supposed to be the best Cornish pasty shop in Cornwall but, this being a Sunday afternoon in early March and because they'd heard I was coming, it was closed.

At Hayle Towans is a bizarre collection of wooden huts squatting amongst the dunes. Some are obviously holiday places but others are permanent dwellings and, because there are no streets, it's easy to feel that you've wandered off the track and are intruding. I did lose the path at a rather more upmarket – but deserted – holiday complex, and in the end decided it would be far easier to walk along the beach. Out towards the water's edge the sand had that lovely firm consistency you feel you can walk along for ever. There's nothing much more difficult to walk through than really dry sand, especially when it's been blown into great heaps, and when it's too wet, you tend to sink into it; but when it's just right, as it was here, the pleasure you get from walking across it is so good you almost feel guilty. I took a delight in leaving boot prints in it as well. Since they were so new, the tread was really well-defined. I toyed with the idea of running round in circles just to make more patterns but resisted stoutly. A good job I didn't have a bucket and spade with me – I'd probably still be there, and I don't even like the seaside much.

At the Strap Rocks, just off Gwithian, the tide had started to come in and I had a momentary panic as I noticed a family much nearer the shore than I was hurriedly packing up to get off the beach. I had to clamber in a very undignified fashion over barnacle-covered black rocks, but I didn't want any onlookers to think that I was making an unplanned evacuation from the beach. I imagined that if I peered intently into the rock pools, the people watching me might think that I was some kind of marine biologist who did this all the time. On each occasion I got down off a rock onto where the beach had been, there was a bit more water than the time before. I like to think I was never in any danger of being completely cut off by the tide but it did cross my mind that I might have to take my boots off and roll my trousers up, thereby exposing my legs to the daylight – and that would have been nearly as bad.

I eventually found some wooden steps which led me safely up to the road at Gwithian where I was afforded the unheard of luxury of being met by Linda, my landlady for the night, and ferried by car to her farmhouse lodgings a long mile away up a rough track. It was nearly dark, I was tired and the straps of my rucksack were digging into my shoulders. Miraculously, I felt better after a hot bath and then a meal and a drink at the Pendarves Arms in the village.

On the Mysteries of Ponies and Farmers' Hats – Perranporth and Newquay

Portreath

Over breakfast the next morning Linda, a proud local, told me about her Cornish-ness and expressed her opinion about some of the local towns. She spoke about Bude (and pronounced it as you would *food* and not *renewed*) as if it were at the furthest flung corner of the Empire which, since it's the last town in Cornwall before crossing into Devon, I suppose in a way it is. I could not have asked for a better welcome than I'd received from Linda and her husband Glyn, and it was with some reluctance that I set off down the long track back to Gwithian, especially since a fine, steady drizzle had set in. Cornish sunshine, Glyn had called it.

By the time I'd crossed the Red River – so called because of the copper mine spoil it washes down to the sea – and reached Godrevy Point, the drizzle had become real rain. The wind had got up again as well and in these conditions the lighthouse out on its island – the inspiration behind Virginia Woolf's *To the Lighthouse* apparently

– looked a fearsomely lonely spot to be. On to the Knavocks, a strangely quiet moorland of burnt heather and owned by the National Trust who, according to a notice here, have introduced six Shetland ponies to the area in order to improve and diversify the wildlife. I saw no sign of them though, which was disappointing because I wanted to ask them how they were doing with the task they'd been set. How, I wondered, would six ponies diversify the wildlife? I suppose they'd start by forming a committee or two and then deciding what sort of animal they considered appropriate. Perhaps, by now, there are herds of caribou grazing here but I suppose I'll never know.

The National Trust own over 100 miles of the Cornish coast and we must owe them a huge debt of gratitude for protecting us from the potential ravages of private ownership for profit. This is not a National Park and there are frequent reminders of the effects of seemingly unchecked urban development. It was reassuring to see so many of the familiar metal signs with the oak leaf logo, and the whole stretch from here to Portreath is in their capable care.

The extravagantly named Hell's Mouth provides ample opportunity for the locals to leap to their doom and I was told that some do. The cliff top is about 200 vertical feet above the waves and it's conveniently situated ten yards from the road. A rather feeble wooden railing would not act as much of a deterrent to the determined but, since there are any number of similar places along this coast, I wondered why this spot in particular should have attracted such a grisly reputation. Much more cheerful was the sight of a café just over the road. Needless to say it was closed, but at least I could stand in the shelter afforded by one of its walls to have a brew and a temporary dry out.

It was when I stopped that I realised how cold it had become. The mostly fine weather of the last two days and the frequent sunshine had lulled me into thinking that spring was well and truly with us, but this wind and rain made me realise that winter's tail still had its sting. I had thought that one of the spin-off benefits of doing the walk from south to north was that I would have the prevailing south-westerlies behind me for the first 250 miles of coastal walking. This was fine in theory, but the weather today was coming from the east and blowing right into my face.

For the next couple of miles the going was easy along a narrow strip of level ground between the cliff edge and the road. I saw not a soul, not even a car passed by, and the only company I had were the ever-present screaming sea birds. You have to marvel at the way they swoop and dive and glide and land on the tiniest, most precarious ledges on the cliffs. I suppose it was the breeding season – theirs, that is, not mine – and there was lots of showing off and even naked aggression. From them, not me.

Just when I was beginning to think that the guidebook had exaggerated the difficulties of this stage of the walk, there were two knee-wrecking downs and lung-bursting ups to negotiate in quick succession. The offshore islands just here are incredibly impressive, with knife-edged ridges running down from their crests straight into the sea. One of these stacks is called Samphire

Island, presumably named after the samphire plant which grows on the cliffs hereabouts and used to be a much prized culinary ingredient. In times gone by it was not uncommon for people to plunge to their deaths while engaged in the almost lunatic activity of trying to gather this delicacy – a task they undertook to supplement their income.

The seaside village of Portreath was going to be good. For once, I said, I will indulge myself in the luxury of a sit down in a warm café with a plate of chips for comfort and a mug of hot tea. As I approached the village across the beach and could see the sea-front properties in the distance, I began to salivate at the prospect of the delicacies in store. But you know that feeling you get when it slowly begins to dawn on you that things are not going to turn out exactly as you thought? Well, this happened to me now. It became sickeningly obvious that not only were all the cafés closed – and would be for centuries it seemed – but there was no shelter of any sort. I tell a lie – there was a phone box and a Gents. At least this toilet was open – eat your heart out St Ives. Neither place offered very cheery accommodation so I slouched against yet another wall which did enable me to eat my sandwiches sheltered from the wind. A vast expanse of puddled tarmac, with a derelict looking camper van and nothing else parked on it, added to the dreariness of this windswept and rain-lashed seafront. The whole effect was neatly set off by the dire warnings of wheel clamping incongruously fixed at intervals to the railings. Lest it be thought that I did not like Portreath, let me say here and now that I did – I'd go back tomorrow. It's just that I did want my chips and my cup of tea.

After completing my al fresco luncheon and having – of course – allowed a suitable time for my food to be properly digested, I set off along more dramatic cliffs with the tall and ugly wire mesh fence of the disused Nancekuke Airfield as a less than cheerful companion. The rain was torrential now but at least it helped swell the stream which spills over a lip of rock at Sally's Bottom to form the first waterfall I'd seen on the coastal path. Places with odd sounding names were a constant source of delight for me on the trip – I'd already been past Ralph's Cupboard and The Avarack and was regretting not having been able to go and look at Praze-an-Beeble and the wonderfully sinister-sounding Barripper. But Sally's Bottom had leapt into the lead as main contender for the coveted Place Name of the Week Award.

The morning brought another change in the weather. The heavy rain had given way to a dank, hanging mist which, somehow, seemed in tune with the surroundings. The greys and pinks and golds of the granite rocks of the Penwith peninsula had been replaced by a much more austere landscape of tall cliffs of dark crumbly slates, steeper and more imposing than the ones I'd seen further west. The tingle of excitement I always get when venturing into new places was intensified by the knowledge that the ground in this area is riddled with potentially dangerous, disused mineshafts. I did not see any unfenced ones though, but there were some covered with conical mesh hats, which I later discovered had been designed to let the resident bats in and out. The lean, angular shell of the buildings at Towanroath Shaft came and went in the drizzly gloom and the walking was excellent and easy across St Agnes and Newdowns Heads.

I encountered more industrial dereliction at Trevellas Porth where the remains of the Blue Hills Mine were difficult to pass without having a good old rummage about. It was when I saw places like this, especially when they were deserted and I could hear the song of the wind blowing through the strange bits of twisted metal and stone, that I began to understand the attraction of industrial archaeology. Perhaps one day I'll come back and have a more leisurely look.

The area around Hanover Cove is very strange indeed. To the right is a disused airfield, its concrete runways slowly sprouting straggly grass and generally returning to nature, but on the left is a succession of improbably tall, steep cliffs. I don't know why it should be so, but people like me who have no particular head for heights are irresistibly drawn to peer over the edge of these places. The wind had not relented at all, although it had swung round so that it was now blowing in from the sea, and the water below me was slamming into the cliffs in a tantrum-like frenzy, the like of which I had not witnessed since my daughter was a toddler and used to throw truly spectacular wobblers. The sight of dozens of seabirds being blown about like confetti below me was also strangely unnerving. Just past the granite outcrop of Cligga Head, there was some really alarming oo-er walking on a narrow path above the tormented ocean. I found myself running through my repertoire of early Beatles' songs in an effort to take my mind off the possible consequences of a slip.

By the time I reached Perranporth the mist had all but cleared to be replaced by brighter, but wetter, conditions. Most of Perranporth was closed too but I was at least able to eat my packed lunch in a shelter in a park. It was notable for being the place where I first took part in the Ritual of Changing the Map. I'd got so used to Landranger 203 *'Land's End'* that when I got 200 *'Newquay and Bodmin'* out of my sack it actually felt different in my hand. The other one had become battered and twisted to the shape of my pocket and I could not help feeling a little disloyal as I consigned it to the rucksack for the rest of the trip. It soon became apparent that I would attach momentous significance to being able to put one map away and replace it with another.

From Droskyn Point just above the town, I had had a full length view of the long stretch of Perran Beach and the sands provided an exhilarating walk through the spray as far as some low cliffs just before Ligger Point. Here was an extraordinary collection of brightly coloured plastic containers of all shapes and sizes, bits of old rope, and wood bleached white by the sun. It wasn't so much the quantity of this stuff that was surprising, more the fact that it was all concentrated in one place. I assumed this was jetsam – or is it flotsam? – but, whatever it was, along this otherwise spotless stretch of coast, it looked as out of place as a mackerel in an oak tree.

Behind this beach are the highest sand dunes in Britain and somewhere in amongst them are the ruins of St Piran's Oratory, apparently built in the seventh century and then soon after covered over by the shifting, whispering sands. St Piran is the guy after whom Perranporth is named and is also the patron saint of Cornwall and Tinners. Why he gets two things to be patron saint of I don't know.

Perhaps it's to make up for the rough crossing he'd had from Ireland. He is supposed to have been chained to a millstone and thrown into the sea by the then Irish royal family. I can just imagine him trying to reason with them: 'Hey, fellers. I've got a better idea. Why don't you get me wafted over on a leaf like St Ia?'

I did not know it then but the following day would be St Piran's Day and the local radio station made much of it during its breakfast time programmes. He even has his own flag – black with a silver cross to represent Cornwall's metal wealth – which is flown from public buildings on March the fifth.

The walk along the perimeter fence of Penhale Camp with its sinister and unnecessary warnings to keep out was not spectacularly attractive. The notices spoke of High Voltage, which I understand, and Non-Ionising Radiation, which I don't. Is this better for you than the Ionising type? Or is it the Non-Ionising sort which makes your teeth fall out and your ears bleed?

Holywell looked sad and a bit neglected and it was near here that I had my first confrontation with a dog-owner. I only said 'Hello' to the woman but her dogs reacted as if I'd tried to make off with her belongings. She attempted to explain their snarling and yapping by saying that they weren't used to strangers. Oh, if only I'd known – I'd have sent her a photo and a CV. Another lady, a few minutes later, directed me across Cubert Common as a short cut to Crantock. My boots were beginning to rub seriously now and I hobbled the last couple of painful miles through the rain to my digs.

I had my evening meal and drink at 'The Old Albion', a pub claiming to be seventeen million years old. I didn't ask why it was named after a Midlands football team, but I'm sure there's a perfectly good reason for it. My eavesdropping entertainment tonight came courtesy, first, of a committee meeting of some sort where one of the participants said, of an absent colleague, 'I don't mean to be derogatory, but she's really quite nasty.' I wondered whether there were ever any circumstances in which you could describe someone as nasty without being derogatory. Then a group of young dentists sat near me and spoke loud and long about the shortcomings of the NHS. It was quite an education for me. I did not know, for example, that not all dentists dispose of the suction tubes each time they use them. Did you? There's a thought for you the next time you're sat reading *Bella* or *Woman's Own* in the waiting room.

At intervals along the Cornish coast are river estuaries which have to be crossed somehow. There are three ways of doing this. The easiest involves getting in a boat and being ferried across. Purists, of course, would not stoop to such a thing so they are left with the choice of walking upstream to the nearest crossing point and then back downstream again, or swimming / wading across. This latter option strikes me as so ridiculous that it doesn't bear thinking about. The ferry at Hayle no longer operates and the one across the Gannell between Crantock and Newquay does not start until May. The walk inland to Trevemper to cross by the main road looked to be a very unappealing alternative, so it was with great relief that I heard Sue, my landlady, tell me over breakfast that the tide would be out and the tidal footbridge at Penpol Creek would be passable. Well, I didn't know what a tidal footbridge was. The guidebook said it may not be usable for up to two and a half hours before and after high tide and I had visions of some terrifying edifice I'd have to race along in the few minutes available to me. It turned out to be nothing more than a bit of duckboard raised a couple of feet above a muddy creek and held no terrors even for a bridgeophobe like me.

Newquay was much the biggest place I'd visited so far but, on this grey, drizzly morning, it was quiet and I liked it. I walked down streets of endless guest houses, many of them closed and some of them displaying For Sale notices. The vast array of shops was welcome and it gave me a chance to spend hundreds of pounds in the chemist's shop on plasters of every description for my feet which, by now, were giving me serious gyp. I mean, what was I thinking of, setting off on a thousand mile walk in a brand new pair of boots anyway? I'd worn them once round the house and that's all. Sometimes, I wonder just how stupid I can be.

The popular beaches were completely deserted as I left the town by way of Lusty Glaze and Whipsiddery, two places sounding more like deviant sexual practices than seaside areas. The walk out to Trevelgue Head gave me another great view of the rough sea and the line of cliffs stretching ever northwards towards Trevose Head. Apart from the descent to Watergate Bay and the climb back on to the cliffs from that dispirited looking place with its burnt-out hotel, the walking was more or less level all the way to Griffin's Point and Mawgan Porth. Along this part of the coast, the land is farmed right up to the cliff edge: there's just enough room for the path to be squeezed in between the fence and the drop into the ocean. There were difficulties in one or two places where the continual erosion of the cliffs had swept the path away and it had had to be diverted slightly further inland. I suppose the fields must be getting smaller and smaller as each year goes by. John Hillaby had a lot of trouble with farmers hereabouts turning him back and saying there would never be a coast path. Well, there is now. I can't praise the architects of this long distance trail enough. Only for a short stretch near Newquay, where a headland is part of a hotel complex, does private land force you to move away from the shore. It's too easy to take for granted our freedom to tramp along this fantastic coast and we owe a lot to all those involved in negotiating access rights and gradually piecing together the South West Way.

Up on the cliff edge north of Watergate Bay I met a farmer repairing a wall. He told me that at fifty years of age he'd just achieved his lifelong ambition – to have his own farm. He didn't own it: the National Trust bought it but he was the tenant and his own boss. At least, as he said, the National Trust were spending an enormous amount of money on new fencing and drainage, money which he could not have found. I was glad I'd met this farmer. It must be a great thing to achieve an ambition as he had done and his example was an inspiration to me when things got tough. One thing did puzzle me about him – and others like him – though. How do they keep their flat caps on in this howling wind? There's me in my expensive foul weather gear hanging on to my hat and pulling the hood drawstrings ever tighter, while these blokes just seem to carelessly perch their caps on the tops of their heads. I thought long and hard about this and came to the conclusion that they actually go into hospital for an NFU-funded operation to have threads tapped into their skulls. The caps are then surreptitiously screwed on when you and I aren't looking. Either that or they use velcro. Or black magic.

Griffin's Point used to be a favourite nesting place for Cornish choughs. This member of the crow family disappeared from Cornwall in the 1970s, partly as a result of changing methods of farming affecting the availability of food, but, happily it has made a return. I imagine one of the other reasons it died out is because it didn't know how to pronounce its own name. Chatting up members of the opposite sex would have been nigh on impossible for it. 'Hi there, I'm a chow,' it might say, totally confusing its neighbour which called itself a choff and therefore thought of itself as a completely different species altogether. Tragic. Strictly speaking, the 'new' chough is thought to have come from Brittany, so they now have the added complication of a language barrier to deal with. Tits have had no such problem of course, which probably accounts for why there are so many of them about.

There was a big hotel place at Mawgan Porth full of people drinking tea and looking warm but bored, and it was a relief that the walk above Bedruthan was as dramatic as anything I'd seen on the whole coast. The tide was in and the succession of giant granite stacks thrusting out of the grey churning sea like petrified grim reapers was an impressive sight. A colleague had once been here on a family holiday in summer but I found it incredible that this place could ever be the scene of children laughing and playing in the sand. Hamish Brown complained that the Cornish landscape is no longer a wilderness and is too accessible. How wild does he want it? This could have been the Gateway to the Underworld. Just fantastic.

Arrival at Porth Mear brought shelter from the gale and it was good to stand in relative comfort and calm, and watch the sea thrashing itself against the rocks at the entrance to the little cove. There was a flock of oystercatchers standing on the beach here and the way they stand, heads bowed, always reminds me of a group of nuns at prayer.

I had no idea where I was going to rest for the night but I felt I needed a break from the pounding I was getting. My feet certainly did and I was lucky to find friendly accommodation at Porthcothan. I mentioned to my hosts that the sheep up on the cliffs nearby were almost the first I'd seen in Cornwall and my hosts said that they were there to keep the grass down. There used to be horses up there for grazing apparently, but not being so sure footed, they kept falling into the sea – a distinct design disadvantage for a coastal animal.

Wreckers and Rocking Vicars – Padstow and Tintagel to Hartland Point

Cambeak

I awoke to brilliant sunshine, the first since St Ives, and set off with Padstow my not too distant target for the day. The going was easy now along a fretted coastline of low cliffs, above which are more of the herringbone-pattern dry-stone walls which had become a familiar feature over the last day or so. All dry-stone walling is miraculous but these are masterpieces. Slices of shaly rock are placed end on at 45 degrees to the ground, with the next course sitting on top and facing in the opposite direction. The pattern is repeated several times and then the whole thing is topped off by a row of thicker stones standing vertically. Every one of these walls – called stone hedges by the locals – had become, over the years, a vertical rock garden and they were a joy to behold.

The blue sea and white surf at Treyarnon and Constantine Bays made a fine sight as I continued to make good progress towards Trevose Head. If you look at a map of England's South West Peninsula you will see that there are a few points where the coastline abruptly changes direction. Trevose Head is one of these and I thought it would be a major landmark achieved when I reached it.

Just before arrival at the Head is a thing marked on the map as 'Round Hole'. I was intrigued to know what this would be as none of my books gave it much of a mention. I was totally amazed to find that it is, in fact, a Round Hole. In general, this part of the coast, north of Porthcothan is slightly less well endowed with natural wonders and spectacular and terrifying formations than it is further south, so it came as something of a shock to find that the gently graded path heading purposefully across a well-manicured emerald green sward was suddenly confronted with this gaping monstrosity. It must be about fifty yards in diameter and I suppose at the bottom is the sea. I didn't dare peer over the edge to look.

There were one or two people about as I rounded the headland near the lighthouse on Trevose Head and I had to stop for a last look back along the superb shoreline that had led me this far. I know I have banged on about some of the terrors this coast could hold for a walker, but I never felt it to be actually hostile. Sailors probably think differently, however. Between 1823 and 1848 there were 150 shipwrecks between Cape Cornwall and Trevose and, despite the incredible bravery shown by generations of lifeboat crews, more stories and legends have grown up around those who saw shipwrecks as an opportunity to grab something of value – the wreckers. A couple of centuries ago Cornishmen saw nothing wrong in going down to the site of a ship in distress and helping themselves to what they could. After all, wasn't this just another fruit of the sea, like fish? The landed gentry even claimed that anything found in a vessel washed up on their shores was legally theirs. The tales of wreckers attaching lights to donkeys or whatever to confuse sailors and lure them to their doom are examples of human nature at its most desperate, and I prefer to side with the point of view that such people probably only existed in fiction.

After rounding Trevose Head, there followed a less satisfactory section; firstly, because I was heading south again and, secondly, because the immediate surroundings had become almost suburban. 'Keep Out' notices, caravan and holiday chalet parks, more signs saying 'No This', 'No That' and 'Bugger Off', and miles of barbed wire. The hamlets of Harlyn Bay and Trevone Bay were closed, which came as no surprise, although I was a bit miffed to find even the Gents at Trevone Bay shut as well.

The headland pushing out northwards to Stepper Point marked a return to wilder and lonelier country once I'd got past yet another Round Hole, even bigger than the one near Trevose. My guidebook said it should be approached with caution. As a Statement of the Bleeding Obvious this took some beating. A few minutes later came some spectacularly layered cliffs where alternating bands of harder and softer rock had produced ledges ideal for seabirds – razorbills and guillemots according to my book but, to be honest, they could have been anything vaguely gull-like. I reached the daymark tower on Stepper Point from where I had a view across the Camel estuary to yet more miles of cliffs marching off into the distance.

Padstow is attractively laid out around its harbour and used to be famous for the Doom Bar, a sandbank barring entry to the harbour for all but the smallest craft and put there by a dying mermaid after she'd been shot by a foolish local. Now, however, in our age where every area has to be linked to some sort of celebrity, it is much better known as the home of the chef, Rick Stein.

In my quest for strange and terrifying ales, I managed to get a pint of St Austell Tinners Bitter in the pub where The Who's *Happy Jack* was one of the songs on the tape that was being played. 'And they couldn't prevent Jack from feeling happy,' it went. But for some reason I felt a bit down. Although one of my feet was now much better, the other had got worse, and felt as if it was being squeezed in a vice. My notebook for the day reads, 'Can't keep pushing on like this.' For the first time since I left Kendal, I went to bed feeling at odds with myself and the world.

Did I say something about purists and ferries before? Well, I'm no purist and, in the morning, I shambled down to the riverbank to catch the ferry over the river to a place called Rock. The tide was so low though that the little boat could not land at its usual spot and it deposited me, the only passenger, on a glutinous sandbank below Brea Hill a little further downstream. I began to wonder whether this had been some sort of practical joke as I nearly disappeared up to my waist in a pale yellow quagmire. It was a bit like crossing deep fresh snow but squelchier, and it was hard to resist the thought that it was called the River Camel because everyone who crossed it got the hump.

With my foot still causing me the sort of pain I'd previously only imagined in my worst nightmares, I decided to miss the headland of Pentire Point and use little lanes and field paths. This at least made a change from clinging to the coast all the time even though the scenery became rather nondescript. The only real splash of colour amongst the faded greens of the fields was provided by a rusting yellow van in a farmyard.

I reached the coast again at Port Quin, a National Trust owned harbour with no village any more, even though up to a hundred years ago it was still a busy little place trading in slate (outwards) and coal (inwards). There were also lead and antimony mines and, of course, fishing. The village died the moment all the men were drowned when their jointly owned fishing boat capsized and, seeing no future there, the women and children packed up and left.

Inland again on a very pleasant track to Roscarrock Farm where there was a manor as long ago as the days of Edward the Confessor – Honest Ted, to his mates. If I'd been a *Poldark* fan, I would have been enjoying an orgy of excitement at this lonely building. It was Nampara in the *Poldark* television series and, apparently, Ned Hoskin was hanged here. I was ignorant of all this, but Roscarrock will live in my memory as the place where I finally sat down and sorted out the problem with my foot. Having tried various plasters and bits of cushioning in all manner of different positions, it dawned on me that all I needed to do was not tie the laces as far up the boots as I had been doing. Guess what? Miracle cure. I had not a scrap of trouble from the boots after that – they were superb – and I wonder why it had taken me so long to try such a simple and obvious remedy. This is one of the drawbacks of walking on your own – the lack of somebody alongside you to make sensible suggestions when you are too thick to work things out for yourself.

With the aches and pains now almost vanished, I marched across fields to Port Isaac, an improbable looking village of steep, narrow streets and old buildings all hunched up on a rocky headland. It looked as if it would have repaid a leisurely exploration but I wanted to reach Tintagel that night; I reckoned it was about 100 miles from the start and it would be a satisfying end to the first week's walking. I sat on a bench to eat my lunch and was joined by an aged and overweight labrador, which went through an obviously well-rehearsed repertoire of pleading looks. Having paid a small fortune for my food I wasn't about to share it with this mutt, however sad-eyed, and I resolved to remain cold-hearted while it ran through its entire routine.

The stretch of coast between Port Gaverne and Tintagel is reckoned to be one of the toughest and, because I'd made such slow progress as far as Roscarrock, I decided to cheat and use lanes and footpaths again. This involved nearly two miles of walking along a fast stretch of main road which I did not enjoy one little bit. It was busier than I had anticipated and, after six days away from speeding traffic, I felt very vulnerable. I might as well have been carrying a sign saying, 'Please drive very fast and try to knock me down'. It was good to turn off for Treligga and then across some of the muddiest fields I've ever encountered to Trebarwith – very quiet and almost medieval-looking – and Treknow (with a silent 'k'). Nearly every place name in this part of Cornwall begins with Tre; it means hamlet or settlement and is more evidence of the Celtic connection with Wales.

Whether my efforts to secure accommodation in Tintagel had been successful remained to be seen. I had been informed on the phone that yes, they had a room but I'd better 'come and see what you think' of it. Having spent much of the day wondering what I could expect, I discovered when I arrived that my room was still being cleaned and had just been decorated. 'Don't touch the walls, they're wet,' I was told. It turned out I was the only guest in this rambling hotel which had just changed hands and was clearly being smartened up for the coming season.

On a cold and windy Friday night, Tintagel's main street was deserted apart from a few local youths congregating around a telephone box. As teenage lads have done for generations, they were making desperate efforts to impress their female counterparts with a colourful courtship display of smoking, slouching and pointless swearing. I ate very well in a place claiming to have the Best Mixed Grill in the West but have to admit to not liking Tintagel much. It had the air of a frontier town. If a poncho-clad Clint Eastwood had ridden down the main street I wouldn't have been a bit surprised. Dodging the tumbleweed, I peered into shop windows displaying little other than King Arthur tat — Tintagel, after all, is reputed to be Arthur's birthplace and, by jingo, it's going to make the most of it.

In the pale light of a cold grey morning, the village looked less alien than it had the previous night. My landlord hoped I'd make it to 'Johnny Groats' and I met a chap who later that day would be playing rugby for Cornwall against Cumbria in the semi-finals of the Rugby Union county championship. Outside a cycling and camping shop over the road was a sign presumably doctored by the local wags. It promised the exotic sounding 'CAMP G-SPOT AND LEISURE', an attraction I had more trouble resisting than the so-called Arthurian Experience, housed in the building next door, where 'the classic legend is told by Robert Powell, highlighted by laser, music and sound. AS SEEN ON NATIONAL LOTTERY LIVE HERE FEBRUARY 95'. I mean to say.

I walked past the Old Post Office, a building which dates back to the 14th century, to reach the coast path again at Tintagel Castle. It was Geoffrey of Monmouth who first portrayed this site as the birthplace of Arthur in his *History of the Kings of Britain*. Whatever the facts of it all may be, there is no doubt that the rocky headland on which the castle stands is an impressive place. The narrow neck of land connecting the promontory to the mainland is almost completely severed, giving the place an air of inaccessibility and remoteness.

The four or five miles to Boscastle gave the best walking and most dramatic scenery since Bedruthan: tall cliffs, impressive rock stacks and deep narrow inlets to cross, the best of which is the imaginatively-monickered Rocky Valley. I took a peek through a hole in an unusual rock formation known as Ladies Window and passed a large group of overseas students going towards Tintagel. There were so many of them that it set me to wondering when I had last seen anybody actually on the coast path. Apart from the odd person out with their dog, I don't think I'd seen another walker since the previous Sunday afternoon about eighty miles before. This was a recurring feature of the trip in its early stages: except at weekends, or at car parks, I was unlikely to come across anybody else.

Boscastle is a gem. The natural harbour is impressively long and narrow and the booming noise of the sea pounding into a hole in the edge of the cliffs and then being squeezed out again by the force of the next incoming wave was startling. The young Thomas Hardy met his bride-to-be, Emma, along this part of the coast and he wrote an autobiographical story, *A Pair of Blue Eyes*, about this period of his life. In the last century Boscastle was a trading port of some importance and boasted, amongst other things, a wine depot belonging to the wonderfully Dickensian-sounding Sloggatt and Rosevear. The coming of the railway to the Delabole slate quarries, just a few miles away, changed all that though and Boscastle swapped slate for tourists as its main source of income.

By the time I was climbing out of Boscastle on to Penally Hill, the weather had become much sunnier and, for the first time on the walk, I felt uncomfortably warm and was beginning to be a little concerned about the effort I was having to put in to climb out of all these coves. Most of the ascents are only a couple of hundred feet and I wondered how on earth I would manage when it came to Snowdon and Scafell Pike. The big difference between coastal walking like this and hill walking though is that, as Hamish Brown says, on a mountain walk ups and downs are long, whereas on the coastal path they are 'constant but irregular, rhythm-destructive and hard work with the weight of a rucksack'.

More dramatic scenery near Pentargon waterfall preceded some oo-er walking and steep climbing above Firebeacon Point and on to High Cliff. At 729 feet above the sea this is the highest cliff on the Cornish coast path but, because it is not as steep as some of the lower ones which had come before, it did not give me the willies as I thought it was going to. The next headland though was Cambeak and this was a different kettle of fish. Jutting aggressively out into the Atlantic, it looked like the head and neck of some enormous reptile about to spring from its lair in the cliffs. Even my little guidebook which had given very little away about the scariness of much of this coast said 'at Cambeak prepare to be terrified by the dangerous nature of the cliff edge.' It was with a massive sense of relief that I saw lots of notices instructing walkers to keep off the headland because of erosion. Feigning bitter disappointment at this prohibition I made the easy descent to Crackington Haven and the best cup of tea I'd ever had in my life.

Searching for accommodation, I turned inland and spent the night at Dizzard. As I passed through the hamlet of Coxford on the way, I noticed the following inscription carved on a stone sundial outside one of the houses: 'Nothing treads so quietly as the foot of time.' I thought it profound and significant at the time, but now I've no idea why. Reminds me of those brilliant ideas you get in the night but have forgotten by morning. Somebody once told me he had the sense to leave a pen and paper by his bed so he could write down the next one of his frequent brainwaves. In the morning he found he had written 'The skin is mightier than the banana.' Which must go to prove something, I suppose.

Before setting off the next day, I booked the next night's accommodation at a village in – fanfare and drum roll please, maestro – Devon! It came as something of a shock to think that I would be actually leaving Cornwall at all – it is such a long county with an even longer coastline that I'd begun to think I was stuck in a timewarp, destined to walk the Cornish cliffs for ever.

The day dawned sunny and warm and undemanding walking along the cliff top brought me to a spot overlooking the spectacular chevron geology at Millook where the rock strata in the cliffs have been folded into an unlikely zigzag pattern. A rather untidy and dreary area near Wanson Mouth was crossed on the way to Widemouth Bay, a holiday beach with no visual amenity at all. This was as dispiriting an interlude as I'd had, past more 'Walkers will be Shot' notices, and across a crowded car park full of people busily reading the Sunday papers. The low cliffs of Upton and Efford Downs brought a return to better scenery and I was delighted to see an octagonal building with the points of the compass engraved on the appropriate side.

Bude provided toilets and a café and I would forgive this town anything for being the home of my favourite limerick:

'There was a young lady of Bude
Who went for a swim in the lake.
A man in a punt
Stuck a pole in her ear,
And said, "You can't swim here, it's private."'

As it was, the place was welcoming and airily attractive, especially around the canal basin, the Bude Canal having been constructed in 1823 to take sand to farms inland. (Why anyone would want to take sand to a farm is one of those little mysteries that I think are best left unanswered.)

A stroll over Maer Down led to Northcott Mouth which was a shambles of half-renovated property and litter, and it was about here that I noticed that the climbs up to the clifftops were getting progressively stiffer. The beach scenery was excellent in the afternoon sun but there were more piles of rubbish on the descent to the cove of Warren Gutter, where bits of paper had blown into the scrubby vegetation and remained suspended from it so that, from a distance, it resembled bunting at a street party.

The little bay and beach at Duckpool were almost idyllic. I had the place to myself and felt a little bit guilty that no-one else was around to be able to see the perfect pattern of sunlight and shadow on the silver waters of the Atlantic. A long, tiring haul on to the cliffs above Lower Sharpnose Point brought me to the huge dishes of the satellite tracking station at Cleave Camp which had been in view seemingly for days. From a distance the white discs against the blue sky made an attractive picture but close up they were just ugly, as was the inevitable fence surrounding them.

After another swooping descent to Stanbury Mouth I decided that, having regard to the lateness of the hour and the knowledge that I had two or three more of these monstrous headlands to negotiate, I would cut inland to Stanbury Farm and then use fieldpaths and lanes to cross the Devon border. This decision probably did save a little bit of up and down work but many of the farm tracks were quagmires. The walk across fields to Tonacombe and the Tidna Valley was excellent, though. This was rural England as you imagine it should be. The sea had slipped from sight behind the headland of Higher Sharpnose Point, the bright green fields were full of contented looking sheep and cattle, and daffodils and primroses were carpeting the floor of the woods. Wait a minute! Woods? Hang on, I'm in a wood. Momentous or what? So far as I could recall, these were the first woods of the whole walk. I suppose I must have seen the odd tree somewhere but, apart from a couple of palms at St Ives, I couldn't think of any.

At Morwenstow is a superb church and churchyard with leaning lichen-covered gravestones. The setting sun cast an almost magical light upon this quiet corner and arrival here was one of the great moments of the walk. You know, one of those occasions when you think to yourself, 'Whatever else happens to me, they can never take this away.' The walk through the churchyard involved crossing the last of the Cornish stone stiles, dozens of which I'd had to deal with so far. They consist of a short step up onto a flat rock, a long stretch over an end-on slate slab onto another stone, and then a short step down. Nicely designed, good to look at but probably a nightmare for short-legged individuals. Unlike English football in the 1960s, Morwenstow is not well-known for its stiles but is famous for the Reverend Hawker who was vicar here for over forty years from 1834. He built a hut from driftwood on the cliff edge and would go there to meditate and write poetry. He was also partial to the odd pipe of opium, apparently.

'Been writing poetry again, Reverend?' his parishioners would ask, as the good vicar rolled home with glazed eyes, singing snatches of Jefferson Airplane songs.

I wanted to see Henna Cliff which, after Beachy Head, is England's highest sheer drop into the sea. It would also be my last chance to be on the Cornish part of the coast path so I hurried across a gently rising field to the edge where the views in both directions more than repaid the small effort. Those of you who have walked any of the National Trails of England and Wales will be familiar with the acorn symbol used on waymarks and signposts. There are places on the coast path where the way is not at all obvious and the waymarks are a great help and comfort. Being familiar with Lake District cairns, it took me a little while to get used to looking for these wooden stakes with the yellow arrows but they soon became good friends. Well, when you're on your own for a long time you can make friends with almost anything, and these little chaps are especially welcoming with the names of the places they are indicating carved vertically into the wood. This is a nice touch which stops as soon as you cross into Devon.

The excitement of being in a new county was so great that I took a twilit photograph of the first Devon sign I saw – on a public footpath after an alarmingly steep climb out of the Marsland valley – and it was almost dark when I arrived at the appropriately named hamlet of Welcombe. My hosts took good care of me and told me in the morning that the only thing they knew about Kendal was that it was the home of the mint cake, but they'd never eaten it. I happened to have some with me and left them some to try. (If there has been a recent increase in mint cake sales in North West Devon I think I ought to be getting royalties.)

If the last couple of days had been spring, the next one was almost summer. A brilliant blue sky and not even a breeze. The cliff top walk was stupendous – this is what I'd imagined coast walking to be like – high above the sea with the views limited only by the haze, almost level, and nobody about. I saw a raven on a fencepost – which surprised me because I had always thought them to be mountain birds – and then what I think was a peregrine falcon. On the other hand, there were virtually no seabirds now, and the contrast with the scenery further south and west was heightened by the presence here of beaches. Very rocky ones admittedly, and very unusual as well. From the lofty vantage point of the cliffs you can look down on a landscape almost like corduroy. Low rock ridges running out to sea at right angles to the shore line, they could have been formed by someone running a giant comb across the rocks when they were still molten.

The seventy-foot double waterfall at Speke's Mill Mouth was impressive and is the highest on the coast path. More switchback walking followed past Hartland Quay, over the Abbey River and across Titchberry Water to finally reach Hartland Point, where the coastline takes a sharp right turn to head purposefully eastwards. Of far more significance to me was the fact that when you stand facing seawards on the headland of Hartland Point you have the Atlantic Ocean on your left but the water on your right is the Bristol Channel.

It is fitting that the cliffs here are as wild as anything I'd seen so far. Whatever else the Atlantic coast had been, it most certainly had not been disappointing and I felt glad and rather relieved that my walk along it had ended with this crashing final chord rather than with an apologetic fade-out.

CHAPTER TWO — THE BRISTOL CHANNEL

THE GOOD, THE BAD AND THE UGLY

Introducing the Boys — Clovelly, Bideford and Barnstaple

Alwington, near Bideford

Against expectations, and despite the ninety-degree change of direction, Hartland Point did not mark any significant change in the scenery and quality of the walking. The imposing high cliffs just marched on into the haze and off the edge of the world and the footpath continued to be easy to follow through the grass. Once past the outlandishly ugly structure at the RAF station, the going was nearly perfect. John Hillaby had long since abandoned the coast in favour of an inland route over Dartmoor, and Hamish Brown, travelling north to south, opted to cut the corner from Clovelly to Morwenstow. I am glad that I persevered with this part of the coast path because in retrospect I think it was one of the best.

I had lunch overlooking Shipload Bay, the only sandy beach along this stretch of coast and, from my splendid viewpoint a hundred feet above, watched a photographer down on the beach playing a bizarre game with his tripod and the incoming tide. The rules appeared to be loaded in favour of the sea. Stick the tripod in the sand, move away to compose the shot and then dash back to remove the apparatus before the water grabbed its legs. It all seemed absolutely Canute-like in its futility.

As I idly sat and watched the world not go by, I tried to recall all the places I'd been through so far and was surprised to find that many of them were already becoming dim memories. In something of a panic I started to mutter to myself the names of the villages I'd visited and the other important features I'd seen. 'Land's End, Sennen Cove, Cape Cornwall, Pendeen Watch,' I went. 'Gurnard's Head, Treen, Zennor Head…' I found that this actually helped pull things back into order from the jumble that it was all becoming; I was almost paranoid about forgetting places and therefore the events associated with them, so I found this banal mantra of place names very comforting. Now I'd discovered this new game I would not let it go and it stayed with me for the rest of the walk; I eventually became oblivious to the funny looks I got from people as I chuntered on through my ever-growing list of increasingly distant places.

Almost imperceptibly the character of the walking changed as the path headed eastwards. The countryside becomes less wild, and rough grazing and sheep give way to pastures and herds of cattle. A succession of big wooden stiles have to be crossed and, at times, the track is on the landward side of the clifftop hedgerows so that I had to walk through the same fields the cattle were in. I don't know about you, but I find young male cattle very troublesome to deal with; their mums are OK, and I have no problem with their sisters. But these swaggering yobs were a frequent nuisance: 'The Boys' as I came to know them. Fuelled by testosterone and pure malice, they would trundle over to where I was walking and try to pick a fight. Sometimes I attempted to sneak through gates or tip-toe over stiles in the hope that they wouldn't see or hear me but this subterfuge was usually futile.

I can't remember being this apprehensive about any group of living things since the days of the Teddy Boys when I was a lad. There we were, playing football in the park, a bunch of harmless eight- or nine-year olds, when the Teds would arrive in their drainies and drape jackets. Anybody who can remember Teds will also remember the way they walked – a peculiar leaning-back waddle, which would have been funny if they hadn't been big and hard and out to cause trouble. Well, that's exactly what The Boys are like. Sometimes, you just have to tough it out with them and, like most bullies, they back off, but on other occasions there's a ring-leader determined to make your life a misery. I have never regarded myself as frightened of animals but The Boys' problem is definitely getting worse, and it's not just me. A walker – a local man – was attacked by a gang of them on the Dales Way at Windermere just after I finished this walk and was left injured whilst they all went off laughing, presumably in search of some cinema seats to tear up. One of the great things about the Cornish coast is that, in general, the path is too exposed and rough for cattle, so these Boys in Devon were the first I had come across. Although they did not actually threaten me with flick-knives, they were quite plainly not keen on my presence and wandered along menacingly behind me to make sure I got through their fields pretty smartly.

I walked on past a small memorial to the crew of a Wellington bomber which had crashed on these cliffs in 1942 and then, after crossing the stream at Mouth Mill, I entered the Clovelly Estate. For the first time since leaving Land's End, I was in formal woodland complete with summer houses and follies such as the elaborately carved Angels' Wings. Having passed Clovelly Church, where Charles (*Water Babies* and *Westward Ho!*) Kingsley's father was rector, I found my digs in Higher Clovelly, on the main road a mile or so above the famous village.

To get to the pub for my evening meal I had to wander down the whole length of the steep, cobbled street of this unique place. Clovelly has a horrible reputation as a tourist trap but, on this Monday evening with darkness just about to set in, there were very few people about. The little cottages are built right up to the edge of the street and the residents must get heartily sick of visitors like me staring in the windows as they walk past.

The pub was full of Popeye types – gravel-voiced individuals with huge tattooed forearms and speaking authentic seafarers' gibberish ... and the men were no better either. The atmosphere had a slightly menacing air about it in a nautical sort of way and I had my food and vanished into the night before I was press-ganged onto a man o' war and sent off to the Spanish Main.

I had been the only guest at the B&B when I arrived back from the pub but, by breakfast, three young Australian women of almost stunning beauty were there as well. From their conversation it sounded as if they were 'doing England' – like I was, I suppose, only a bit faster. They were going to see Clovelly today and then go on to Bath. I marvelled at their confidence and have to confess to envying them their money.

'Where for Easter, Natalie?'

'Oh, Egypt I think, then the U.S.'

Not bad, eh?

The lady who ran the B&B was everybody's idea of what a West Country landlady should be, so much so that the Australians took a photograph of her. Rosy-cheeked and cheerful with a repertoire of clucks and coos and an accent like clotted cream, years of experience had given her that peculiar ability – shared only by doctors, in my experience – to ask a question and then answer it herself.

'Have you got faarr to go, moy dearr? Yes, I expect so. Another cup of tea? Thaat's roight, then. It's been noice meeting you, do come again.'

And before I knew what was happening I found we'd all been neatly shepherded off the premises and left blinking in the sunlight outside.

The day's walk started with an almost level tramp through some splendid woodland along the Hobby Drive which was constructed to provide work for unemployed fishermen and French prisoners during the Napoleonic Wars. It is so named because it was built as the hobby of Sir James Hamlyn Williams. This sounds so unlikely it must be true. He'd have been great on Blind Date wouldn't he?

'An' I believe you have an unusual hobby, Sir James?'

'Yeah, that's right, Cilla. I build roads with French prisoners.'

'Well, you must have a lorra lorra laughs. That's our James from Clovelly.'

The Hobby Drive was devoid of any other human life but the woods were home to dozens of pheasants, alarmed at my approach. The excellent track took me to Buck's Mills, a sort of wannabe mini-Clovelly strung out along a steep lane going down to the sea. From here to Bideford, the South West Way follows the coast east and then northwards to Westward Ho! before heading south again along the Torridge estuary. (There is a shortcut option of using the ferry from Appledore to Instow, but you will not be amazed to learn that it was not available to me as it does not operate until May.)

I really did want to see Westward Ho! Anywhere named after a novel and with an exclamation mark in its name can't be all bad, but I also wanted to get beyond Bideford before nightfall so reluctantly decided to give it a miss. I cut inland at Buck's Mills, crossed the ghastly A39 main road at Horns Cross and headed off along narrow twisting lanes towards Bideford. There is a marvellous church tower just east of Horns Cross with apparently no village for it to belong to. A tiny cluster of buildings marked as Alwington on my map appears to be far too small a community to justify such an imposing edifice, although the same is probably true of the better known church at Stoke, near Hartland. It must have been a feature of life around here to build massively impressive churches. Primroses and daffodils grew on the banks of these little lanes and it was strange to think that, even in this spring weather, the daffodils here were only at about the same stage in their growth as the ones on the shore at Sennen Cove had been more than ten days ago.

    I liked Bideford instantly. The biscuit-coloured brick that most of the town was made from looked warm and welcoming. Just behind the church was a building with a facade constructed from quite unusually decorative bricks and there were lots of interesting little nooks and crannies. It was becoming clear to me that I could not possibly get the maximum benefit from this walk. There just wouldn't be the time. How could I see all I wanted to see, yet still maintain a reasonable average mileage every day? The answer, of course, is that I couldn't. So, nearly every time I left a town or village, I did so with the slightly uneasy feeling that I should have stayed longer. This happened in Bideford where, amongst other things, I saw signs to the Pannier Market. Its Charter was granted by Henry III in 1272 and, according to the leaflet extolling its virtues, it now sells 'Everything from Antiques to Aromatherapy!' This is fine if you want to buy an anvil, or apples or an armadillo, but completely hopeless if it's sealing-wax or treacle you're after.

I crossed the medieval Long Bridge to pick up the Tarka Trail which coincides with the South West Way from here to Barnstaple and makes use of a disused railway line. The old Bideford railway station has been pleasantly renovated and made a good place to stop and have a snack. It is about twelve miles along this track to Barnstaple and it's as level as makes no difference so I thought I could make it by dark, especially since I appeared to have found what John Hillaby calls the 'supercharger'. This, he says, is where you can maintain normal cruising speed without effort and still have something in reserve. After eleven days on the road, and now that the difficulties with the feet had been resolved, walking had become easy, even with the weight of the rucksack.

'Pride goeth before destruction, and an haughty spirit before a fall,' says the Good Book – and quite right too. It was on this stretch that I first noticed a twinge in my left shin just above the ankle. Thinking it was nothing and would pass, I carried on walking at the fair old lick I'd adopted. The house and garden of Tapeley Park were a blur as I shot past, caring little that it is owned by the Christie family who founded Glyndebourne in 1931 – and then presumably gave the world Julie, star of *A for Andromeda* and *Don't Look Now*, and Lou who brought even greater glory to his forebears by taking *I'm Gonna Make You Mine* to number 2 in the charts of 1969. On through Instow, where I saw the first ice-cream van of the trip, and then along a drab section past the old Yelland power station and the Isley Marsh Nature Reserve with its double line of electricity poles. An air of slight desperation had crept upon me as I realised I still had some way to go, and the uninspiring surroundings did not help. The shore was now mud and where the power station used to stand was a gravel wasteland awaiting re-development. Helicopters were going about their noisy business from Fremington Camp and the traffic on the A39 was close enough to be seen and heard.

Once over Fremington Quay things improved. I caught my first sight of Barnstaple and, from this distance seen through the evening haze, it looked like somewhere on the Adriatic coast. I know this sounds fanciful, but it did. Honest. The marshes on my left were now grassy rather than muddy and were the home of thousands of wading birds and Canada geese and mallards. There were some stately white birds standing in the pools and the only ones I could see in my bird book that looked anything like them were spoonbills but I wasn't near enough to see them properly. They were probably herons.

I've always been amazed by the vast knowledge of the countryside travel writers seem to have. You know the sort of thing: 'I walked through an avenue of poplars and listened to the cree-cree of a lesser-spotted warbler nesting in the purple ragwort. Bluebells danced in the breeze and sticklebacks lazily fed off passing dragonflies.' I thought that by doing this walk information like this would become mine, but I never considered how this process was going to take place. If I didn't know a hen harrier from a hole in the road before I set out, what made me think I'd know now? Anyway, big white birds which weren't seagulls or swans. That'll have to do. Sorry.

The town centre of Barnstaple was reached by crossing another Long Bridge – over the Taw this time – and I got to my lodgings after dark and very tired. Barnstaple is the capital of North Devon, one of its main industries being the collection of gravel from the shallow waters of the estuary opposite Appledore. I don't know what the gravel is then used for – scattering on school playgrounds across the country so that when children fall over it really hurts, I suppose. I often wondered where it all came from. I had seen Barnstaple described in less than glowing terms but I thought it looked thriving and there was an optimistic air about the place. John Gay, author of *The Beggar's Opera*, went to school here but now much is made of the area's association with Henry Williamson and Tarka. I celebrated my arrival at this metropolis by treating myself to my first Indian meal since I'd set off. Chicken Tarka I had – it's like a vindaloo but a little otter. One little known fact about Barnstaple is that the health centre there used to have a sign reading 'Family Planning. Please use rear entrance.' I don't know about you, but I think that's rather splendid.

I spent a pleasant evening at the hotel talking to Elaine, the new owner, about this and that and listened while she told me about her previous career as a secretary to a Formula 1 motor racing team. It was meeting people like this, who had made significant changes to their lives and appeared to be all the better for it, which sometimes kept me on the rails, because there were times on my walk when the future looked a bleak and scary place.

On Mud, Mist and Minehead – Exmoor to the Quantocks

Culbone Church

From Barnstaple the coast swings out westward again to Croyde, a detour which I considered to be not worth the effort, so I decided to cut the corner by heading roughly north-east across the edge of Exmoor to rejoin the coast somewhere near Lynton. It was dull and damp as I left Barnstaple by way of the pleasant Pilton High Street but the bridleway I had decided to use along the Yeo valley turned out to be so disgustingly muddy that it was barely usable. However, rather this than the appalling main road, so I persevered to make painfully slow progress by slithering and squelching through one of Britain's Great Quagmires. Occasional relief was to be had by climbing out of the sunken track on to the earth embankment but this was so overgrown with a particularly vicious type of bramble that the only reason for doing so was just to suffer a different kind of torture. Eventually the track deposited me, looking like a non-kitted-out competitor in a bog-snorkelling championship, onto a tarmac road which was nice and dry but horribly busy for a mile or so, until I turned off for Loxhore and Wistlandpound.

As I climbed the steadily rising lane, the grey drizzle became a thicker and thicker mist until everything was blanketed in an eerie white silence. I could hear the occasional bird, and sometimes a sheep, but nothing else. There was a dead cat in the road and I would not have been remotely surprised to have come across a gibbet. This was definitely 'We don't get many strangers round these parts' country. The picnic area at Wistlandpound Reservoir made a convenient stopping point but it was deserted and gloomy, and through the murk it was impossible to see where the water ended and the sky began. The sense of isolation and loneliness was heightened by the plaintive quacking of a solitary and unseen duck which sounded to me very like mocking laughter. It was good to get moving again and to leave the road for a short stretch across Rowley Down on Exmoor where I crossed a 1,000 foot contour for the first time on my journey. I arrived at the Fox and Goose in Parracombe earlier than I had anticipated and had a long wait until I could eat and drink at seven o'clock.

Until about a quarter past the pub was empty apart from me, the landlady and a young lad playing solo darts. Then, all hell broke loose. It was Lynton and District Ladies' Darts League Individual Finals – and it was Parracombe's turn to host this prestigious annual event. Anybody who has ever witnessed a Ladies' Darts evening will know what they entail but, because this involved participants from every team in the league, it was even busier and livelier than usual. After the quiet, restrained evenings I had become used to, this came as a shock to the system. The effect of all these darts players and spectators and supporters was extraordinary – almost like a physical blow. I went to bed with my head reeling from the excitement – nothing to do with the unseemly amount of beer I had consumed you understand.

Jean, the landlady, told me the following morning about the problems a village like Parracombe had to face. Being in a National Park, it was subject to rigid planning constraints, it had limited employment opportunities for its residents and was in danger of being overrun with tourists in the summer. A familiar tale which I am sure you could hear repeated from any number of places in any of our rural areas. So far, the village looks to have fared very well. It still has a shop and post office and a thriving school but the big fears now are whether houses which come on to the market will be bought to be lived in or used as holiday homes because, if the latter, that will surely sign the death warrant for the village as a viable community. Just ask people in certain places in the Lake District.

From Parracombe I headed north into the Heddon valley, a picturesque area of tumbling streams in a wooded gorge, and dry stone walls reminiscent of those back home. A walk along narrow winding lanes through the splendidly named Kittitoe and Mannacott brought me to Martinhoe with its eleventh-century church, but not before I had caught sight of the sea, and beyond that, Wales! This was an exciting moment. Despite the good weather I'd had along the coast so far it had been hazy, so this first, distant glimpse of a land I knew I should soon be walking through was a Big Event.

Suitably fired up, I descended through an area of gorse and spiky woodland to Woody Bay, so called because there is a bay and it's woody. The locals never tired of telling me that Elkie Brooks lives here. I don't blame her, it's very nice. By the time I was passing high above Lee Abbey, about to descend to the Valley of Rocks, the soreness above my left ankle, which I first encountered on my walk towards Barnstaple, had returned, and I limped down the slope to watch a large collection of randy feral goats desperately intent on doing what randy goats do. Castle Rock, rearing almost vertically 800 feet from the sea was impressive, as was the paved and deceptively genteel sounding North Walk leading to Lynton.

Built on a clifftop, Lynton is another unassuming place, with a welcoming feel to it. After Poldark and Tarka, I was now in Lorna Doone country – and again, it was lost on me I'm afraid. I've never read *Lorna Doone* either. At the bottom of the cliff is Lynton's baby sister, Lynmouth, and the two places are linked by a unique water-operated cliff railway. There are just two cars, joined by a cable, and when one is at the top the other is at the bottom. The one at the top has its tank filled with water, the weight of which makes it heavy enough, as it descends, to pull the lower car up. When it gets to the bottom, the tank is emptied. I wanted to know how the water is transported back to the top car and decided I would treat myself to a journey on this amazing contraption. Guess what? Closed for repairs. So I never did discover the secret. I decided, after much thought, that there must be another railway nearby, electrically operated and buried underground to make it invisible to the eyes of prying tourists. At the dead of night, when electricity is cheaper, this railway which was constructed solely for this purpose, is put into operation and carries all the water back to the top of the cliff.

To my surprise the Youth Hostel at Lynton was almost full. There was an Australian family staying there, a couple of Americans studying veterinary science in London, and a clutch of Duke of Edinburgh youngsters who were going to be camping on Exmoor for the weekend. Their supervisors were friendly, hearty people who showed obvious concern about my leg injury which had worsened to the extent that I was now walking with an L-I-M-P, pronounced limp. One suggestion was that it was tendonitis, a form of repetitive strain injury. If so, this was bad news as the only cure is rest, apparently.

This was my first stay in a Youth Hostel since I was a teenager and I was vastly impressed. It was clean and cheerful and welcoming. Sue, the warden, told me how much she enjoyed the job of looking after the place but it looked like a lot of hard work to me — cooking, doing the laundry, taking bookings and so on — and I was glad to be off in the morning just in case I started to feel guilty and offered to help out.

A blue sky and a strong cold wind greeted me as I walked

down the steep hill to Lynmouth, the most picture-postcardy place I'd seen since Clovelly. The harbour walls are built from thin pieces of stone placed vertically, an unusual arrangement which I had also noticed near Parracombe. Although it has an almost timeless look about it, Lynmouth was virtually completely rebuilt after the horrific flooding of August 1952 when nine inches of rain fell in twenty-four hours on the already sodden moorland above the village. As one person described it, the ground just exploded, and the waters of the East and West Lyn swept trees, buildings and people into the sea. Thirty-four folk died in the disaster and four of the bodies were never recovered. Although it happened all those years ago, it is what Lynmouth is famous for to people of my generation and it brings home to you just how fragile we are.

On this pleasant spring day, though, I was in more danger from the drivers on the A39 – yet again – as it climbs out of the town. The coast path here has to share the road for a short while and it is not at all agreeable. Soon, however, the track branches off to cling to the clifftops for some wonderfully invigorating walking across the headland of The Foreland. I left the path to climb to the trig point at the top of the slope and had trouble regaining it through a sea of thick, ankle-wrenching heather. The traverse through the gorse high above the shining sea made for stunning walking. This is where 'Exmoor Meets the Sea' and there is a feeling of airiness which I had missed over the last few days. The cliffs are high but not terrifying and the going is generally easy.

All too soon I entered the woods of Glenthorne, Embelle and

Yenworthy which are impressive admittedly, but after a while I wanted a change from the restricted views they offered. For mile after mile little changed and I saw absolutely no-one. A spring called Sister's Well offered some relief from the monotony, as did a National Trail Registration Point nearby. This is a wooden box where walkers on the coast path are encouraged to write down their comments on the forms provided and leave them in the box. There were no forms though, so people had taken to scrawling on the box itself. One comment said 'Hills too steep for children', to which someone had replied with rapier wit: 'Leave the fuckers at home then'.

Somewhere here I crossed into Somerset. After ages spent in Cornwall, Devon seemed to have slipped by pretty quickly. Keats called Devon a 'splashy, rainy, misty, snowy, foggy, haily, floody, muddy, slipshod County'. Well, I would maybe agree with the 'muddy' but I think it was the pleasantest of places. There had been several recent landslips along the path here – you could almost see geology happening before your very eyes along this coast – and one of the resulting diversions took me very close to a family of deer, another bit of great excitement to a townie like me. Culbone Church was a surprise. I knew it was on the path and had read it was the smallest complete parish church in England, but I was not prepared for just how small it is. Nestling in a sunlit glade, it made an obvious stopping point and I was disappointed that it appeared to be locked. Nearly all the gravestones in the little churchyard bear the name 'Red' and I was later told that there used to be a leper colony here.

An odd walk through the almost surreal tunnels and grottoes of Lord Lovelace's estate took me to Porlock Weir but, with my leg now sore again and swollen, I had to go on to Porlock itself before I found lodgings. It was a man from Porlock who disturbed Coleridge as he was writing *Kubla Khan* but no-one bothered me as I was writing up my notes in my lonely garret that evening.

Past the ochre-coloured thatched cottages in the olde worlde hamlet of Bossington, the path goes out to the coast again and then follows a steady thousand foot climb to Selworthy Beacon. Unfortunately the mist had descended and there were no views to be had. However, this was as close to 'proper' fell-walking as I'd come on the trip so far. I felt as though I was up on a hill and was reminded of the fells back home, a feeling given added piquancy when I heard a skylark – my first of the year. I know what I said before about my woeful and shameful ignorance of the natural world but even I can recognise the wonderfully mellow song of the skylark as it flies high in the sky. To anybody who has walked on the grassy hills of the eastern Lake District, the sound is evocative and absolutely unmistakable. So there. Or maybe it was a meadow pipit.

It was a steep descent to Minehead where the South West Coast Path officially ends (or begins). A wooden sign rather inconspicuously placed against a house wall says it is 613 miles to Lyme Regis but does not give the distance to Land's End. I reckoned I had come about 215 miles, about one-sixth of the total distance I thought I had to cover. I had been following the coast path – more or less – since I set out fifteen days ago, and it was with mixed feelings that I embarked on a new stage of the journey. Obviously relieved that I had come this far but sad that I was leaving what I regarded as the real coast for the last time until the north of Scotland.

Walking into Minehead was a new kind of experience. It was Saturday lunchtime and the town was busy with residents, holidaymakers and, above all, crowds of Welsh youths in red rugby shirts. They were on tour apparently, and were due to play a match in the afternoon. As far as I know Rugby Union is a fifteen-a-side game, so either this lot had come down with at least eight teams, or they'd all brought their mates along. They had also brought their mums and sisters and grannies and cousins – not many dads that I could see – and they were all wearing the same red jerseys.

Most of the likely looking eating establishments were full, as were the pavements and roads. I certainly hadn't expected this horror. It was like Oxford Street just before Christmas. As well as feeling hemmed in and claustrophobic, I also felt somewhat overdressed with my boots and rucksack. I should have expected Minehead to be like this because I had seen it described as 'bustling', which is often brochure-ese for 'overrun with people'. If a place is even worse than bustling, it's called 'vibrant'. Well, Minehead was vibrant, with knobs on. Still, it was all perfectly good-natured, and I eventually managed to find a fish and chip shop with a place to sit and some plaice to eat.

The railway station here though is a delight, and a must for steam railway buffs. The West Somerset Railway runs steam trains to Bishops Lydeard from where a bus will take you the few miles to Taunton. I shambled round the station for a few minutes watching small boys aged forty-odd shovel coal and pour oil and scrub metalwork and sell tickets. Some of the staff are volunteers who cheerfully give up their weekends to do tasks they would run a mile from at home – sweeping up, cleaning lavatories and being polite to children. I spoke to one volunteer in the pub that night and he told me he was quite happy just to come down and do anything that was required. I don't think many of them graduate to the important jobs like fireman or driver. Even on this cool, blustery day in mid-March, business seemed brisk and it was good to see so many noble steam locomotives being well cared for and put to good use. Diesel and electric locomotives may well be more efficient, but you'd have to be a real killjoy to resist the nostalgic pull of an old-fashioned steam train. The smell of the smoke wafted me back down the years to a time when I thought nothing of waiting for hours on a draughty platform just to catch a glimpse of a train. Mind you, there are people who do that now – wait for hours on draughty platforms, that is. Commuters, they're called.

Sticking with the coast for as long as possible, I left Minehead along The Strand and walked past the garish collection of amusements known as Somerwest World. The unsubtle primary colours of the Big Wheel and the perimeter fencing did nothing to relieve the greyness of the day; indeed, the fact that much of the place needed a lick of paint only underlined the bleakness that had been carried in on a strong, rain-flecked westerly wind. I think

Butlins run Somerwest World and the adjoining holiday camp, and it was with some amazement that I recalled a family I'd met at Porlock who told me that they had been to Butlins forty-six times in the last year. Not necessarily this one, you understand. Just any Butlins. But think about it – forty-six times! It's scarcely physically possible, is it? Perhaps there's an award for Services to the British Holiday Industry. If there isn't, there should be.

A rather squalid footpath makes an inauspicious, snivelling departure from the road down by the side of the golf clubhouse, but things improve again with an open walk along the shingle of Warren Point. According to the OS map, the beach here is called Madbrain Sands, another for my growing collection of magnificent place names. If ever you're on a walk and things get boring, just look at the map and amuse yourself by trying to find the strangest name you can. It's something to do while you eat your sandwiches.

A quietly rural walk took me across the railway to the backwater of Marsh Street and on to Dunster which must be one of England's great villages. Dominated by its castle built high up on an isolated wooded hill, Dunster is an apparently haphazard collection of old cottages and interesting buildings such as the Tudor Yarn Market. This is a roughly hexagonal affair with a gabled roof supported on wooden pillars, and it is where the local cloth – amazingly enough, called Dunster – was bought and sold. I don't know what this cloth was like but just consider the accidents of history and the train of events which made the local cloth from Nimes, in France, so famous. If things had been otherwise, we might now be wearing

Dunster jeans and jackets, and not denim. The village would be internationally famous and would no doubt boast a theme park or two. As it is, the place is busy enough, as evidenced by the large car park and the Exmoor Tourist Information Centre.

With my leg now painful again, I rather stupidly followed my old friend, the A39, for a mile or so to Carhampton, a village which was no doubt peaceful once upon a time but is now sliced in two by the horrible and invasive road. By crossing Ker Moor, I reached the shore again at the enticingly-named Blue Anchor but, after the wild and spectacular scenery of the South West Coast Path, it was difficult to feel much affection for this place. Maybe the scowling grey weather did not help, but the collection of shabby huts and unattractive caravan sites looking out across a road, a concrete foreshore and then dark mud did nothing to cheer me up as I hobbled along. To add insult to injury, part of the coast path had been closed due to landslip and I was forced to use yet more busy road. Just as I was beginning to feel that this was a hopeless sort of place altogether, I cut back through woodland to a low cliff top path and saw a fox. It was quite unimpressed by my presence. I'm not even sure it saw me, as it walked sedately across the meadow into the shelter of the trees.

I had to negotiate my way through more caravans to drop frustratingly down to the Washford Valley and the railway once more. With impeccable timing, I just missed seeing one of the steam trains – I heard it and I saw the smoke, but that's all. The height just lost had to be regained by climbing up to St Decuman's

Church on the edge of Watchet. Now St Decuman was something else: he made St Piran and St Ia – remember them? – look like beginners. He came over from Wales as a missionary and was beheaded by a pagan for his trouble. Most people, I suspect, would have become discouraged and given up at such a turn of events, but not St Decuman. Undaunted by this minor setback, he retrieved his head and carried it to a well where he dunked it in the water and was then able to fix it back on to his neck. The holy well is still there for all to see and, had I not been quite so done in by then, I would have gone into the church. I did not visit nearby Watchet either, despite its being the place that inspired Coleridge to write *The Rime of the Ancient Mariner*. Watchet, of course, is twinned with Oraisle (France) and Smashyafaysin (Ukraine).

It was with great relief that I finally hobbled into my digs at Williton. I felt refreshed after a shower and a meal but unfortunately my leg was no better and I was forced to take the advice of an ex-runner I got talking to in the bar. Rest it, he said. So I did. There was no way I could have walked on it the following day and I had a frustrating time reading the Sunday paper. I couldn't help feel it was a day wasted but was convinced that I would be on the road again on Monday. Disaster! Although I set off, I managed only about a hundred yards before grinding to a halt. The day's rest had apparently done no good. My leg, a few inches above the ankle, was very swollen and very painful. It was the act of putting my left foot on the ground and lifting it again that was causing me so much trouble and, since I had to do this rather a lot, it was impossible to carry on. Feeling very sorry for myself, I caught a crowded bus to Taunton and then a train to stay with Dee's mum in Wiltshire. Desperate to find a cure for the ailment, I went to the casualty department of the local hospital.

'My leg's all swollen. What can it be?' I asked the doctor.

'You've got a swollen leg,' came the answer.

Encouraged by this dazzling display of knowledge and patient care, I had four days doing not very much apart from changing the ice pack on my leg every few hours. At least I was well looked after and I caught up with all my washing and minor repairs. I also had the chance to reflect on how foolish I had been. All the books I'd read and all the people I'd spoken to had warned about taking regular rest days. It's obvious really. You can't expect to just set off and walk for mile after mile, hour after hour, day after day without giving your body a chance to adjust to the new regime. I suppose it's a bit like running in a new car engine, and my foolishness was threatening the success of the entire project.

On the Road Again –
Over the Quantocks and Sedgemoor

Bicknoller Post, Quantock Hills

Suitably abashed, and with all my clothes smelling a little sweeter, I arrived back at Williton ready for the crossing of the Quantock Hills. More spring sunshine welcomed me as I made my way through the very English countryside around Sampford Brett towards the miniature mountain range of the Quantocks. Not that they are mountains really – they are too grassy and rolling and their highest point is not 1,300 feet above the sea – but they do form such a definite ridge, and there is a distinct mountain country feel about the approach to them. Dunkery Beacon on neighbouring Exmoor is considerably higher, but Exmoor is more of a sprawling high landmass. The Quantocks are neater and more abrupt, and I found the climb up Weacombe Hill quite stiff. An enjoyable, springy walk along what Wordsworth called 'smooth Quantock's airy ridges' took me past a group of Duke of

Edinburgh Award lads to the trig point on Black Hill. There followed a short descent and more easy walking by some fine beech trees to the Triscombe Stone which is said to be a 'wishing stone'. I do not know what a wishing stone is but presumably it has some sort of supernatural power to grant your wish if you touch it or sit on it or something. I should have tried it because my leg was already starting to hurt again. The views from the top of Will's Neck – at 1,260 feet, the summit of the Quantocks – were superb. I could see much of Somerset, from Exmoor and the Brendon Hills right round to Hinkley Point power station on the coast and the line of the next day's walk across the Somerset Levels.

The short cropped turf and dark brown heather of the immediate surroundings, and the bracken and very woolly sheep I had seen earlier on the crest of the hills, along with the keen wind that was blowing, strengthened the impression of being high above the world and all would have been very well if it had not been for the recurrence of my injury. To get a nasty pain in the Quantocks is no laughing matter – it's a bit like being shot in the Trossachs but lower down. In a fit of pique, I took off my boots and walked down to Hawkridge Reservoir in trainers. I don't think it helped but at least I felt I had done something positive.

This area around Aisholt and Nether Stowey is very much Coleridge country and he wrote some of his greatest hits here. He was also visited by his mate, Wordsworth, and the two of them would wander off and compose stuff, little knowing that nearly two centuries later, teenagers throughout the land would have to commit half of it to memory. This is not the last time on the walk that we'll tread the same ground as these two fellows – they'll crop up again in the Wye Valley and the Lake District and Scotland. There's no denying they had taste when it came to landscapes. Wordsworth, in fact, was one of the world's great walkers. De Quincey, that well-known opium eater – and not so well-known former editor of *The Westmorland Gazette* – calculated that, by the age of sixty-five, Wordsworth had walked about 180,000 miles. How he did this calculation and, indeed, why he would want to is not recorded. Maybe he'd been to see the Reverend Hawker in that little hut at Morwenstow to share a pipe of something exotic.

It was road walking for the few remaining miles to an excellent farmhouse B&B near Bridgwater and, although I was enjoying the break from the switchback nature of the coast path, the surroundings were a little uninspiring and there was a lot of traffic about. I had seen signs warning of Migrating Toads back near Hawkridge Reservoir and I wondered how the little fellows would manage trying to cross these busy lanes. Unless, of course, the notices had been put up to alert passing pedestrians and motorists to the dangers of giant toad mutations who terrorised the neighbourhood on their way to and from their breeding grounds in the outfall from the nuclear power station at Hinkley Point.

A spectacular sunset, which lit up the underside of the clouds with vivid pinks and golds, promised good weather for the next day and so it proved. Clear and bright but cool enough to be pleasant for travel, it was the sort of day to beckon a walker onwards. Like

Bideford and Barnstaple – and everywhere else beginning with a 'B' – Bridgwater looked interesting but, coming so soon after my enforced break, I felt that I could not afford to devote the time to it I would have liked. These are the sort of towns that would have made ideal places for a rest day if I'd planned the thing properly instead of going off like a bull at a gate. Still, there we are.

It was market day in Bridgwater, and a fruit and veg stall had been set up in front of the statue of one of the town's most famous sons, Admiral Blake, born here four hundred years ago. Blake was one of Cromwell's hard men who went off and beat the Dutch and Spaniards in one of our early periods of wanting to rule the world, and behind the statue is the slender spire of St Mary's church impressively rising nearly 200 feet above the rooftops.

Bridgwater was the biggest place I had been through so far. There are large areas of modern housing, factories and a mainline railway station, the town having grown up originally as a port on the tidal River Parrett. When I crossed this river though, it was a despondent looking thing of mud-banks, brown water and wrecked supermarket trolleys.

An oddly-vibrating footbridge led me over the M5 motorway and into the farmland of the Somerset Levels. Ever since the planning stages of the walk I had been looking forward to the journey across these flatlands, partly because I thought the lack of gradients would make for rapid progress, but mainly because it would be a journey through a totally unfamiliar landscape. Well, I was right about the second reason, but it was a surprisingly strenuous trek along the banks of the King's Sedgemoor Drain, a canalised continuation of the River Carey. For the dozen or so miles from Bridgwater to Walton Hill near Street, I did not cross a single contour line. Never had I seen land so flat. For mile after mile I had the Drain for company and little else. There were no people and no livestock. In fact, the only moving things I could see were the families of swans and ducks and the occasional heron in the reeds and rushes of the water's edge.

In the distance was the spire of Westonzoyland Church which overlooks the site of the Battle of Sedgemoor, reckoned to be the last 'real' battle fought on English soil. I don't know what a real battle is – is there such a thing as an artificial one? – and I wondered about the Battle of Clifton Moor in Cumbria, since I thought that was England's last. Whatever, the Battle of Sedgemoor seems to have consisted of a few peasants, armed only with pitchforks and who had been persuaded by the Duke of Monmouth to take on the forces of King James II. Trying out a new sweeper system, the peasants were annihilated by the regular army which used a more traditional flat back four. Like all good leaders, Monmouth ran away but was captured and beheaded. The peasants who survived the battle were tried by Judge Jeffreys at the infamous 'Bloody Assizes' in Taunton. One hundred and fifty were executed and more than 800 were sent as punishment to Barbados. I'll repeat that, just in case you weren't paying attention. For being naughty boys, they were sent to Barbados. 'Oh no Judge Jeffreys, don't send me to Barbados.' And this was in a time when the penalty for stealing bread was hanging. Ah, the good old days. All this excitement and bloodshed seemed light years away from the almost total lack of activity here today. On and on I trudged through a strangely tiring countryside of long grass, nettles and dock leaves and innumerable rickety stiles.

For three hours, the most exciting thing that happened was when the Drain took a big left turn, causing all the angles and perspectives to shift slightly. The spiky and rather sinister-looking metal sluice gates which punctuate the flatness from time to time made their own faintly menacing contribution to the strangeness of this area. There is a haunting, peaceful quality to the walking though, and I had my lunch in almost completely undisturbed silence with only skylarks and the very distant rumble of traffic as an accompaniment. All of a sudden there was movement by the water's edge on the muddy bank of a tributary of the main Drain, and a sleek, dark brown animal scuttled along through the reeds. I watched this creature for the minute or so it took to disappear from view and, searching through my incredibly unextensive mental data bank of British mammals, came up with 'otter'. It was too big to be a rat or a vole, but I thought otters were nocturnal. Perhaps something had disturbed it, or perhaps it wasn't an otter at all. Could it have been a mink? Or a stoat? Oh, if only I knew all this stuff.

For ages I had been able to see a white windmill away in the distance on Walton Hill and it was a little soul-destroying to realise how painfully slowly it was getting nearer. Cradle Bridge marks the spot where I left the Drain at last and from where I got my first glimpse of Glastonbury Tor, looking improbably tall and conical from this angle. Now on a tarmac lane, I headed across the gloomy expanse of Butleigh Moor to the foot of Walton Hill, which is one of the Polden Hills, a narrow ridge rising a modest 269 feet above sea level. Such is the effect of the incredible flatness of the Levels, however, that from a distance the hills look as impassable as the north wall of the Eiger. The reality was different, of course. A simple climb took me past that windmill, now sailless and converted into a dwelling, onto the crest of the hill from where the view stretched back across Sedgemoor and ahead to Street and Glastonbury.

Street is the home of C & J Clark, the shoemakers who took over K Shoes in Kendal. There is a footwear museum here now and the town is neat but, despite its bypass, overrun with traffic. A short walk along a very busy main road led to Pomparles Bridge over the River Brue and the final climb of the day on to the aptly named Wearyall Hill. By this time the sun was low in the sky behind me and Glastonbury was bathed in a golden light which, given the town's almost mythical reputation, seemed appropriate somehow.

One of the most famous of all England's small towns, Glastonbury is the legendary last resting place of King Arthur. Centuries ago, when the surrounding land was more prone to flooding, the higher ground the town is built on would have given the appearance of an island – hence the association with Avalon. The Abbey is one of Britain's very earliest Christian sites and is said to have been founded by Joseph of Arimathea. On Wearyall Hill is a Glastonbury Thorn, a thing that flowers at Christmas and which is supposed to have sprouted from Joseph's staff when he struck the ground here. The most striking landmark to the casual observer is the Tor, a great cone visible for miles around. The town itself contains some interesting buildings, and it was busy with locals and visitors and some New Agers. In the late evening there was a slightly threatening feel to the town centre though, and the local paper carried a report that persons unknown had lit a fire in the tower on top of the tor. The heat was so intense that it caused the stone flags to crack and the building had to be closed for repairs. I suppose the morons responsible will be happy when open access to places like this finally becomes a thing of the past.

The walk across Queen's Sedge Moor to Wells was remarkable only for the stench emanating from the ditches along the roadside and the first view of the Mendip Hills and the city of Wells. Even from a distance Wells is dominated by its cathedral, but the first notable building I came to as I approached England's smallest city was the Bishop's Palace with its moat whose swans are supposed to pull the bell rope when they are hungry.

I am no expert on ancient buildings and I would not normally worry unduly if I missed seeing an old church or two but Wells Cathedral is just something else. The sight of the huge West Front stops you in your tracks. It is difficult to comprehend how anything man-made can be so huge and yet so intricate at the same time. Hamish Brown says it is beyond praise so I'll just leave it at that. If you've never seen it, go and have a look. Apart from its cathedral, there is plenty to see in Wells. I was there on market day and it made a relaxing change to have an idle hour or so just wandering around soaking up the atmosphere and the warm sunshine. I even had a cup of tea in an old-fashioned tea shop. I walked along Vicar's Close, reputedly Europe's oldest complete street and, as I was leaving Wells, heard through an opened window the lazy sound of someone practising their piano scales which boosted the already strong sensation that I had been transported back in time.

Gorges and Bridges –
Cheddar, Bristol and the Severn

Clifton Suspension Bridge, Bristol

A walk past a thoroughly modern fence, designed to keep walkers from plunging over the edge of a hugely intrusive quarry, jolted me out of the reverie I'd drifted into and it was a relief to enter the sanctuary of the Ebbor Gorge, which was donated to the National Trust in 1967 and is now a nature reserve. At first, the track is broad and level as it leads into the Reserve and the only excitement to be had was from helping two old ladies get their even older male companion over a gate because he wasn't sufficiently nimble to climb the adjacent stile. They also had with them a small, impossibly fat and equally ancient dog, which waddled along behind them. One of the ladies warned me about the treacherous nature of the terrain I was about to enter but, as it turned out, there was nothing more fearsome than a limestone gorge narrow enough at one point for both walls to be touched at the same time. The path steepened considerably and it was good to be so close to rock again after several days spent walking across the soft underbelly of England's green and pleasant land.

A short ascent took me out of the confines of the gorge and on to the flat windswept fields of the Mendip Hills. Knowing that Bristol and Avonmouth were only a day or two away, it was especially gratifying to discover the feeling of quiet spaciousness this plateau possesses. Yes, it's all farmland so one's freedom to roam at will is limited, but the cooling breeze and the dry stone walls – the first since goodness knows when – lent a distinctly upland quality to the walking. From here to Cheddar, passing through the village of Priddy – with its unusual thatched hurdle shelter on the village green – was all pleasant and undemanding apart from the numerous Mendip stone stiles I had to cross. These consist of big limestone slabs requiring an ungainly scrabbling movement to surmount them – not easy with a big pack.

The one very serious blot on an otherwise good stretch of walking was the recurrence of the leg injury. It was back with a vengeance, and the long descent to the village of Draycott was purgatory. Instead of the easy stroll I had anticipated, I had to try all manner of unnatural walking positions to make any sort of progress at all. The only way I could avoid the excruciating pain was to walk backwards down the slope so that the tendons were not being stretched quite so much. This eased the pain considerably but made navigation somewhat more difficult. I wondered whether anybody had ever completed an entire end to end walk in reverse and decided they probably had – it seems to have been done in just about every format imaginable. I limped into Cheddar very late after a bizarre walk past some ramshackle looking places with corrugated iron roofs and the apparently obligatory scrap cars and barmy dogs chained up in the gardens.

Later, as I was hobbling through the village in search of a pint, a group of youths drove their car through a puddle so that I was splashed with dirty water. The hoots of laughter that followed left me in no doubt that this was done deliberately. Now, I'm not one to bear grudges but, if you're reading this lads, may the fleas of a thousand camels infest your armpits. There is no doubt that that evening in Cheddar was the low point of the whole journey. My leg was painful and had not, it seemed, responded to the rest it had been given a few days before. The pub I was in felt hostile and there was a drunken squabble going on between a persistent man and a woman clearly unimpressed with what was on offer. Despite being famous for its cheese and strawberries, the village appeared more geared to the trinket buying tourist than the hungry one and, had I been in a place where public transport was more readily available, I might well have caught the first bus or train home.

On such chance occurrences, though, are many things decided so, having nothing better to do, I returned to my B&B where I fell into desultory conversation with Anne, the owner. My talents in many directions are extremely limited but one thing I can do very well is whinge. If whingeing ever becomes an Olympic event, I would like it put on record here and now that I offer my services to the British team. I may be too old to take part in the Games themselves but what a coach I'd make. So, I had a good old whinge about my leg and it's just as well I did because it turns out that Anne's mother, who popped in briefly to talk about a dog show or something, and instead had all her planned conversation derailed by this Moaning Minnie in the corner, suffers from some arthritis-type disease and is an expert on Mystery Leg Ailments.

'Just keep changing your footwear,' she said. 'If you were wearing boots today, put your trainers on tomorrow morning. But change back to your boots at lunch time. Don't wear the same footwear all day.'

Well, I don't know how sound or scientific this advice was but she seemed so confident that it would be a success, I went to bed feeling more optimistic than I had done for some time. As I had worn trainers on the walk from Glastonbury to Cheddar, I put the boots back on in the morning. After all, there was to be a serious ascent from the village to the top path along the rim of the Cheddar Gorge. Gingerly I set off up the steep path. Not a twinge.

I reached the edge of the gorge from where there are some alarmingly dizzy views down to the road 400 feet below. Because of the verticality and the strong wind I was briefly reminded of the Cornish coast path. A tall wooden tower on the edge of the cliffs is known as Pavey's Lookout Tower and was apparently built by a local baker who thought he could fly across the gorge. Despite the blustery conditions and the leaden skies, there were good views back to Glastonbury Tor and across the Levels to the distant Quantocks. A brisk march brought me to the end of the walk along the gorge more quickly than I had anticipated and it dawned on me that, for the first time since Bideford twelve days previously, I was having no trouble whatsoever with my leg injury. Not a sign of it – miraculous.

Thanking all the gods I could call to mind, I walked on through Black Rock Nature Reserve and then into the strange, rather forlorn area excitingly known as Velvet Bottom. This is a surprising countryside of old industry where the legacy of the lead mines, worked here for nearly two thousand years, is poisoned land on which little grows, and stock have to be strictly limited in the time they can safely graze. There used to be four artificially created lakes here for filtering the minerals, each at a lower level than the one before. Walking upstream as I was, meant that height was gained in a series of steps, as if on a giant staircase. A little further on are the remains of the stone flues used to smelt the lead, and it did not require a huge leap of the imagination to hear once again the merry chatter of workers being exploited in the name of profit and progress. There are a couple of small reedy pools hereabouts and the mournful sound of the water lapping against the banks added to the general feeling of desolation.

I was glad to escape this odd little spot and reach the windswept top of Beacon Batch, the summit of the Mendips 1,072 feet above the sea. A concrete trig point, a few boulders and a sea of heather told me that here was a real fell top. The views were wide-ranging and it was with some excitement that I saw the two great bridges over the Severn. All being well, I would soon be crossing the easternmost one of these as my way in to Wales.

An easy descent to Blagdon was spoiled by the number of unfriendly-looking, barricaded houses adorned with cheerful notices reading 'No Admittance', 'Dogs Running Loose', and 'Keep Out'. The second one is particularly sinister. What does the postman do? Or the meter reader? Or the poor double-glazing salesman? I mean, we've all got a living to make. It's obvious that these people have made their pile, have spent some of it on a swanky house in commuter land and are desperate to shut themselves off from the uninvited part of the rest of the world. Why? What are they afraid of? Ordinarily, I don't suppose I would have noticed but nearly every property had some warning sign or other. A pity, because Blagdon is nice. It straggles down the hillside towards the lake and, near the village centre, is a shop where I bought a splendid pie from a friendly chap. Village Shop of the Walk Award goes to that one in Blagdon.

On through a typically English countryside of horse riders and hedgerows and the very English villages of Butcombe and Winford, the walk used a combination of muddy bridleways, quiet lanes and footpaths. Unexciting scenery but plenty of exciting decisions to make regarding crossing fields where public footpath signs were missing or damaged and where there were gates which should have opened but didn't. It always adds a frisson to the day if you think you might get challenged or shot at by an irate landowner, especially in an area where people think nothing of telling you they have dogs running loose in their garden. I don't think I've ever knowingly traipsed across private land if there has been an alternative available, but I do start to get annoyed when what is marked as a public footpath on my map and clearly fits in with the detailed description in my guidebook is barricaded with string and barbed wire. Still, no time here to get on my high horse. It only upsets me.

As does the sight of an out of control dog bearing down on me. At least this one at Winford had a human on the end of a lead, so I did not feel completely at risk. Even so, the dog gave a pretty alarming display of ferocious barking which was made to look even more fearsome by its owner's obvious inability to control it. 'No!' he shouted, 'No, Nooo, No!' while the dog ignored him completely, at the same time producing vast quantities of foaming spittle through the growls. 'It's all right, he won't bite,' said Mr Dogwalker. How does he know? It looked to me as if, given half a chance, the animal would have had my arm off.

Saying that your dog won't bite is beaten into second place in the League Table of Fatouous Remarks by Pet Owners only by the brilliant 'He's only playing'. This one is usually reserved for special occasions like when a Rottweiler has just buried its teeth in the back of your leg. Why do people want such terrifying animals as pets? If I had my way, dog owners who can't control their charges, would be made to walk around with some really harmless thing on a lead like a hamster or, better still, something inanimate like a sponge or a bag full of wet sawdust. The whole walk was beginning to degenerate into an obstacle course through dogs and doggy poo.

The twin rewards for the steady pull up to Dundry and its masts are the sudden view of Bristol spread out below you and the sight of the spectacularly intricate gothic tower of Dundry Church. From here Bristol looks impossibly large but at least I could make out quite clearly the Clifton Suspension Bridge under which I would soon be walking. After a pleasant tramp across Highridge Common and through the park of the Malago, there was some very uninspiring walking through more dog crap, empty lager cans and wind-blown crisp packets to cross a graffiti-covered railway bridge which finally led me to the River Avon.

A day spent in Bristol would have given me the chance to see some of the sights of this historic city and provided me with a rest day which, given my new resolve to take a break every few days, was about due. Bristol is famous for its docks, the great church of St Mary Redcliffe, Isambard Kingdom Brunel, *SS Great Britain*, the Clifton Bridge, WD & HO Wills, the University and two under-achieving football clubs – it is supposed to be the largest place in England that has never had a Premiership team. Well, anyway, for various reasons to do with accommodation and my desire to get to Wales before having a day off, I saw very little of the place. It is also true to say that, after more than three weeks in mainly rural surroundings, I did not really relish the prospect of a day in a big city.

Torrential rain accompanied me on my walk out of the metropolis along the banks of the Avon where I got chatting to a woman who had been walking at Hartland Point the previous weekend and whose ambition was to walk the Pennine Way. She was looking for a companion to do the walk with her and I hope she found one. The Clifton Bridge is as awe-inspiring as I imagined it would be. As graceful and elegant a structure as you could wish to see, it spans the Avon gorge nearly 250 feet above the water. Like many high places it has been a magnet for attempted suicides, some of which have failed, none so spectacularly as the young lady a century ago whose petticoats ballooned out like parachutes, causing her to descend slowly and land gracefully and completely uninjured on the muddy riverbank. She went on to live to be eighty-five. Just goes to show. Poor old Brunel died five years before the bridge was completed, but at least he was spared the sight of the graffiti plastered in huge white letters just beneath the bridge on the black rocks of the gorge.

After an hour or so I left the river bank to pass a reservoir, a big house that looked like some corporate HQ with impressive cedars in the grounds and the strangely sad and rather creepy remains of Ham Green Hospital. Some buildings were in a state of almost total collapse and decay, whilst others looked occupied. I saw two people in the gatehouse which made the obvious dereliction in the gardens and service roads seem even stranger. The usual 'Keep Out' signs were given added impetus by the words 'Infected Area'. I did not hang around and sped off to Pill, a strange village clustering around a muddy creek of the Avon. There was a large collection of broken cookers, bent bedsteads and dilapidated settees standing outside one row of houses as I approached the Avonmouth Bridge; the sight was so unexpected that I wondered a few hours later whether I had actually seen this linear scrap heap at all.

When people asked me after the walk what the most memorable parts of the journey were, I did not usually mention crossing the M5 Avonmouth Bridge but I should have. Long after many sections of the journey have faded into a blur, this half hour horror is still vivid in my memory. For anybody unfamiliar with it, the Avonmouth Bridge is a mile-long concrete monster carrying the M5 across the Avon. To my untrained eye, it appears to be of no architectural merit at all. You wouldn't say it was ugly – it's just there: a long, level thing leaping across the river on a few concrete sticks.

The noise from the motorway traffic was incredible. As an old campaigner at Who concerts in the late sixties, I thought I would be immune from anything less than an atomic explosion, but I was wrong. You know when people say they can't hear themselves think, well that's what this was like. Worse than the noise, though, is the movement under your feet. When you drive across it you don't even realise you're on a bridge at all but on foot it's a different story. The whole structure bounces and sways alarmingly. There I was, despite the noise, trying to remain cool and sophisticated several million feet above the river but I simply could not adjust to the sensation of the ground shifting under my feet. You have to try to get the rhythm right, so that your foot hits the ground on the up-bounce. A few strides of this and all is OK, but then another juggernaut would thunder past and alter the rhythm so that you'd miss the beat and hit the ground on the down-bounce. This would cause me to stumble and it provoked an odd feeling, almost like sea-sickness. On top of all this, a contract killer on a moped narrowly missed finishing me off completely. With all the noise I did not hear him as he crept up behind me to go by with only inches to spare.

Having just cheated death on the bridge, it was almost a relief to negotiate the huge roundabouts and main roads that lead to the Avonmouth industrial area which was just noisy and dirty. There was an awful lot of traffic and not much in the way of a pavement. A sign saying 'Welcome to South Gloucestershire' was happily placed at the exact spot where things improved – a sudden and almost total transition from urban excess to rural peace.

The path followed the very edge of the Severn estuary underneath the imposing structure of the second Severn crossing at Severn Beach, once a holiday village but now more intent on reinforcing its sea defences. On I went across a military rifle range and through meadows to the original Severn Bridge near Aust. They say we all have our demons and the Severn Bridge was one of mine; I'd been having panic attacks and sleepless nights about it for days. I had heard about how it sways and bounces, and local people had told me lurid tales of why the second bridge was built.

'It's not safe you know,' they'd said. 'They've found cracks in the concrete and the steel hawsers are perished with the salt in the air. It should really be closed completely.' And so on and so on.

And that's ignoring the terrifying statistics. The two towers are 400 feet high and the total length is well over a mile. It did not help when I learned that a lot of the construction methods employed were considered to be revolutionary at the time. I know it's been there for many years but, as you approach it, you cannot help noticing how frail it looks. It's just a narrow strip of crumbling concrete suspended a couple of hundred feet above the water from a few strands of rusty wire. I know it's pathetic but I wasn't half nervous as I set off along the footway that runs to the side of, and a little below, the road. And it did sway and it did bounce. But, oddly, by the time I had passed the halfway stage, I realised I was actually enjoying this elastic walking. There was none of the noise and menace that the Avonmouth Bridge had thrown at me and the views, both seawards to the Somerset coast and ahead to Wales, were interesting – one full of memories and the other holding out the promise and excitement of lands still to be discovered. What an impressive way to enter a new country. Croeso i Gymru!

CHAPTER THREE – WALES

WITH A LITTLE HELP FROM MY FRIENDS

White Castles and Black Mountains – Chepstow to Hay

The church at Llangattock Llingoed

For years I had been a little bewildered by the cliché of referring to various parts of the world in terms of the size of Wales, as I didn't really know how big Wales was. But I was about to find out as I was going to walk the whole length of the country from bottom to top. While I was doing this I wanted to discover the answers to some of the mysteries associated with this fascinating land of legend and fairytale. Was King Arthur's Merlin really born in Carmarthen? Who were the Druids? Why is the cave in the cliffs below Chepstow Castle said to be the temporary resting place of King Arthur and his knights? Is there any truth in the story of the dog, Gelert? And why do Wales always get ridiculously difficult opponents in the World Cup qualifiers?

For the moment, though, my priority was to get to Chepstow where I was to meet up with friends Adrian and Chrissie. I had been offered the chance to spend a couple of days at their place in Tintern just up the Wye valley, and the prospect of a rest and a couple of days where I could return to convivial company in the evening was too enticing to resist. Chepstow has a long history dating back to Roman times. It owes its growth to being the lowest bridging point on the River Wye and was important as a port right up to the nineteenth century. Where Wells has its cathedral, Chepstow has its castle – a massive structure which dominates the original part of the town and is one of the oldest surviving such buildings in Europe.

In the shadow of the castle is the delicately ornate cast iron road bridge built by Rennie in 1816 to span the Wye. To demonstrate that there was no end to his talents, he then went off and invented the indigestion tablet. In the railings of the parapets of his bridge are the county names of Monmouth and Gloucester and it was strange and rather disappointing to be leaving Wales so soon after arriving. The River Wye at this point was a fearsome thing as its brown swirling waters raced beneath the bridge – it was certainly announcing itself as a river of some importance. Adrian walked with me from Chepstow to Monmouth and I realised that this was the first time I had had a travelling companion since I set off nearly four weeks previously. Most welcome it was too, as we set off in a steady drizzle – 'good wetting stuff' as it's known in the Lakes where people are connoisseurs of that kind of thing.

When I was compiling my mental list of Things Not To Be Missed on the walk, the Wye Valley was one of the first places to come to mind. The river has carved a deep trench in the limestone plateau of the western part of the Forest of Dean, producing a spectacular landscape of tall, steep and copiously wooded cliffs. John Hillaby had called the Forest of Dean 'the most beautiful assembly of trees in Britain' and that was good enough for me, even though I was to cross its edge only.

As an added bonus, there was the prospect of walking along the Offa's Dyke Path. This was opened as a National Trail back in 1971, so there would be the old acorn waymarks again, not seen since the South West Coast Path. The ODP is one of the few such trails not to follow a natural geographical feature. Instead, it is based on a man-made one – the ancient earthwork of Offa's Dyke. Although the path does not follow the Dyke throughout its length, it does so for much of the stretch just north of Chepstow, and an impressive construction it is. Even the most inexpert of people can readily appreciate the scale of the undertaking when you stop to think that the task facing King Offa was to build his Dyke from one end of Wales to the other.

There are still arguments as to whether the work was defensive or just to mark a boundary. Both explanations strike me as a little odd. If you had been asked to mark a boundary you'd use little posts wouldn't you, or something similar – you certainly wouldn't dig a great ditch and throw up a 25-foot high bank on one side of it. On the other hand, if the Dyke is really a defensive earthwork, it's a bit feeble in certain places. I don't think it would have kept out a family on a Sunday afternoon ramble, let alone a marauding army. A third possibility is that it was built by the English as a sort of tangible reminder to the Welsh not to try anything fancy in the way of invading. Will we ever know? The Dyke is thought to date from the late eighth century, and it was with some amazement that I realised I was walking along something constructed over twelve hundred years ago – before the Battle of Hastings, and before the castle at Chepstow was put up, even before the first episode of *Last of the Summer Wine* was screened.

Before we reached the Dyke itself though, there was a short climb to the top of the 200 foot vertical limestone cliff known as Wintour's Leap, so called because a Royalist sympathiser by the name of Sir John Wintour evaded his pursuers by scrambling down the cliff here. These days you're quite likely to see rock climbers but there were none about on this dank and gloomy Wednesday. The river far below looked really impressive as it surged dark and menacing towards the sea, and the great loops it makes as it fights to find a way through the plateau made it easy to see how it got its Roman name of Vaga, the Wanderer.

Somewhere along this stretch, in amongst the trees and the hanging mist, we came across The Man With the Best Job In the World. We've probably all met people from time to time and thought, 'I wouldn't mind doing what they do for a living,' but this chap was the Real McCoy, the cat's pyjamas. He was Dutch and worked for a travel agency over in Holland. It was his lot in life to be sent to various parts of the globe to recce walks and trails that his company were thinking of using for their holidaymakers. He had been given the southern part of the Offa's Dyke Path and the Wye Valley Walk to suss out, and what he had to do was follow the official guidebooks and report back to his bosses on the state of the terrain underfoot, the adequacy of the waymarking, the quality of the recommended accommodation and such like. Can you imagine what this job must be like? No wonder he looked so cheerful when we caught up with him. His English was good enough to understand expressions like 'Meaningful multicultural exchange of topographical data' and 'Lucky bastard' but, as he pointed out, it was a difficult and demanding job that had to be done by somebody. Fleetingly, I contemplated doing him in and assuming his identity but remembered in time that my Dutch was on the sketchy side and that I would probably have had to become a PSV supporter.

We also met an old chap doing what he called his 'avoiding a heart attack walk'. He apparently walks the same stretch every day, rain or shine, to keep things moving and he didn't look a day over sixty. He told us he would soon be celebrating his twenty-eighth birthday and we wished him well as we parted company.

From somewhere near the rocky plinth of the Devil's Pulpit you get your first view, through the trees, of the ruins of Tintern Abbey (oh, yes it is an abbey, I'd like to hear you cry, but you're probably not that juvenile), another astonishing structure but one in desperate need of a roofing job. Whereas the castle at Chepstow impresses by virtue of its solidity and sheer size, Tintern Abbey is like the West Front at Wells Cathedral and Brunel's suspension bridge over the Avon – massive, yes, but so delicately wrought that the effect is one of almost fairytale fragility. Rebuilt in the thirteenth century on the site of an earlier effort built by the Cistercians, the present building can be overrun with tourists and is, perhaps, for that reason best seen from this fine vantage point high up in the woods. The Devil's Pulpit is just another good viewpoint with a bit of rock which has come to be associated with Old Nick – he's supposed to have shouted at the monks or something from here, but wouldn't you have thought he had better things to do? I know they say that the Devil has all the best music, but he's got all the best geographical features as well – there are several Devil's Bridges, there's a Devil's Beeftub, a Devil's Cheesewring and a Devil's Kitchen. That's without thinking too hard about it. I suppose there must be a Devil's Microwave and a Devil's En-suite Master Bedroom somewhere as well.

We descended to river level again at Brockweir. Adrian told me that the Wye is tidal to this point and all this area was, up until a hundred years ago, the scene of intense industrial activity in the form of iron smelting. The ore was mined locally in the Forest of Dean and the swiftly flowing streams on the eastern banks of the river were used to power the mills. The Wye itself was the main transport artery and gangs of men used to pull boats known as trows if the tide was unfavourable. It's such a peaceful spot now that I found it hard to take in that this place was once the Trafford Park of its day.

Up in Highbury Wood we followed a marvellous section of the Dyke – an unmistakable ditch and embankment complete with properly gnarled trees. If the word 'gnarled' had not existed, it would have been necessary to invent it just to describe these trees. Just before the steep descent to Redbrook we had a cracking view up the valley to beyond Monmouth. This was the first long distance view I'd had today and it quickened the pulse to be able to see the country the next day's walking would be leading me through.

Like so many places I had already passed through, Monmouth was dominated by traffic problems but is a town of great charm and interest. The weather had improved as the day progressed and the late afternoon sunshine gave the town a friendly, welcoming feel which Chepstow had lacked in the cold, grey drizzle of the morning. Monmouth is the home of Henry V (I don't know whether it was Part I or Part II) and Charles Rolls, of Rolls-Royce fame. There are statues to both of them in Agincourt Square; I thought it a rather bizarre coincidence that Henry V should have been born in a town with a square bearing the same name as one of his greatest battles.

Just as an aside, Henry V — who was king of England remember — had an army consisting of 'English nobles and yeomen, wild Irish fighters, skilled Welsh archers, German artillery experts, Flemish sappers, Dutch and Portuguese'. Sounds a little like your average Premiership football side. Also in Monmouth is a truly splendid thirteenth century gatehouse — unique in Britain — built on the bridge over the River Monnow, and it was through the archway of this edifice that I left the town to resume my journey north.

At Monmouth, the Offa's Dyke Path parts company with the line of the Dyke itself to head westward towards the Black Mountains. The path took me across some of the pleasantest country I was to meet anywhere on the walk. It is mainly rolling farmland dotted with tiny villages with enormous names such as Llanfihangel Ysturn Llywern, Llantilio Crossenny and Llangattock Lingoed, each with a superb little church and one with a very ancient inn called The Hostry. This was all excellent stuff, almost perfect. The bright, cool weather was ideal, there were newborn lambs, wild flowers were growing everywhere and the countryside, although obviously well-kept, was hillier and a notch or two wilder than the manicured fields of Somerset.

This land of plenty was still able to spring one more surprise though — arrival at the hilltop site of White Castle. This was one of the gems of the whole trip. I had no idea what to expect — the map just says 'White Castle' in Olde English lettering. There was absolutely nobody about so I had the whole place to myself for an hour or more. There are huge walls and a moat and towers you can go to the top of by climbing the stone spiral staircases. I could play King Arthur and his Knights and there was nobody there to stop me. It was brilliant. Rudolf Hess thought so too apparently, because he used to visit it while he was a prisoner at Maindiff Court nearby. I wonder if he played at being King Arthur as well.

The storm clouds were beginning to gather over the increasingly ominous outline of the Black Mountains as I approached my lodgings at Pandy. My landlord there told me that the next day's walk over Hay Bluff would be easy after today's. I found this hard to believe since tomorrow would see me reaching a height of 2,300 feet, by far the loftiest point so far on my journey, but he said that the walk from Monmouth had involved crossing 87 stiles while the next stage was plain sailing once the height had been gained. It was good after passing through so much of lowland Britain to be on the fringe of mountain country again. Gorse was evident once more and there was that raggedy, spiky, almost irascible feel to the landscape which you only get in hilly areas.

I confess to having felt a little apprehensive about the walk along the Hatterrall Hill ridge on to the Black Mountains. After all, the ascent from valley level was almost 2,000 feet and I had found many of the relatively modest climbs of the coast path and the Quantocks pretty hard work. I need not have worried too much though. After a steep start, the way was up a long but very gentle incline which followed almost exactly the border between Wales and England. Beautiful cotton-wool clouds in a bright blue sky gave added depth and colour to an amazingly huge view eastwards over Herefordshire.

As I gained height and passed the second and third trig points on this long ridge, a cold wind grew in strength and I had to keep moving to keep warm. The immediate surroundings were, by now, not inspiring; the ridge becomes broad in the beam and flattens out considerably so the views are restricted to the peat-hagged moorland near to the path. But after so long spent walking at low levels, the sensation of spaciousness was almost palpable and I felt surrounded by sky – this was definitely no place for agoraphobics. Conditions underfoot had deteriorated and the crisp, dry day almost certainly eased the difficulty of crossing this soggy moor. Rather oddly, the high point of the ridge at 2,306 feet has no name, and it's a further three-quarters of a mile to reach the slightly lower top of Hay Bluff (Sunday name, Pen y Beacon) which has another trig point and a height of 2,219 feet. This is a seriously good viewpoint from where I could see the line of the next day's walk heading west along the Wye valley from Hay and, beyond that, there were exciting glimpses of distant purple hills. Further round to the west, and closer at hand, were the scarps of the Brecon Beacons and, nearer still, the jutting noses of the other Black Mountain ridges.

The top of Hay Bluff is a great place to be but I was cold and didn't linger too long. A knee-jarring descent down a gully, or *rhiw* – no, I don't know how to pronounce it either, but I thought the use of a Welsh word casually tossed into the text might lend this section much-needed authenticity and verisimilitude and might even impress you – led to the very busy car park on the Gospel

Pass road. The sight of so many people milling around reminded me that today was Good Friday and, because my night's stop was to be in the holiday town of Hay-on-Wye, I was relieved that I had booked my accommodation in advance. An uneventful, though surprisingly steep, walk across farmland took me to Hay only after I had had a late afternoon siesta in a delightful wooded dell just above the town.

Capital of the second-hand book trade is what Hay is known as. Not a wildly inviting title to confer on a town, especially one as attractive as this. The word Hay is a corruption of the old Norman word 'haie' meaning hedge, the town having grown up in a hedged enclosure in hunting land. Why a French word though? Pretentious, *ou quoi?*

I arrived late in the evening and left early in the morning so did not get the opportunity to venture into any of the dozens of little places selling bargain books of every type and price, but I was able to do some window shopping as I had an evening stroll round the narrow streets of the town centre. The tall clock tower was particularly striking – no pun intended – and there are very similar ones in other towns in mid-Wales. Hay was the scene of many of the jolly struggles which used to take place between the Welsh and English and also witnessed the 'Revolt of the Housewives' in 1795 when, as a protest against the high price of corn, a group of townswomen liberated the contents of a flour wagon and re-distributed it to the poor people of the parish.

Hammer Films, Owls and Red Kites – the Wye Valley to Rhayader

A perfect morning in the Wye Valley near Hay

Perfect weather greeted me as I awoke on Easter Saturday and, as I had a long day ahead of me, I was grateful for this inducement to hit the road early. It was time to leave the Offa's Dyke Path to pick up the Wye Valley Walk and, in so doing, I just missed the village of Clyro, the home of Francis Kilvert who was curate there for seven years from 1865. Kilvert was a young man when he arrived in Clyro and he fell in love with the area and its people. He began to keep a diary in 1870 and the parts that survived were published in the late 1930s. *Kilvert's Diary* is now regarded as a classic and, almost inevitably, the area round here is known as Kilvert Country.

The river scenery for the first couple of miles through Wyecliff Wood and beyond was outstanding. The trees were beginning to show the first signs of spring colours, the meadows were a vivid green and the blue sky was reflected in the still waters of the Wye as they meandered languidly seawards. I reckoned that if you were designing your own ideal piece of British landscape to enter into the World Landscape Championships, you'd have to have this stretch of the River Wye in it. This was another good game – piecing together bits of scenery, as in a gigantic three- dimensional jigsaw, to make the best landscape you could come up with. The coast at Wicca Pool in Cornwall and the River Wye here at Wyecliff Wood were dead certs so far.

My feeling of well-being was disturbed, first by three dogs which ran out of a garden by the footpath, barking ferociously and jumping up at me. I was not remotely amused by this latest example of irresponsible pet ownership – I was on a waymarked public footpath which looked well-used and these dogs would have posed a serious worry to a young person or someone shorter than me. Or perhaps it was just me that provoked this hostile reaction in our canine and bovine friends. John Hillaby reckoned it was something to do with the shape of a man with a rucksack on his back which upset dogs and horses. Maybe he had a point.

A few minutes later I passed a stone with an inscription commemorating some local bloke who 'killed a lot of salmon at this spot'. The use of the word 'killed', although presumably apt, struck me as a little odd. Why did it not say 'caught' instead? Maybe he didn't fish for them at all. Perhaps he shot them, or used a depth charge or passed 5,000 volts through the water. Just after negotiating one of the many stiles hereabouts, and whilst

I was still muttering about the bloody dogs and the man killing the salmon, one of the strap buckles on my rucksack shattered causing the whole load to slew alarmingly to one side. Displaying a resourcefulness I didn't know I possessed, I fashioned a temporary repair by tying a horrible granny knot in the strap.

The pastoral loveliness of this stretch did not last for long and there was a taste of things to come as I crossed the brambly expanse of Brynrhydd Common near Llowes, a village whose church contains a Celtic cross which is supposed to have been thrown over the river by a witch called Maud de Breos after she discovered it in her shoe. A woman with feet this size is obviously not to be trifled with and it will come as no surprise to learn that she also built Hay Castle in a single night. Her flagrant disregard for the Building Regulations and the fact that she could not possibly have let the plaster dry properly before the first coat of emulsion almost certainly explains why the castle is now in ruins.

A level trek through the Norman village of Glasbury and across the impressively long stone bridge at Boughrood brought me to a lengthy stretch of wooded riverbank and then to the forlorn graveyard which marks the site of a private chapel, forming part of the Llangoed Estate. Where the old, leaning gravestones at Morwenstow and Culbone had a pleasant, almost welcoming atmosphere about them, this place was sinister and, although I was pleased that the sun was still shining, nothing could relieve the stifling melancholy hereabouts. This must be the place where all those Hammer films were made – you know, the ones with black-plumed horses pulling ghostly carriages back and forth across the same piece of heathland while a buxom wench from the nearby village walks towards her doom. Why don't they just run when they hear the sound of hooves? They must know it'll all end in tears. Anyway, that's what this place was like. Except, there was no buxom wench, unfortunately – or plumed horses, or a huge camera crew.

The path crosses the river again by way of the splendid Llanstephan suspension bridge, apparently one of the very few wooden-decked suspension bridges left in Wales. As you approach, the bridge looks to be fairly frail and narrow and I was astounded to see a car drive over it. As an experienced survivor of the horrors of the motorway bridges of the Avon and the Severn, this little chap could not scare me but even so, I was glad that I saw the warning notice about maximum weights and speeds only after I'd crossed it.

Easy walking continued to Erwood, an unremarkable place which was, however, the spot where one Henry Mayhew found some respite from the creditors who were pursuing him and whilst having a drink at the Erwood Inn conceived the idea for the satirical magazine, *Punch*. It's amazing when you stop to think about it… all these places in Britain that I'd never previously heard of, and all with some quirky tale to tell. Dentists throughout the land should make a regular pilgrimage to Erwood to honour the man without whom their waiting rooms would have been so much the poorer.

After all the gentle walking I'd done so far today it came as a shock to the system to find I had two stiff climbs onto Twmpath and Little Hill Commons. The country was wilder now with bracken and gorse and tiny newborn lambs, and there was not much in the way of wild flowers. The retrospective views down the Wye valley were superb, but I was disappointed to see how close Hay Bluff and the other Black Mountains still looked. Ahead, there were no towns to be seen and no landmarks to give direction or scale to the seemingly endless hills, through which the valley followed its twisting course. There was yet more climbing onto open hillside near Bedw where I passed some hill ponies which came right up to the field fence to fix me with the sort of penetrating stares normally mustered only by the very hungry.

This was the longest day's walking so far – I reckoned it to be about 22 miles from Hay to Builth Wells – and the going generally gets tougher as the day goes on. The descent to Builth seemed endless and threw a nasty steep uphill in my path long after I thought I'd done enough to earn my night's recuperation. A rest and then a pie and a pint of Albright's in the White Horse improved things, even though the locals were disappointed to see the Welsh football team unsurprisingly losing a World Cup qualifying match they had to win to stay in the competition.

Builth Wells is about the same size as Hay-on-Wye but, despite its rather fancy name with its connotations of Victorian gentility, it is more down to earth and less crowded with sightseers than Hay. The Builth part of the name comes from the Welsh *buellt*, meaning 'cow pasture', and the Wells was added in the eighteenth century when the chalybeate springs began to attract visitors who believed that the waters would cure their ills. Chalybeate is an iron-based mineral and the waters derived from it are supposed to be a defence against anaemia and general debility but 'taking the waters' is an activity that should be supervised. Over a hundred years ago, a local guidebook said, 'Better stay at home than subject one's organisation to the careless use of these waters.'

Whatever else you might think about Builth, there is no doubt it offered the most eccentrically appointed accommodation on the whole walk. The Owls Guesthouse was perfectly OK and normal in most respects. I got a friendly welcome, the breakfast was spot-on, and it wasn't expensive – but the interior of the place had been turned into a homage to owls. As you might expect, there were plenty of pictures of owls, and pretty standard stuff like owl-shaped ash trays, but everything was owlish: the duvet cover and pillowcases had an owl design on them; the clothes hooks were in the form of owls; there was an owliform toilet roll holder; there were stuffed owls, and there were soft toy owls. Even the signboards outside were shaped like owls. There must have been hundreds of owly things about the place. It was fantastic. The owners – both disappointingly normal looking – said that it was like it when they took the place over; all they've done is add to it a bit. I can thoroughly recommend it, especially to anyone fed up with staying in the standard hotel room. Several million points out of ten for being different. May the gods smile on them when the Euro-owl is introduced and they're allowed only their official quota.

There is no denying the high quality of the way out of Builth and along the river bank past Penddol Rocks, where the river is at its most playful as it cavorts among huge moss covered boulders.

Just a little further upstream, in what looked like a very ordinary field where I stopped for a breather, I was struck by the sounds I could hear – sheep and their lambs, the river, songbirds and a very loud woodpecker. (No owls though.) There was not a single discordant note and it dawned on me that the walk would have been worthwhile for the sounds alone.

An excellent track high above the river offered fine views north and east across the valley to the impressive Doldowlod House and the hills beyond. Although I could feel the miles disappearing under my feet, Rhayader, my target for the end of the day seemed to get no nearer. After the unexpected and rather incongruous sight of a herd of Scottish highland cattle – you know, the big woolly ones with ferocious looking horns – the only obstacle that stood between me and Rhayader was a worryingly unstable suspension bridge over the River Elan, one of the Wye's major tributaries. Digging deep into my reserves of courage I ventured onto this ramshackle affair which, despite an alarming tendency to slope and sway, carried me safely over the water.

And so to Rhayader. I was excited about arriving here because it had, I thought, a splendidly Welsh looking name, and I was a bit disappointed to find it is an anglicised version of its real name which is Rhaedr Gwy – Waterfall on the Wye. Like Hay and Builth, Rhayader has a clock tower, but the place had a more mountainous feel to it. Local people will tell you that all roads out of the village lead to mountains and there is a sense of isolation here not present in the other settlements I'd visited.

Expecting to hear Welsh spoken, I was somewhat taken aback to find that the owners of the B&B were from Walsall so instead of a Welsh lilt I got a West Midlands twang. Still, I suppose it indicated some northward progress – gone now, the West Country burr which had accompanied me all the way from Cornwall to Chepstow.

The Elan Valley near Rhayader was the scene of furious activity a hundred years ago as it witnessed the construction of a string of huge reservoirs, built to satisfy the growing demand for water for Birmingham. Although this massive civil engineering project provided work for two thousand people, there was the inevitable opposition from some local people and the presence of the huge sheets of water still rankles. My journey took me over a very lonely and rather indefinite ridge well to the east of the reservoirs and I could catch only distant glimpses of them.

When I say very lonely, I mean very, very, very lonely. Once out of Rhayader and up on the moorland, I saw nobody for hours. It was yet another brilliantly sunny day and I saw some red kites wheeling above me. I know they were red kites, because I'd seen signs saying this was Red Kite Country. On and on I walked, across a trackless landscape of tussocky grass and the odd standing stone when I saw, in the distance, a lone walker heading towards me. Rather like in those Western movies when you see two people approaching each other, it took hours for us to actually meet. So overwhelming was the effect of seeing another human being, I couldn't help addressing the stranger with 'Dr Livingstone I presume?' This chap had been camping in the Elan Valley and was on his way back to civilisation at Rhayader.

On the Pleasures of Shopping and Needlework – Mid-Wales

Mynydd y Cemais, between Plynlimon and Snowdonia

After this encounter, not another soul. It was nice to be out in open country again without having stiles and gates and bridges and fences and farmyards to deal with. Apart from a couple of very old looking cairns, the only man-made structures I saw close by were a series of what looked like concrete standing stones. Does anybody know what they are? My best guess is that they are boundary markers of some sort – the concrete might associate them with the water works. The distant views were exclusively of hills and, from this lofty vantage point, I was beginning to get a real impression of just how hilly Wales is. It was, though, a pity that so many of the skylines were cluttered with wind farms and little did I know that I was soon to come very close to a whole collection of these madly whirling white towers.

A fenced-off area of forestry forced me away from my intended direction and through a disgustingly wet area where my left leg disappeared in bog and was only retrieved after much struggling, grunting and foul language. It's always as well in moments of crisis to remember all you've read in learned tomes and heard from experts and remain completely calm. So why is it, I wonder, that my first reaction to any minor problem is usually blind panic? I just had enough time to wonder how long it would be before my well-rotted remains were discovered in this morass. Maybe I'd have become famous, like Cro-Magnon man. The frame of my rucksack would have become welded to my back so that anthropologists would have puzzled as to why this specimen had extra bits coming out of his shoulders.

The right of way indicated on my map appeared to have been obliterated by forestry operations so I made use of the time I needed to study the map properly by drying out my completely soaked left boot and sock. Once I'd found the forest track it was plain sailing down to the valley and the little village of Llangurig, the highest settlement on the Wye.

Before I set off on my journey I'd attempted to learn a bit of Welsh – mainly to be able to pronounce and understand place names a little better. It looks much more fearsome than it sounds but I regret to admit that I did not make as much progress with the language as I had hoped. The only pieces of conversation I considered I had mastered with any degree of fluency were the Welsh for 'May I sit here?' and 'I am an American nurse', phrases which, were I use to them together were more likely to get me beaten up than chatted up. Oh, I don't know though. Anyway, the thing is that at Llangurig there is a building proclaiming itself to be a Tourist Information Centre but which seemed to me to just sell sheepskins and trinkets. I marched into this place and asked if they had any details of accommodation in Llanidloes, a few miles further on. Recalling all I had learned from my Teach Yourself Welsh course, the word Llanidloes held no terrors for me. Yet, for some reason, when I asked the lady she looked at me blankly and I had to repeat the question. It turns out that my crime was to place the emphasis on the first syllable, like this: *Lla*nidloes. She replied by placing the emphasis on the second syllable, like this: Llan*id*loes. See? Different, eh? Apparently all Welsh place names have the emphasis on the second syllable. (This is Number 37 in an occasional series of Jacko's Handy Hints – you'll thank me one day for that one). The lady couldn't help anyway – they only dealt with accommodation in Llangurig – so I pressed on over the low hill out of the Wye valley into that of the Severn and so into Llanidloes.

This is a totally splendid place with a magnificent timbered market hall which, since it was built four centuries ago, has been used as a courthouse, meeting place, jail, library, working men's institute and now houses a museum. Llanidloes, known locally simply as Llani, was once one of the busiest industrial towns in Wales. It was the main centre for the cloth and knitting industries and what started as a cottage industry had, by the mid-eighteenth century, become factory based. So great had the demand for knitted products become, that people could be seen knitting as they walked along the streets. Do you believe this? It sounds incredible doesn't it? Unfortunately, because of its isolated position and poor lines of communication, the industry declined as the market was flooded with cheap Welsh flannel from – believe it or not – Rochdale. Not in an area normally associated with social upheaval, Llani is no stranger to industrial unrest and mayhem. The Chartists, who had promoted a programme of social justice in the middle of the nineteenth century, were big in Llani and, provoked by the town mayor, one of their meetings exploded into riot and occupation of the town by 'the mob' for nearly a week.

Shopping is not my favourite pastime but it was a pleasure in Llani. First, there is a National Milk Bar, a kind of throwback to what caffs used to be like in the fifties and sixties. For one and threepence you can buy a cup of frothy coffee, have spaghetti on toast and listen to Little Richard on the jukebox. What more could anybody want? These Milk Bars are, I think, peculiar to Wales and the sooner they are exported to the rest of the known universe the better. Even more exciting than the Milk Bar was the greengrocer's which appeared normal in most respects but had a hand-written notice pinned to one of the shelves behind the counter. The message this notice contained has baffled and troubled me ever since I read it. I should have asked what it meant but didn't like to. It was so bizarre that to enquire as to its significance would have felt like an intrusion into someone's private grief. It read – and I swear this is true – 'Owing to short people on this side, we will not be keeping apples on the top shelf.' Now, does that seem odd to you, or is it just me?

As if all this were not enough, Llanidloes has its own Catholic saint, Richard Gwyn, a schoolmaster who refused to take the oath of supremacy in Good Queen Bess's time and was tortured to death for his trouble. All in all, I reckon Llani was one of the great places I visited.

It was April Fools' Day when I left the town to cross the Severn by the Long Bridge. I thought it strange that the Severn and Wye should be so close at their mouths and also so close in their infancy. Both, in fact, have their source within a couple of miles of each other on Plynlimon, a sprawling mountain not far from here. My route followed the valley of the Clywedog to the great dam and reservoir of Llyn Clywedog. On the way, I passed through the partly restored ruins of the Bryntail lead mines which, like the woollen industry, peaked in the nineteenth century and then fell foul of the lack of decent transport facilities.

Despite – or perhaps because of – the previous day's hill walk, I was finding any uphills difficult and it took a massive effort to haul myself up to the road above the huge dam 200 feet above the mines. There followed an easy and quiet walk along the lane bordering the reservoir and it was with some surprise that I noticed there was no 'tidemark' along the lake shore. Perhaps, after all, the weather had been wetter than I thought.

The lane took me through the Hafren Forest and to a road junction where all three roads were rather confusingly signposted to

Llanidloes. Taking care not to make the elementary error of turning round and following the road back along the way I'd just come, I continued past the tiny settlement of Llwynygog and on to Staylittle, allegedly so called because the local blacksmith was so quick at shoeing horses that travellers only had to stay a little. Hmm.

After all the road walking that I'd done that day, it made a pleasant change to climb up onto open hill country before the final descent to the Star Inn at Dylife where I managed to arrive just in time to buy a drink. Dylife – pronounced a bit like *deliver*, not *die-life* – appears to consist only of a large churchyard, the aforementioned Star Inn, a very few houses and a big area of abandoned mine workings. Over a thousand people worked these mines but, as economic conditions changed and the inevitable lack of profit set in, the workers moved away leaving virtually a ghost town. The churchyard, with its weathered, leaning and cracked gravestones, was a particularly eloquent memorial to a once thriving place. Perched as it is more than 1,000 feet up a remote valley, it is hard to envisage Dylife ever thriving again.

Two friends, John and Angela, have a place near here and they had offered to put me up for a few days, an offer I was glad to accept. They came to meet me at the pub and, once again, it was great to have company and to be able to just chill out without having to move on. Although I was enjoying the journey immensely, there was a feeling sometimes that I had to keep moving, rather like some fugitive from justice. It had been just over a week since my last rest day so to be with friends and have a day off mooching around the shops and market stalls of Machynlleth was just what I needed.

Machynlleth is the capital of this part of mid-Wales. It has posh shops and ordinary shops and the almost obligatory clock tower. It is also the place where Owain Glyndwr, a nobleman who led the Welsh in a long and bloody rebellion against the English, set up the first Welsh parliament in 1404. Predictably, I suppose, it all ended unhappily when Owain disappeared less than ten years later, still regarded as a hero by his followers, and the rebellion was put down. He clearly had the interests of his followers at heart though, because I noticed that, very sensibly, Owain had had the parliament building erected just opposite the off-licence.

As well as having a day off and being able to stay with friends, I was to be joined for three or four days' walking by another mate, also called John. This was walking John as opposed to the other John who has the place in Wales and who, come to think of it, also walks and cycles and is, in fact, a multi-faceted and multi-talented individual but, as far as my journey was concerned, he didn't walk. So, you see, there's these two blokes, both called John. For the sake of argument, let's call them John the Walker and John the Resident. Well, John the Walker had been planning to spend a little time sharing the route with me. His job dictated that this time would have to be during the Easter break and, because I had no real schedule for the trip, I don't think we had much more than a vague idea that it would probably be somewhere in Wales that we'd meet up. As events unfolded, it could not have turned out much better for me as I was about to embark on three days of tricky route finding across a confusing landscape in generally worsening weather.

Raring to go after my rest day and all excited that I had some company again, I set off from Dylife with John the Walker on a damp, grey morning which quickly deteriorated into a wet, grey morning and a cold one at that. A freshening wind blew the rain and mist away and the middle part of the day was spent in sunshine giving thrilling views ahead to Cadair Idris, the Rhinogs and the Aran ridge. My original route from the mid-Wales hills to Snowdon would have taken me over Cadair Idris and the Rhinogs but I was put off the latter by the dire warnings that the way was long and the going particularly tough. So I opted for the softer option of the Arans which, at over 2,900 feet, were going to pose a sufficient obstacle I felt. To see these three great mountain ridges in one broad panoramic sweep in the distance was a bonus and, seen almost end-on from here, the Aran ridge looked especially enticing. I felt rather pleased with myself that, with my prior knowledge restricted almost entirely to what I'd seen in books, I had chosen what appeared to be the best-looking route. Oh yes, I was pleased all right. Even a tricky bit of zig-zagging through a forested area couldn't hold us back as we steamed onward to a lunch stop overlooking the road at Bwlch Glynmynydd.

But then, of course, it all went haywire. First we lost the path in a very dense conifer plantation and had to wrestle our way through thicker and thicker undergrowth and then later we must have missed a path junction, because we ended the day by descending a steep hillside over the wreckage of recent forestry work, clearly not the intended way, to our rendezvous with the other John.

The following day, we took our leave of J the R and his forty-year-old Land Rover which had ferried us hither and thither over the last couple of days. We'd grown used to its endearing habit of not wanting to start and its many up-to-the-minute features such as tyres on the wheels and hand-operated windscreen wipers. It had been fantastic to stop with John and Angela – their hospitality was just what I needed after the lonely days of mid-Wales. As well as the company and the good food and all that, I was also able to spend a happy evening repairing the damage to my rucksack; I sat there with needle and thread engrossed in this newly discovered skill and was pleasantly surprised to discover that the repair appeared to be a success as we climbed out of Commins Coch across yet more confusing country with indefinite or non-existent tracks.

Eventually, after much trial and error and splashing through bog and stream – so much for expert micro-navigation – we arrived on a track not marked on my map. It was the width of the M6 and led us right up to, and past, a dozen or so of the great white windmills I had seen so many of on my trip. Up until now I had only seen them from a safe distance on the skyline – lots of them. It seems that in Wales, now that building reservoirs is considered passé, They – with a capital 'T' – are having a competition to see whether more land can be lost to conifer plantations than to wind farms. I would say that the wind farmers have the edge just now. I suppose it's a bit like it was in the Wild West when the cattle farmers were constantly at odds with the homesteaders who wanted to grow crops. Perhaps we'll see a modern version of *Shane* where a silent stranger in a buckskin coat – played by Mel Gibson – arrives in a Jeep to protect the hard hit foresters from the evil wind farmers, led by Alan Rickman. Or perhaps we won't.

Anyway, I don't want to alienate the pro-wind farm lobby, so I'll just say that, from a distance, these slender white towers have a certain appeal and lend a quality to the landscape that wasn't there before. And we discovered that close up, too, they are fascinating things to look at. The single rotating sail or blade appears impossibly large and looks ready to strike the ground on each revolution. The effect of watching them is almost hypnotic and they appear to rotate at different speeds depending on the angle you see them from. But the noise! You know that bit at the end of *The Pit and the Pendulum* where Vincent Price, by now completely barking, watches as that great blade thing swishes to and fro? Well, the noise was a bit like that. It was so loud that, calling a temporary halt to our Don Quixote-like journey, I tried to record it on a dictaphone thing I'd been carrying around with me but the batteries had gone flat. Technology, eh.

In the afternoon persistent and sullen clouds, later giving way to persistent and sullen rain, made for fairly demanding walking across rough, wet moorland, most of it trackless. It almost goes without saying that there was nobody else about and, of the whole journey, this was one of the strangest and most puzzling areas to navigate. After passing by the forlorn skeletons of a couple of abandoned farms we followed an improving track down to the Dyfi valley and so to our lodgings at Minllyn. Yet again, we were given a friendly welcome and were able to avail ourselves of an excellent drying room which, after the soaking we had had, was much appreciated. I'm still not sure whether he was telling the absolute truth or not, but our landlord informed us that the warmth in the drying room was provided partly by heat from the beer pumps. In other words, the more beer we drank, the drier would our clothes become – a tremendous piece of marketing know-how, I thought.

We had entered the Snowdonia National Park just before the end of our day's walk and, relatively untrodden and quiet as it is, this corner of it seems very wild. Steep wooded hills rise abruptly on both sides of the fast flowing River Dyfi which, at Dinas Mawddwy, just to the north, is formed from a Y-shaped confluence of valleys, so that there are hills ahead too. In the glowering, sodden weather that greeted us, the whole effect was one of almost elemental wilderness. Even with my limited knowledge and powers of observation, I could recognise the buzzards as they circled their territory. Well, when I say I could recognise them what I mean is that I could recognise them as buzzards – I couldn't recognise them individually as Brian and Barbara Buzzard or anything like that, but it was a start.

Meeting the Man from Manchester – the Aran Ridge to Snowdon

Cwm Orthin

This was to be the day of the Arans, that high ridge which we had seen from afar in gloriously clear conditions a couple of days previously. It was thirty-six days now since I had set off from Land's End and, even though I had planned a route to take in upland Britain, I had so far spent only a part of one day above 2,000 feet, and that was a fairly gentle walk along the Black Mountains. Well, today would be different. At 2,971 feet Aran Fawddwy is a big mountain by English and Welsh standards; it's higher than Great Gable and Bowfell in the Lakes and Lliwedd on the Snowdon Horseshoe, but I wonder how many of the thousands of people who ascend those mountains have given much thought to Aran Fawddwy. Apart from anything else, it's not too easy to pronounce – something like Vowth-oo-ee, I think. There has also been bitter wrangling between the various interested parties over access and there now exists a kind of uneasy stand-off where walkers can get onto the mountain at certain places only and, once on it, are kept pretty much to well-defined routes. Apparently until quite recently the Arans were almost totally neglected by visitors, but the explosion in popularity of outdoor pursuits has led to a big and sudden increase in the number of people heading into this area. Freedom of access to high ground strikes me as a basic right in our crowded country but I can understand the problems caused by irresponsible behaviour and the pressure put upon people who have to live on, and work, the land leading into the hills.

None of this was uppermost in my mind though as we walked along the quiet lane up into Cwm Cywarch. This was real mountain country – at last. The gaunt grey crags of Craig Cywarch hung almost impossibly vertically from the ragged folds of cloud swirling above us and I felt just a little apprehensive as we prepared to venture up into the unseen and unknown mountain world.

'Going up the Aran, is it?' asked an old shepherd in the valley bottom and, after a little while, we certainly knew we were going up – a relentless ascent relieved only by a view of a huge stone compass somebody had constructed down in the valley. The summit ridge was in thick mist so we had quite a struggle finding the trig point on the top. There then followed what would normally be a fairly straightforward walk northwards over Aran Benllyn, a sizeable hill in its own right but why it was named after a brand of cough medicine remains a mystery. The much curtailed visibility, together with a gale force wind and persistent rain, made the journey a bit more interesting. Every few yards it seemed, we came across a fence with crossing points provided in the form of massive twin ladder stiles, one stile alongside another. Strange things, these. For a start, it appeared that the paths that led from them were not heading where we wanted to go which, according to my map, looked the obvious direction to be travelling. And secondly, why were they double stiles? One for people going up, one for people going down, maybe? Perhaps because of the restricted access, all the people on this hill are channelled into this one area so they might get busy in summer. We came to the conclusion that they were His and Hers stiles, constructed this way to preserve decorum by denying chaps the opportunity of looking up ladies' skirts.

A long, gradual descent led us out of the cloud and down into the village of Llanuwchllyn with views ahead of Bala Lake (or Llyn Tegid), the largest natural lake in Wales. It was as well that our accommodation had been booked ahead because at this time of year and in these weather conditions the place did not look like holiday country. Ken, our host for the evening, had stopped doing B&B some time ago when his wife died but had taken pity on us and let us have a room. Understandably nervous about letting two strangers into his house, he had apparently informed the police of our impending arrival but he treated us with great courtesy. I think he was glad of the company and he took a delight in regaling us with tales of his youth in sunny Manchester.

Ken was keen to be up early he said, and asked us whether that would be all right, and could we be away promptly so he could get on with what he had to do? Yes, we agreed, that would be fine. As it turned out, it was Ken who had trouble getting up. We couldn't wake him and were briefly worried that he had expired in the night. For all that, Ken was a star. He'd made a big effort for us and what he charged would barely have covered his costs. He was an interesting man, the type of character who really made my journey worthwhile and it was with great sadness that I learned a few months after I'd finished the walk that he had died. His son found a letter from me amongst Ken's possessions and very kindly rang me to let me know the news.

After walking with me for the morning through frustratingly bright sunshine so that the Aran ridge was completely clear of cloud, John returned to the bosom of his family in Kendal leaving me at the summit of the road from Llanuwchllyn to Trawsfynydd. Solitary walking is great and I did intend this trip to be a mainly solo one but I was certainly glad of the company when I had it. Walking up the Wye from Chepstow to Monmouth with Adrian was good, and the two or three days that John had spent with me could not have been better timed. Apart from the companionship, I had the reassurance of another opinion when things looked dicey in the mists and murk of the mid-Wales mountain and moorland.

It was a little unsatisfactory and I felt I was cheating a bit to use a road for almost a whole day but I could see no easily available alternative in linking the Aran ridge with Snowdon. True, it looked as if there was a way over the Arenigs and the Migneint but the route looked long and without places to stay, so the road appeared the best option. As it turned out, it was mostly free of traffic and passed through attractive countryside giving outstanding views westward to the Rhinogs and back to the Arans. It was late on Sunday afternoon when I passed through the village of Trawsfynydd and it was almost completely shut. The nuclear power station built on the lakeshore near here was in the process of being decommissioned and this presumably has had an adverse effect on the local economy. Many of the dark grey houses along the main street were for sale and certainly, when I was there, the village looked to have turned its back on a hostile world and seemed content to sit there and brood. A group of lads playing football in the street struck a threatening posture but, noticing the logo on their shirts, I ingratiated myself with them by pretending to be a Liverpool supporter and discussing their prospects for the last part of the season.

More open walking followed across a bleak moorland, where lie the remains of a Roman fort and amphitheatre, apparently unique in Wales. The gorse and daffodils were at the same stage of growth as they had been at the tip of Cornwall five weeks ago, and the Moelwyn Hills formed a misty and rather formidable looking barrier which I would have to cross the next day on my way to Snowdon. After passing the splendid waterfalls of Rhaeadr Cynfal which, judging from the architecture of the bridge and the presence of steel cables and iron railings, must have been a favourite haunt of trippers in Victorian times, it was only a short step to my B&B in Ffestiniog.

This is Llan Ffestiniog, not its more famous but much younger upstart brother Blaenau Ffestiniog. Stiniog, as it is known locally, is not a pretty place in a picture postcard sense but appeared to be well looked after and welcoming in a way that Trawsfynydd did not. Over the centuries, Ffestiniog has witnessed bands of baddies chasing bands of goodies, or vice versa. Our friend Owain Glyndwr was chased here by the English in 1404; the Yorkists chased the Lancastrians in 1468, Lancashire having set Yorkshire an impossible target of 300-plus in forty overs on a turning wicket at Liverpool; and Cromwell's army chased the Royalists a couple of hundred years later. Ah, happy days. I'm pleased to report that nobody appeared to be chasing anybody else while I was there. In fact there was hardly anybody about at all.

Walking down to the village in the evening, I could see the estuary near Porthmadog and was surprised to realise how close to the sea I had come. A claw-shaped cloud appeared to be squeezing the last rays of light from the setting sun and, content with the thought that tomorrow promised to be fair, I enjoyed a curry at the wonderfully named Balti Towers. A man in the pub chatted to me about job prospects and local life in general. Inevitably, he mentioned the effect that the closure of the power station at Trawsfynydd had had and, when he learned that I lived near the Lake District, asked me whether conditions there were any better. In general, this part of North Wales has suffered more than the Lakes in recent years as a result of industrial decline, and my feeling is that the tourist industry here has not yet made the most of its potential. Whether that is a good or a bad thing I'm not sure. Avoiding badly eroded footpaths and overcrowded villages is usually easier in North Wales than it is in the Lakes and there seems to be less pressure on space here.

Totally ignoring the promise of the previous evening, the morning dawned murky and cool with the Moelwyns wrapped in mist again. I had been told that Cwm Orthin was the key to my crossing of the Moelwyns so off I set on what was to become one of the most interesting walking days of the whole journey. I left Ffestiniog across some shaggy fields that had resisted all attempts at being tamed and wandered through the wooded dell of Coed Cymerau, now a nature reserve. The damp, misty conditions lent the place an air of mystery and excitement. This is what I thought Wales was all about! Great, moss-covered rocks sprouted from the steep ground, trees grew from any precarious foot-hold they could find and the Afon Goedol flowed noisily down its boulder-filled valley. The only jarring note was the water in the stream which was a milky white colour, presumably something to do with all the slate quarrying going on nearby.

A steep pull led me up to the track of the Ffestiniog Railway which must be one of Britain's Great Things. Built in the 1860s to carry slate from the quarries at Blaenau down to the sea at Porthmadog, the railway was closed in 1946 and left to rot. A bunch of enthusiasts got together though, and by 1955 a little piece of the line had been re-opened. Work is still going on but you can take a ride now all the way from coast to quarry and back, and marvel at the engineering skill required to construct a railway through such a hostile environment. Even better is the fact that some of the locomotives are the original steam engines, now over a hundred years old and restored to their former glory. Unfortunately, I displayed the same impeccable timing as I had with the West Somerset Railway at Minehead and managed to miss seeing any of the trains except from a distance when I was walking along the opposite shore of the Tanygrisiau Reservoir. One train whistled for me though, and that sound echoing back off the slopes of the Moelwyns, together with the sight of the plume of smoke rising to mingle with the mists will stay with me for a very long time.

Tanygrisiau – pronounced a bit like *Tannie-greesher* – village is extraordinary. It did not grow gradually and evolve like most places, but instead sprung up almost overnight in the manner of a Klondike gold rush town. The Blaenau quarry system had extended this far so the cottages, chapels and schools were built to accommodate the workers and their families. The name Tanygrisiau means 'under the stairs', a reference to the cottages being built below the steep inclines and tramways used to transport the rock. An incredibly steep road leads from the main part of the village up into a 'suburb' dwarfed by towering slate tips at the entrance to Cwm Orthin. This quarry is still very much in business and a rather bizarre attempt had been made to soften the visual impact by constructing an ornamental garden, complete with Chinese-style bridge, in the midst of the surrounding mayhem. Picking my way gingerly around sinister looking machinery and across piles of greasy slate, I reached the bottom of the Cwm and could see the track snaking away up the hillside at the far end.

This was great stuff again. You would have to be made of wood not to feel some admiration for the people who lived and worked up here. There's a derelict chapel, its isolation somehow highlighted by the pair of Scots pines now growing alongside it; the trackside fence is one of those affairs constructed from upright slate slabs and held together with wire, and a little higher are the ruins of some quarry buildings. The lake itself, unsurprisingly called Llyn Cwmorthin, looked dark and unwelcoming in its bowl beneath the crags of Allt y Ceffylau. Some nice people had written 'English Out' in whitewash on the slate walls at the ruined buildings so I did my best to oblige by hurrying on up to the skyline where there were more ruined quarry buildings to investigate, this time thankfully free of graffiti.

An interesting walk through a tangled and confusing countryside of strange, baffling gradients led me past Llyn Cwm Corsiog to the day's highest point, a col between the hills of Cnicht and Moel Druman. Here I lay down and watched various people in the distance, flirted briefly with the notion of stashing my rucksack for a quick ascent of Cnicht, and gazed across the Nant Gwynant valley towards Snowdon itself which, had it not been for the mist, I would have been able to see. 'I could get used to this,' I thought as I sat and enjoyed the best packed lunch I had had on the whole journey, provided by the people I'd stayed with at Ffestiniog. What a magnificent cheese and chutney sandwich they did for me. Best Packed Lunch of the Journey Award – no question.

After several hours of watching Snowdon fail to free itself from the clouds, I thought that I had better get moving before I seized up completely and set off through yet more bandit country, down a steep gully and past what my map calls in Olde English a Burnt Mound. Any ideas? It was a longer and wearier descent than I had anticipated to reach the Youth Hostel at Bryn Gwynant which, rather incongruously, after the day I'd had, was packed.

A Big Hill, a Big Bridge and a Big Tunnel – Snowdon to the English Border

The Llangollen Canal

The next day was to be the first of the Big Ones – the ascent of Snowdon – and what a beautiful, cloudless morning it was. This was the first really good weather I'd had for over a week and it could not have been better timed. I had thought before I left home that, given its gruesome reputation for rain and cloud and given that it was still early in the year, I would do well to just get over Snowdon in anything other than foul conditions. Well, here I was plodding up the Watkin Path into Cwm Llan, feeling overly warm. I left the main track just above the waterfalls and struck up a disused quarry tramway and then open hillside to the foot of Snowdon's south ridge. From here to just below the summit of the mountain the walking was stupendous along a narrowing, increasingly impressive ridge. Despite the plunging views down into Cwm Tregalan, I felt comfortably at home in this terrain – no oo-er walking here. The weather helped, of course, and I could not believe my good fortune as the views opened out in all directions. On the way up I met a lad who told me he'd lived in the shadow of Snowdon for all his twenty-seven years but had never so much as set foot on the mountain before. Well, he was here now and his sense of wonderment at what he was seeing was a joy to behold.

Snowdon's top is called Yr Wyddfa – the Burial Mound – but I could barely make it out beneath the seething mass of humanity swarming about the summit cairn. I'd said I'd get to the top so I had to wait my turn to teeter about briefly on the topmost rocks before skulking away to try and shake off the crowds. I just don't know where they had all come from. True, I had seen some people down below me on the Watkin Path, but nothing like this many. They must have all arrived from the Llanberis side of the mountain – I don't know if the mountain railway was running or not, but I had not heard the 'manic hooting of engines', as one writer has called it.

Less than five minutes away from the summit, just above the start of the stony descent of the notorious Zigzags, I found a quiet, airy spot to have my sandwiches. I regret to say that I was bullied into sharing them with an aggressive seagull which could obviously recognise a good thing when he saw one. No matter, I thought. If David Attenborough can bond with gorillas, I can do the same with seagulls.

The descent beneath the surprisingly big cliffs on Snowdon's north face was stunning as the afternoon sun bathed the screes below the shadowed gullies and pinnacles in a warm golden light. The Zigzags and the Pyg Track to Pen y Pass have been much 'improved' in the last few years by the construction of stone staircases to ease the worst of the nastily eroded bits. I suppose most hill walkers will have an opinion on these 'made' paths; I know some people feel they are an intrusion into what, essentially, is a wild environment. My view is that, in certain places – and this is one of them – there is no alternative, unless we start banning people from the hills completely.

From the crowded car park and café at Pen y Pass, I had to get to Capel Curig. To avoid walking along the main road, I hauled myself up to the hidden lake of Llyn Cwmffynnon from where a trackless route across a squelching moorland brought me to the new path running parallel to the main road to Capel Curig. I had imagined that this path would provide easy, roughly level walking all the way. Will I ever learn? Designed by someone with a warped sense of humour, it had been waymarked by some white posts planted in the ground just far enough away from each other to be invisible until you had gone a few yards from the last one. So, I had to guess which direction the next one was likely to be in. Sometimes I was right and sometimes I wasn't. One day the route will be trodden out and there will be no difficulty. In the meantime, I can strongly recommend you to go and take part in this 3-D version of a Join the Dots puzzle. The views back towards Snowdon were magical, though, and the classic set-piece picture of the Snowdon Horseshoe seen across the twin lakes of Llynau Mymbyr at sunset was unforgettable.

Having had a thoroughly good time wandering through the mountains of Eryri what I had to do now was find a way eastwards to rejoin the main south–north axis of my route. Using a mixture of field paths, back lanes and quiet roads, I crossed a peaceful, unfrequented countryside of hills, pasture and sheep. I walked past Ty Hyll – the so-called Ugly House – where the Snowdonia National Park Society has its headquarters. I think they must be the local equivalent of the Friends of the Lake District and, from what I had seen, they must be doing a grand job. Our National Parks are unique in that they remain part of the living, economic fabric of the country. People still live in them and have to work. The Parks are not museums or wild life reserves but have to change and adapt like everywhere else. They just have the added complication of being such precious, irreplaceable bits of the country. So trying to balance the wishes of all the different players must be incredibly difficult. Somebody must be doing OK though – I thought Snowdonia was brilliant.

On I went, along the 'other side' of the famous Swallow Falls. To see the falls from the main road you have to pay. This side you don't but then, because of an impenetrable screen of trees, you don't get the classic view of them either. Betws-y-Coed was the busiest place I'd seen since Monmouth but a few minutes later I was having lunch, totally alone, by the tumbling waters of the Penmachno Falls.

The lanes around Ysbyty Ifan were edged with dry stone walls, on top of which were hedges and then, for good measure, a post and wire fence. Ysbyty is the Welsh word for hospital and Ysbyty Ifan had one of the very old types of hospital, a hospice run by the

Knights of St John for pilgrims on their way to Bardsea Island. I think there's a church there now. It's certainly no use turning up there for an X-ray or to have a foreign body removed from your earhole. I was rather taken with Ysbyty Ifan; it's a plain enough looking place, but attractively sited in a fold of the hills and I was especially pleased to be asked by a very Welsh lady whether I was the gentleman staying in the holiday house. It was the only time on the whole journey I was referred to as a gentleman and I was so overwhelmed I briefly considered abandoning the whole venture just so I could bask in this glory a little longer.

Hidden valleys, lonely farms with sheep, sheep and more sheep, and doubts as to the correct way to go were characteristics of the rest of the journey as far as the Deeside village of Cynwyd, British headquarters of the Keep Vowels Out Of Place Names Society. I had a scary encounter with some more Boys at one farm and I did have one or two moments of frustration where footpaths had been blocked off or misleading signs had been erected. I was beginning to realise that you don't have to travel far from the popular walking areas in this country to feel as if you're treading virgin territory but there was a sense of adventure, and even daring, that you don't get by walking the well-trodden way.

Fortunately, I rarely felt the need to measure my progress against any pre-determined timetable. When I did bother to think about it, I just knew that every step was taking me nearer to my goal. So when I arrived at one col to be confronted by an impressive range of big purple hills, I was mortified to discover they were my old friends, the Arans. Blimey, how long ago was that? 'Going up the Aran, is it?', Ken and the blasted ladder stiles. To get to Snowdon had necessitated a big detour, almost a U-turn. Even though I would not have missed Snowdon for anything, it was sobering to be so close to somewhere I had been nearly a week before.

From Cynwyd, with its irresistible fish and chip shop, the way followed forest tracks across the slopes of Moel Fferna, another 2,000 foot mountain I had intended to ascend. However, the sight of acres of thick heather between me and the nice track I was on and the summit did enough to dissuade me from bothering. The way into Llangollen was down a stupidly steep road with a plethora of signs warning motorists to 'Turn Back Now' etc, etc. Since the road had long ago degenerated into a rutted, bouldery track which would have tested the suspension of a Moon Buggy, I thought the signs were nearly as unnecessary as those advising people to keep away from the radiation at Penhale Camp in Cornwall. Still, there's no accounting for some folk. Perhaps there's somebody about somewhere with two heads, both of which glow in the dark, driving round in a car with no bottom in it.

Like Betws-y-Coed, Llangollen was busy and hot. The elegant Dee Bridge spans a turbulent, rocky stretch of water which, for good measure, is right alongside the recently renovated steam railway station. For Great Western fanatics this must be great, but having been weaned on the wonderful LMS I contented myself with a photograph as I found my way to the Llangollen Canal just above the town.

Llangollen is famous for being the venue of the annual International Eisteddfod which must hold a place dear to the heart of many a Welsh man and woman. A little English–Welsh phrasebook we once bought when we were on holiday in Anglesey had curiously little to say on what you might call the normal holiday matters of shopping, being taken ill and being robbed but was cluttered with phrases you might want to use at the Eisteddfod. 'Who is the victorious Bard?' and 'Can you please direct me to the Welshmen Overseas Tent?' were just two of the questions we struggled to resist posing on our visit.

The walk along the canal towards the English border was splendid. Completely level but with good views both distant: up towards the limestone cliffs of World's End, and closer to hand, young ladies sunbathing on the roofs of the many colourful narrow boats plying this stretch of water. I had to cross the truly amazing Pontcysyllte aqueduct, constructed by Thomas Telford nearly 200 years ago to carry this little branch of the canal across the deep gash of the Dee valley. They said he was mad when Telford proposed this typically bold solution to what looked like an insurmountable problem, and I have to confess I'd have been one of them if I'd been around at the time.

First seen through the trees from a bend in the canal a mile or so away, the aqueduct looks impossibly fragile. It's nothing more than a cast iron trough supported on stone pillars, but it's over 300 yards long and more than 120 feet above the valley bottom. I seem to remember that water weighs 10 pounds a gallon and I tried to work out how many gallons there would be on this bridge at any one time. After all, I needed to know whether it was safe. My rucksack was so heavy that I feared I might cause the whole structure to collapse, which would have seriously undermined my popularity with the canal preservation people. The arithmetic involved in this calculation was beyond me though, but for the minute or two I was on the bridge I was more concerned with just getting over it. The gaps between the railings were just wide enough for a person to fall through and I wondered why anybody would want to bring children up here. The other side, away from the towpath, is even more alarming, as there is no barrier there at all – just fresh air between the driver of the boat and the valley bottom. A friend of mine told me – after my journey, I'm glad to say – that she went and hid in the bowels of the boat while her husband had to stay on deck and steer the thing safely across.

Good old Telford. He had a major impact on this area; he also designed the turnpike road (now the A5) through the Conwy Gorge near Betws and across the Nant Ffrancon Pass just beyond. For good measure he built the Menai Suspension Bridge, linking Anglesey with the mainland and which, for many years, was the only road crossing. A real clever dick if ever there was one. I did not know it then, but I would actually be walking through Telford's birthplace in a few weeks time.

Not long after the vertigo of the aqueduct came the claustrophobia of the Chirk Tunnel where the towpath is plunged into darkness for nearly a quarter of a mile. What fun, stumbling and slipping on the wet cobbled towpath, using a rickety handrail as a guide. On emerging into the daylight there's another aqueduct, but only a baby one this time, across the Ceiriog valley and then I entered England again at Chirk Bank. If the Severn Bridge had provided an exciting way into Wales, the Pontcysyllte aqueduct and the Chirk Tunnel had more than matched it as a dramatic way out.

CHAPTER FOUR – THE NORTH WEST

HOMEWARD BOUND

Say Cheese! –
From the Dee to the Mersey

Raw Head on the Sandstone Trail

In the six weeks since I'd left Land's End, time and distance had seemingly flown by as my journey took me through new and unfamiliar country. Some areas, like the Cornish coast and the Wye Valley, I had read and heard about, but others had been a surprise – they simply jumped up and took me unawares. Places like

Morwenstow and White Castle and Cwm Orthin had provided wonderful, breathtaking moments of pure joy. In a sense, this was about to change as I embarked on the next stage of my journey, as I have lived most of my life in the north west and thought that a lot of the ground I was to cover would be well-known.

After a rest day staying with friends in Wrexham, Kev ferried me back to Chirk on a cool, grey morning and told me that the cloyingly sweet smell I'd noticed from the canal bank there came from a chocolate factory. Unfortunately there was no sign of Willy Wonka or Veruca Salt as I set off along the Maelor Way, a fairly recently devised footpath linking the Offa's Dyke Path in North Wales with the Sandstone Trail in Cheshire. It seemed a long time ago that I'd walked along the ODP across the Black Mountains to Hay-on-Wye and crossing it again near Chirk made me realise how much quicker it would have been to stick with it, rather than veer off across mid-Wales to Snowdon. Ah, but I wasn't in a race, and just think what I would have missed. The Owls and the Arans and Ken and the Ffestiniog railway and, of course, Snowdon. For all that, the ODP in its entirety must be a marvellous walk. Well done King Offa – the boy done brilliant; it is not generally known but this was the origin of the expression 'Special Offa'.

I thought I'd left Wales but the Maelor Way plays a very amusing game with the boundary between Wales and England as it heads north eastwards across some rather undistinguished countryside. In general the Welsh border runs south to north but just as it has the coast in its sights, it does a very strange thing and shoots off eastwards towards Whitchurch before swerving back north and west to the Dee estuary.

Unlike most borders, this one appears to have little correlation with obvious geographical features. The River Dee is just here, a natural boundary if ever there was one, but it seems to have been almost totally ignored by the administrators or whoever fixes borders. The reason may be that this land was fought and squabbled over for centuries and what we have now is presumably the final outcome of all the to-ing and fro-ing between various Llywelyns, Henrys and Edwards.

The early part of the day was rural and uneventful through a rather ordinary countryside but, armed with a bit of knowledge gleaned from a guidebook, it's amazing how such an area can spring into vivid life. The big flat field I walked across looked just like a big flat field and nothing more. Last year's crop of corn had been chopped to a colourless stubble, puddles spattered the furrowed soil and there were no longer any views of distant hills. But here used to be a Roman fort which probably predated the famous one at Chester and was an important strategic site from where attacks on various innocent parties in North Wales were launched. If the gap between present-day quiet and the clamour of battle seemed a huge one at Sedgemoor, it was an almost unbridgeable gulf here at Rhyn. I had to tell myself that if I'd been doing this walk 2,000 years ago I'd probably have been beaten up by Romans yelling unspeakable things at me in Latin. 'Walkio ergo sum,' I'd have shouted back but it would have done me no good. Thank goodness they've packed up and gone.

Apart from a sinister-looking fenced enclosure containing a few unhappy looking birds and with a dead crow hanging from the wire mesh – this is a pheasantry apparently – all was pleasantly rustic. The woods were carpeted with bluebells and the smell of wild garlic was almost overwhelming. A field full of aggressive looking Boys forced a muddy detour but I soon regained the proper route to pass the impressive timber-framed farmhouse of the cruck-built Sodylt Old Hall. I reached the bank of the River Dee opposite the village of Erbistock where the Boat Inn looked very inviting, but completely unattainable, as there is no way of crossing the river here; there used to be a little ferry but it went out of service sixty years ago.

A little park near the church at Overton was a good spot to rest for lunch and I was able to see the yew trees which, I'm sorry to say, looked like any other yew trees to me. They are, however, according to the old rhyme, one of the seven wonders of Wales:

Pistyll Rhaeadr and Wrexham steeple,

Snowdon's mountain without its people,

Overton yew-trees, St Winifrede's wells,

Llangollen bridge, and Gresford bells.

Overton was pleasant enough but I think the best thing about the place is the name of the bloke who accepted ownership of it from Edward III in 1347: Eirbule le Strange, Baron of Knockys. Brilliant. It was a complicated course I had to wend through gates, over stiles and across a field, where I was chased by two horses, to Penley, an ordinary-looking place apart from its thatched school building. The tall plants along the lane between here and Hanmer are, according to my book, hops. Who'd have thought it?

Hanmer is a bit more like it. A genuinely appealing place with all the trappings of a traditional English village, even though it's in

Wales – an impressive church, a pub and attractive cottages, many of them listed buildings. It's also got its Mere, one of several small lakes in this area, which is home to Canada geese and mallards. But just to demonstrate how various strands of history can get woven together even on a single journey such as this, I thought that the most remarkable thing about Hanmer is that the daughter of Sir David Hanmer, the local squire five or six hundred years ago, married Owain Glyndwr – you remember, the chap with the parliament building in Machynlleth. Amazing isn't it?

Some more something or nothing walking took me past Iscoyd Park, a big house set in its own grounds. I don't know who used to live in it but the German foreign minister Von Ribbentrop stayed here in 1938 and visited Chester races.

I got talking to a chap tending the garden of a little cottage nearby and he commented on what a beautiful country we live in. Although this part of the journey was OK, it was a bit bland after some of the places I'd seen. If scenery was food, the Cornish coast would have been smoky bacon and grainy mustard, Snowdonia would be fillet steak and the Maelor Way sliced white bread. Iscoyd Park was the last – definitely, this time – piece of action in Wales. A few minutes later I crossed into Cheshire to pick up the Sandstone, Trail which was to lead me northwards to the Mersey.

My journey through Wales had been full of interest and incident. The terrain and scenery had mostly been stunning, the weather had been generally kind – apart from the day on the Arans, blast them – and the people I had met had been almost without exception generous and hospitable. I had certainly felt none of the hostility which had supposedly greeted that intrepid traveller George Borrow back in 1862 when he embarked on a tour of Wales and was given a good telling-off for having the temerity to go out walking on the Sabbath.

The first few miles of the Sandstone Trail weren't all that exciting. It was easy walking, first along the Shropshire Union canal as far as Willeymoor Lock and then across the lush pasturelands for which Cheshire is famous. To my untrained eye, this appeared to be by far the most fertile farmland I'd seen on my journey north. Everything looked well fed; the Friesian cattle were fat and contented looking – no frisky, swaggering Boys here – and even the grass and the clover and the wild flowers looked big and fat and sumptuous. So did the opulent, half-timbered, black and white houses. Cheshire is famous for its cheese; some people even believe that the word Cheshire is a corruption of Cheseshire (silly sods). Though this is obviously dairy farming country – before the disastrous foot and mouth outbreak of 1968 it was reckoned to be the most densely stocked dairy cattle area in the world – very little cheese is produced here now. Indeed, the town which believes itself to be the centre of the Cheshire cheese 'industry' is Whitchurch and that's in Shropshire. Well, so what? They tell me Venetian blinds were invented in Japan. Funny old world.

The next twenty miles offered the best walking I'd had since the ascent of Snowdon. First there is an enjoyably bouncy stroll along the sandstone spine of the Central Cheshire Ridge which although it reaches only 746 feet at its highest point, Raw Head, feels much higher because of the flat plains on both sides. The views, particularly west back towards Wales, were outstanding and the going is excellent through bouldery red outcrops, heather and pine trees. The two famous castles here are Peckforton, which is a fake built only 150 years ago but impressive enough to have been chosen as the location for the film Robin Hood, Prince of Thieves, and Beeston Castle, which is the genuine article. Built in 1337 by Rannulf, Earl of Chester on a spectacularly steep rock outcrop rearing 300 feet above the plain, it looks impregnable even now. The village of Beeston appears to be impossibly perfect and I imagine you would have to be impossibly wealthy to live there. The trees on Bulkeley Hill were nearly as gnarled as the ones I'd seen by Offa's Dyke near Tintern, and this whole stretch was just splendid.

After a pastoral interlude across more farmland, dotted with marl pits – pools which look like natural ponds but which were, in fact, dug out by farmers so they could get the marl, a lime-rich clay used as a fertiliser – and linked together by the enticingly-named Pudding Lane, Gullet Lane and Old Gypsy Lane, I arrived at Delamere Forest. In my childhood, Delamere was where you might go for a day out or a school trip. It had seemed an incredibly vast place then, to be ventured into only by the very brave or the very foolish. It is still the only forest between North Wales and the Lake District so we had good reason to feel some pride in it, but it's not all that fearsome really. My guidebook describes the forest as a 'dim, quiet world', and this dim, quiet walker managed to lose the waymarked trail at one point. Resisting the urge to run round in circles shouting 'I'm a teapot', I eventually managed to pick up the route out of the forest without too much difficulty.

From somewhere near Manley I got my first view of the Mersey and its industry and then, after an extremely wetting walk through a field of golden, shoulder-high rape, came a short but miserable stretch past the 'Keep Out – Private' notices of a caravan site and a pig farm. I treated myself to some mild excitement by scaling the short sandstone staircase known as Jacob's Ladder and arrived by the war memorial on the hill overlooking Frodsham. The view from here was one of the most compelling of the whole journey. Pretty it ain't. Admittedly, there is some greenery between here and the rock outcrop of Helsby Hill a mile or two away, but the overwhelming impression is one of industry and urbanisation gone mad. Across the rooftops of Frodsham can be seen the M56 motorway and then the Mersey, on the banks of which is the most extraordinary collection of spires, turrets and domes – not a medieval castle or gothic cathedral, but an oil-refinery complex, a power station and various chemical works. Even from this distance the thunder of the motorway can be heard surprisingly clearly, so it was a noisy view too.

This was an obvious place to halt and I reflected on the Sandstone Trail and how well waymarked it had been. Stiles and gates were impeccably maintained and I can heartily recommend it. The Walkers' Guide produced by the County Council is excellent, too. After a few minutes, the traffic noise got a bit much so I wandered down the hill into the metropolis that is Frodsham.

The First Cut is the Deepest –
Along the Canals to Manchester and Beyond

Under the bridges of Stretford

After the ear-splitting sound of the boats towing some water skiers on the River Weaver, I enjoyed a quiet saunter under a brilliant blue sky along the peaceful, grassy river bank where suburban Merseyside seemed worlds away. I had only waterfowl for company as I continued as far as Dutton Lock, obviously a busy place in its day but now home only to a half-submerged cargo boat. The Weaver is a big river which was canalised to carry freighters for the Cheshire salt industry but there is now no evidence of its glorious past. Like much of what was industrial Britain, the Weaver appears to have lapsed into a kind of contented torpor.

A short walk across meadowland took me to the Trent and Mersey Canal. I would be following canal towpaths for the next two or three days on my journey through Manchester to the edge of the Pennines. Canal towpath walking has been described as the 'ultimate escape into a world that has changed little in over 200 years', so I was looking forward to this next stage in my journey along part of the famous Cheshire Ring, a rough circle of six linked canals more or less following Cheshire's boundaries.

One of the pleasures of hill walking lies in the fact that each step is different from the one before. The terrain is such that you can rarely march over it without having to alter your stride. You find yourself making minor adjustments all the time and this, as much as anything else, appears to act as a sort of lubricant to the joints and sinews and all the other bits and pieces so that no one part of the body gets over-tired. Canal towpath walking is different. Necessarily level and, in general, good underfoot, a towpath will lead you on for mile after mile with no break in rhythm or step required. This takes a bit of getting used to and, just as I was adapting to this new regime, the path ended at the dark and sinister looking portal of the Preston Brook Tunnel. It is over 1000 yards long and appears to have been built too narrow, so there's no towpath and two boats cannot pass. The designer was Thomas Brindley, the Telford of the canal world, so whether he made a mistake with his arithmetic or what, I don't know. In the canal's heyday every barge had to be 'legged' through, which meant that the bargee would have to lie on his back and push the boat using his legs against the tunnel roof as propulsion. Modern pleasure boats have engines of course, but there has to be some complicated timetable arrangement in force to prevent collisions, traffic jams and unseemly brawls.

At the other end of the tunnel lies – unsurprisingly – Preston Brook, once the canal equivalent of Clapham Junction and now a thriving marina. Here the canal becomes the Bridgewater, completed in 1777 and generally regarded as being the first commercial canal opened in this country. Around here the canal appears to act as a barrier to the spread of urban sprawl. On the left, back gardens leading right up to the canal bank and, on the right, just over the water, green fields with contented looking cattle munching away. Past Daresbury – where the stained glass windows in the church commemorate the characters in Alice in Wonderland because Lewis Carroll was born here when his dad was vicar – and on by Moore to Walton, where the canal dives into a shady glade reminiscent of some of the walking along the Wye and the Dee. Once past Lymm, a rather self-consciously attractive village famous in my youth for being the place where successful Manchester United players lived, I got my first view of the Pennines. They were nothing more than a dark smudge on the skyline from here but no less exciting for that.

A few miles further on I reached Broadheath, an industrial area on the edge of Altrincham. The old engineering factories probably grew up along the canal with its easy transport links to Manchester and Liverpool but, with the decline of the traditional industries, new ones have sprung up and there is one of those modern retail park thingies there as well now. You know the places: vast car parks with big supermarkets where cowed and miserable-looking people seem condemned to wander endlessly looking at carpets, car shampoos and complicated devices to fix shelves to walls.

I lived the first twenty years of my life in Sale, just a couple of miles further on, so I was now reaching ground that I knew well but which I had not visited in probably thirty years or more. I was glad to see the old Linotype works still there. This is the home of 'hot metal' – the traditional method of producing printing type – but I don't know whether they still do it there or not. The factory was still clanking and banging though, as were plenty of others along this stretch; the din was phenomenal. The factories of Broadheath employed hundreds of people when I was a teenager and we used to derive much pleasure from reading the job adverts in the local rag to find the post most suited to our fevered minds. There were grinders and borers but 'Full-time body-presser' was the one we most liked the sound of.

I did work briefly in one of the canal-side factories (but not as a body-presser) and was delighted to see the place still very much alive and well. I was into serious nostalgia mode by now, but how could it be otherwise? Revisiting things that had once been so important to me was bound to cause some kind of jolt. The sight of the factory where I worked set me thinking about my former colleagues and I was surprised how vividly I recalled some of them. There was Coop, who used to shout 'Won't be long now, fellers' just before the end of every shift we worked, and who had a dog that was so clever it used to go to the shop and bring a can of dog food home in its mouth. Then there was Jacky, a Belgian chap who insisted on referring to screwdrivers as 'scroove-driers', so that I always had this mental picture of a cabinet affair with warm air passing through it to dry a batch of the mysterious scrooves. And there was Dave, a lad who used to keep us entertained with tales of his life as a fireman on the footplates of British Rail steam locomotives, and whose enthusiasm for classical music opened up a whole new world to me. I probably would never have heard the unsurpassable magic of Shostakovitch's Fifth Symphony if I hadn't worked with Dave.

And so into Sale. There's not much to say about Sale, I suppose. Until the 1850s it didn't really exist but with the coming of the railway it grew into commuter land so quickly that by the turn of the century it was home to nearly 50,000 souls. I always assumed when I lived there that it had existed for centuries and never thought to ask why there were no ancient cottages or castles. In a sense it grew almost overnight, much as Tan-y-Grisiau had done back in the Welsh hills. The difference is that Sale continued to grow as more and more commuters were needed to satisfy Manchester's voracious appetite.

A remarkable thing happened when I got hold of the rusting iron railing running along the canal bank near where I used to live. The rough metal must have acted as a conduit to a world of forty years ago and ripped a great jagged hole in the space-time continuum, because the feel of it was enough to transport me back to my childhood when we used to turn somersaults over these iron bars. This wasn't just memory – I felt as though I was actually there, back in the 1950s.

In Sale I met my brother-in-law Guy and he walked with me along the canal bank as far as Stalybridge. It was felt that, now I was a country hick living in Kendal, I was not equipped to deal with the potential problems of negotiating the canal network through central Manchester where I might be set upon by brigands and thieves. The first part of the walk through Stretford shot by as, deep in conversation, we rattled up the miles. The short section through Trafford Park was different, though. It was incredibly noisy and dirty and looked as an urban canalscape should. Reminiscent of the set from *Eraserhead*, there were bizarrely ugly buildings bristling with sinister looking pipes oozing steam and other gunge, and a huge collection of coloured metal containers stacked up like outsize Lego bricks. Amongst all this noise and grime people were sitting down and trying to fish. I mean to say, what can they possibly catch in this wasteland? We passed underneath the gigantic north stand of the Manchester United Old Trafford where Guy, a City supporter, expressed a certain unwillingness to be photographed and then we had to fight our way through the gritty shambles of some bridge works near Salford Quays.

Will Manchester ever be finished? Ever since I can remember, they've been knocking it to bits and rebuilding it. They're even demolishing things now that I can remember being built in the first place. The stretch from Old Trafford into the city centre, past what used to be the massive Salford Docks, must be one of the ugliest pieces of countryside I encountered anywhere. And I can't ever recall it being any different. The litter is jaw-droppingly awful, but through it all there was an amazing amount of bird life: a swan had built her nest in the most unlikely looking siding of the canal in among floating debris and overlooked by decaying and tottering, derelict warehouses, and there were coots and moorhens. I only know they were coots and moorhens because Guy told me, and he knows what he's talking about.

As always, though, Manchester faces the future with optimism and a positive outlook. It is rapidly growing as a commercial centre and as increasing numbers of young execs move in to work there, the tumbledown cotton wharves and warehouses are being converted into expensive housing. The dark Victorian brick is being replaced by glass and steel and the whole city has an upbeat and almost aggressively prosperous air. We walked on up the 'Rochdale Nine', a long flight of locks right on the edge of the city centre and unsuspected from the streets above, to the inappropriately named Paradise Wharf, a dismal place of filthy water and greasy, unhappy-looking men.

The journey out of Manchester took us along the Ashton Canal through a gorge of redbrick textile mills and past the new velodrome, built when Manchester's Olympic bid was still alive, then on to a Robertson's jam works. This was great! I mean, you somehow expect to see stunning scenery on an end to end walk, but not a jam works. Disappointed not to see happy little people unloading exotic fruits from colourful boats, we had to content ourselves with the olfactory delights of the strong, sugary smell wafting across the water. In the five or so miles between Manchester and Ashton-under-Lyne, there are no fewer than eighteen locks, not a problem to a walker but probably a nightmare for the boatperson. With the Rochdale Nine, that's twenty-seven locks we'd climbed so it came as no surprise to see that the canal had taken on a more upland appearance compared to its cousin at Sale. Where was brick was now black gritstone – the Pennines were clearly not far away.

Owing to an almost unforgivable act of bureaucratic vandalism, a supermarket has been built over the course of the canal at Ashton so we had to do a bit of car park walking to find the start of the Huddersfield Narrow Canal leading to Stalybridge, where there is a completely wonderful bar in what used to be the station buffet. Relaxing over a pint in front of a real fire while we waited for my sister Alison to come and pick us up, I was able to conclude without any difficulty that this had been another of the great days – Sale to Stalybridge. What a long way! Well done Guy – thanks for riding shotgun.

It was a cool, grey morning when Alison and I set out to cross the streets of Stalybridge to pick up the Huddersfield Narrow Canal which would, we hoped, take us to Uppermill. Stalybridge is a textile town on what used to be the Cheshire side of the River Tame, one of many industrial towns and villages in what was known as the Cheshire 'Panhandle', a strange prolongation of the county from Stockport up into the Pennines. Like Llanidloes, which now seemed to be light years away, Stalybridge and its neighbouring towns were big in early attempts to promote workers' rights in the 1800s. The Chartists here organised a two-week shut down of all the mills in North Cheshire and South Lancashire in an attempt to prevent a pay cut. There was also the remarkable Reverend Stephens who was imprisoned in the 1830s for making 'seditious speeches' in support of the downtrodden, and who carried on fighting long after his prison term was over. A monument to this man stands in the park between Stalybridge and Ashton.

Despite its turbulent and fascinating past, the place looked drab on this Friday morning but at least I was able to see something of the town. This was very much the downside of using the canals to traverse Manchester. I can't think of a better way of doing it — there's no traffic noise and fumes, no dangerous roads to battle with and there are interesting things to look at like locks and bridges — but you don't get much of a feel for the towns you are, in a sense, avoiding. I thought I couldn't possibly do this walk without visiting Sale and paying homage to Manchester, but how could I go so close to the centre of the city without making a point of looking at the great Gothic town hall? Or the Bridgewater Hall, the new hi-tech home of the Hallé Orchestra? Or the Hacienda, spiritual home of Madchester? Well, there we are.

The Huddersfield Narrow Canal is, like the Ffestiniog Railway, one of Britain's Great Things, but it still needs a tremendous amount of work to make it usable again. Construction work began on it in 1794 and just four years later all but seven of the canal's twenty miles were complete. Rather crucially, it was the middle seven miles that were missing and it took a further thirteen years to construct the Standedge Tunnel under the Pennines. By the time the canal began to show any kind of profit, the railways had arrived and the canal has seen no commercial through traffic since 1921. But times are changing and there's serious talk of re-opening the canal as a viable freight route. Who knows, it might even take some pressure off the horrendous M62.

In the meantime, restoration work is going on along the stretch between Stalybridge and Uppermill. The scars are new and the concrete is still an eyesore but time and nature will hide all this. The area around the now demolished Hartshead power station is one of almost comical ugliness – a decaying concrete conveyor, black trees and a gigantic electricity pylon straddling the canal all adding their own contribution to the visual feast.

Soon, though, all this was behind us. The surroundings started to become hillier and much more dramatic and then ... Scout Tunnel. This place should have its own theme music – maybe the dur-dur, dur-dur bit from *Jaws* or the music off *Mastermind*. It's only 220 yards long so compared to the Chirk Tunnel on the Llangollen Canal it's a tiddler, but the whole atmosphere here is different. The scenery is about a thousand per cent wilder, the tunnel itself is hewn out of the bare rock, and you can hear the constant and rather ominous drip, drip, drip of water finding its way through the rock above your head. You also get the feeling that nobody has ever been here before. Alison did ask whether the tunnel was open to walkers and with the sort of confidence displayed by the very stupid I assured her it was. It was only when we got to the other end we found that the path had been barricaded by steel mesh so we had to retreat, which obviously meant going through the tunnel again. When we arrived back at our starting point we saw that the fencing at this end had been torn down by some jolly pranksters and dumped in the water.

A detour took us over the tunnel and to Bottom Mossley which, not surprisingly, is in the valley bottom as opposed to Top Mossley which is on the top of the hill. A former colleague lived in Mossley as a child and she used to know one of the all-time great north-westerners, Little Harry Pilling, the finest batsman never to play for England. Seeing Harry and Clive Lloyd bat together used to be one of life's most rewarding pleasures, not just for the success they brought to Lancashire cricket, but also for the chance to witness what was probably one of the greatest ever differences in style and physique between two batsmen. Clive Lloyd, a cricketer of undoubted world class, seemed to stand about six foot eight, and covered the distance between the wickets in three giant loping strides. Harry was four foot nine and could barely see over his pads. His every run was scurried in a desperate race to keep up and in the hope he would not be flattened by Clive who had notoriously poor eyesight and, in view of the height differential, probably would not have had Harry in his line of vision anyway. I never saw it, but rumour has it that Harry was actually 'lapped' on one or two occasions.

As this book was going through the final stages of proof-reading and all the other mysterious stuff that goes on before it gets sent to the printer, I read, with great sadness, of Harry Pilling's death. I did wonder about removing the above reference to him, but decided that I should leave it in, if only to serve as an affectionate reminder for all of you who saw him play. RIP Harry.

Just as Stalybridge used to be in Cheshire, Mossley was in Lancashire and Uppermill was in Yorkshire, but I'm told all three had an affinity with each other and regarded themselves as essentially Pennine rather than belonging to one or other of those counties. Like many other places in the known universe, they have now been gobbled up by Greater Manchester, which has thereby grabbed itself a piece of tourist land. At weekends Uppermill is crowded with visitors who come to feed the ducks on the canal and spend their money in the factory shops and craft centres. It must be one of the pleasantest of the Pennine villages and this whole area of Saddleworth is home to an annual brass band competition where bands from all over the country, and even from overseas, come to impress. They travel from village to village performing their own distinctive type of music and, if the film *Brassed Off* is anything to go by, getting more and more inebriated while they're at it.

King Cotton –
the Lancashire Pennines

Blackstone Edge from Lydgate

One of the reasons for venturing as far east as Uppermill was that I had found a book called *The Red Rose Walk* which describes a route from that village to Arnside, just inside Cumbria. The line it takes passes through much of east Lancashire, an area which, much to my shame, I knew hardly at all. The express route from Frodsham to the Lakes would have been to sneak across Chat Moss between Warrington and Manchester and use canals and riverside paths past Wigan, Preston and Lancaster but I was still enthusiastic enough to want to see as much of the country as possible. So the splendidly indirect line of the Red Rose Walk, as it negotiated its way through and around towns such as Rochdale, Ramsbottom and Accrington, was too good a chance to miss. After all, I might never come this way again. Tom Schofield, the book's author, clearly loves the area and knows its finer points so I entrusted myself to his care for the next few days as I headed on up towards Kendal.

Predictably, since the cricket season had just started, the weather turned much colder as I started the Pennine part of the journey which would prove to be an interesting switchback walk, but one that was in no hurry to free itself from the shackles of Manchester's influence. I left Uppermill along the canal to the old wool wharf and then climbed over Harrop Edge and down into Delph, another of the seven villages making up the parish of Saddleworth. On the steep descent back into the Tame valley Delph, crowded along the river bank and with a tall mill chimney piercing the skyline, looked every inch the typical Pennine village. Not quite so typically Pennine is chewing gum but Edmund Wrigley, who invented the stuff in America, was born in Delph. He was, honest. There you are, another little place with a remarkable claim to fame.

Another, gentler, climb took me to the twin reservoirs of Castleshaw, a cold and cheerless spot on this blustery day. The remains of a Roman fort were discovered here but, unlike the one near Chirk, this appears to have been built for defensive purposes only – to protect the road from Manchester to Glossop. Yet another up and down brought me to the site of Dowry Castle, where there used to be a Victorian mansion. You have to wonder why anybody with money enough to build a mansion would choose to do it here. It was almost unimaginably bleak and inhospitable, although the view from the front room was probably better then than it would be now.

I found the scenery of the west Pennine moors just a little dispiriting. There's an austere grandeur about the dark hills and the steep-sided valleys, but these uplands have not been treated kindly; every skyline appears to carry some intrusive adornment. There are rows and rows of electricity pylons, the ubiquitous radio masts, and concrete motorway bridges. And nearly every valley has its reservoir and main road.

Spring was much later arriving here so it was back to newborn lambs. There were skylarks again and, despite the messiness of much of the surroundings, it was good to be out on the open hill once more, where the going was excellent along well graded tracks. For the first day or two, The Red Rose Walk tends to cross valleys, rather than summits and in order to facilitate accommodation and transport it visits the edges of many towns. It picks an ingenious way through the outer limits of Rochdale and Bury but the recent construction of modern, gentrified housing in some spots has confused things, especially where footpaths may have been diverted and not properly re-signed. This happened near Littleborough after a decent walk across Syke Moor where, I have to confess, I envied anybody who may have been up on the excitingly serrated skyline of Blackstone Edge high above my right shoulder.

Down in the valley by the banks of the Rochdale Canal, where some hardy souls were attempting to play cricket, I met a lady who was cycling the towpath from Rochdale to Hebden Bridge and back. Good luck to her, I say. There was some more rather messy walking under electricity lines from Clough to Wardle by way of High Lea Slack where all the stone step stiles were broken, apparently deliberately, and then further doubts as to the route where more building work was going on near Whitworth Golf Club. Apart from the golfers, there was another group of chaps out here flying radio-controlled model aircraft. What with horse-riding and walking and cycling and sailing on some of the reservoirs, you have to admit that these low hills provide an almost infinite variety of recreational opportunities to thousands of people in the Manchester area.

Healey Dell nature reserve joined the list of unexpected delights on this trip. Risking life and limb to cross an alarmingly busy main road, I entered the Dell from above a splendid stone-arched disused railway viaduct. The railway was constructed to link Rochdale with Bacup and was never commercially viable. Unlike some of the canals which were built in the vain hope of giving the investors some kind of return, this white elephant was born purely out of the desire of an existing railway company to prevent a rival getting a line into their territory. This must be the ultimate madness of rail privatisation, and I was to come across a further example in Scotland's Great Glen. The River Spodden has carved itself a miniature gorge through the rock, and the birch woods added a welcome sylvan touch to the day's walking.

Back on the open hillside again there was a long gradual ascent of the Rooley Moor Road, an old route between Rochdale and the Rossendale valley. This rutted track is clearly a must for mountain bikers because on this Sunday morning I saw hundreds of them. I'd got tangled up with the Rossendale Something or Other, where the cyclists have to complete forty-five miles of tough country in seven hours. As I was plodding uphill, these people were coming down, and gravity and desperation were both playing their part in ensuring that they all went faster than looked comfortable. I had wondered what the Mountain Rescue ambulance was doing at the bottom of the track; now I knew. Each time I thought the last one had gone by, another batch would appear over the skyline and another group of grim-faced, death-defying lunatics would rattle past. All good things come to an end though and by the time I'd reached the trig point on Top of Leach they had all gone.

Top of Leach was grand. Standing a modest 1,556 feet above the sea, it was nevertheless the highest actual top I'd been on since Snowdon. A five-sided column bears the names of the towns making up the Borough of Rossendale and what a fine set of names it is: Whitworth, Rawtenstall, Ramsbottom, Haslingden and Bacup. The views were far-reaching in all directions. Southwards, I could make out the immense sprawl of Manchester and its satellites and beyond that the curiously shaped tops of the Peak District hills. Further west was Cheshire's sandstone ridge, along which I'd been walking not many days before, and the power stations on the Mersey estuary while away to the north, Pendle Hill stood boldly against the grey sky. And was that Ingleborough peeping out behind it? The rooftops of Haslingden and Rawtenstall were clearly visible just to the north and seemed almost within touching distance, but my route turned its back on these settlements and headed south again towards Bury.

At Waugh's Well, a rather strange stone affair looking a little like an elongated fireplace which was erected in memory of Edwin Waugh, a Lancashire dialect poet, I found other walkers for the first time since I'd left Uppermill. The *Manchester Evening News* features a walk to somewhere local each week, and this week's was to Waugh's Well. So, no longer alone on this Sunday afternoon, I trudged down the long slope to Cheesden. I lost the crowds again as I crossed the main road and battled my way on to Harden Moor where there was more footpath sign vandalism and barricaded gates. An easy descent past the remains of Grant's Tower led to a frustrating dead end; my track ended at the M66 because the footbridge across the motorway was being repaired. After I had retraced my steps up a long grass slope, I saw the notice advising walkers of the necessity to make a detour but it was so small, and placed so high above the ground, that I hadn't seen it until it was too late. Oh well, muck or nettles, as they say round here, and the diversion at least gave me the chance to see more of Ramsbottom than I otherwise would have. In my far-off Cheshire youth, Ramsbottom was one of those places that had Lancashire written right through it. The truth is that, until the late eighteenth century there was nothing there at all apart from a 'fair valley of trees and daffodils with a fine river meandering through lush meadows'. Robert Peel, founder of the Metropolitan Police, was born not far away and opened a printing works and, during the first half of the 1800's, the Grant brothers — they of the ruined tower who had come down from eastern Scotland in search of fame and fortune

– built a state-of-the-art mill and the church of St Andrews. They were enlightened employers and were used by Dickens as the basis for the Cheeryble brothers in Nicholas Nickleby. The 'fine river' was the Irwell which, by the end of the Industrial Revolution, must have been one of Britain's most polluted waterways. Some quick-thinking civic dignitary is reputed to have told Queen Victoria that the pieces of used toilet paper floating in the water were, in fact, 'No Fishing' notices. Times are better now though, and the Irwell once more supports wildlife and runs through pleasant parkland just east of the town.

Once I'd extricated myself from the clutches of yet more new housing which had sprung up to smother the footpath, I reached Holcombe Brook and the steep ascent onto Holcombe Moor where the unmissable and strikingly ugly Peel Monument stands sentinel over the Irwell valley. This square, turreted tower was built in 1851 and stands 128 feet high and I'm told it's sometimes open to the public. Not the day I was there, though. Are you surprised?

An easy stroll across Harcles Hill leads to a small stone monument marking the site of the Pilgrims' Cross where travellers on their way to Whalley Abbey would rest and pray. It's interesting to note that this monument was erected in 1902 to replace the original which was destroyed by vandals. So vandalism isn't a new phenomenon after all. The menacing Army Firing Range notices just add to the general feeling of desolation, which isn't helped by the sad Ellen Strange stone, commemorating the discovery of the body of young Ellen, supposedly murdered here by her boyfriend, Billy.

The trees of the Alden valley offered welcome relief but the heavy cloud cover finally gave way to the rain that had been threatening for some time. Fortunately, it didn't amount to much more than a shower as I made the long haul up to the head of the Musden valley, a surprisingly wild place with the by now familiar, abandoned and derelict farmsteads. The Musbury Quarry with its ruined chimney was eerily reminiscent of the Geevor tin mines on the Cornish coast, and there was another descent to the reservoirs on the outskirts of Haslingden. I seemed to have had this little town in view for days and I felt a bit more satisfied once I'd climbed up and over Haslingden Moor towards Accrington. By this time the rain had returned with a vengeance and there were more route-finding difficulties at a farmhouse that was being renovated. The builders appeared unconcerned by my arrival in their midst but I remain unconvinced by the accuracy of the directions they gave me, especially in view of the fence I had to climb and the bull I had to pretend to ignore.

I'd lost count of the number of messy exits from so-called civilisation on this walk and here at Baxenden, near Accrington, was yet another fine example, with some exceptionally ferocious dogs chained up in a farmyard and then the white-knuckle experience of crossing the A56. Running to dodge fast traffic while carrying a big pack is an interesting game but not one I'd recommend. Things improved mightily with the short ascent to the trig point on the top of Great Hameldon, then deteriorated again for a very scruffy walk across a disused rifle range to a small conifer plantation where the footpath traversed ground so deeply furrowed that it was like walking across a giant piece of corrugated iron. The mournful wreck of Miste Farm with its sightless windows and rotting roof timbers spoke volumes about the tough times some farmers have, but I was soon cheered up by the dramatic and totally unexpected gorge at Childers Green where some strangely honeycombed rock had been weathered into odd turrets and pinnacles.

Crossing the Calder valley with its lines of communication – road, canal (Leeds and Liverpool, this time), railway and the M65 motorway – marked a change in the nature of my journey through east Lancashire. None of the well-known former cotton towns lie north of this valley; they're all between here and Manchester. The list of them reads like a football league table from 1897: Oldham, Rochdale, Bury, Bolton, Darwen, Accrington, Blackburn and Burnley. The Red Rose Walk had threaded a sinuous course between many of these places, knocking on the doors as it were, but never quite crossing the threshold.

I was looking forward to the more scenic delights that awaited but there was no denying the interest in the ever-changing landscape I'd walked through over the last three or four days. These open moorlands were also home to curlews and lapwings. Curlews are shy birds and are a dull brown colour, so they're not often seen by unobservant walkers like me, but there's no mistaking their grief-stricken call – a mellow, liquid whistle which I always think is the saddest sound in the world. (I have to tell you that not everyone agrees with this assessment – one walker I chatted to reckoned vacuum cleaners make an even sadder sound than curlews. Takes all sorts.) Lapwings, by contrast, are cantankerously exhibitionist individuals who make an angry clatter when disturbed. Their erratic, almost random, flight pattern makes them look from a distance like paper bags being blown about by the wind. Of all the birds I encountered on the journey lapwings were my favourites, partly because I know what they are but also because I never tired of watching their aeronautical prowess. I did not know it then, of course, but weeks later with the end of the journey in sight, I was set upon by a vicious mob of these feathered hooligans, an experience so alarming that, had it happened near the start, I might have packed up and fled back home.

Based on figures derived from tax returns, Lancashire before the Industrial Revolution was ranked poorest of all of the thirty-eight counties assessed. Compared to the drier east and the more prosperous south, there were virtually no prehistoric monuments or ancient buildings of any note. Even the Romans referred to the place as Britannia Inferior – the longer this walk went on the more the Romans were beginning to annoy me – and the generally miserable climate made life here a claggy mess. But ironically it was that same climate which was largely responsible for changing all this when the cotton mills sprang up. The damp air was an essential raw material in the spinning process – too dry and the spun cotton would snap. Power to the mills was provided first by the fast flowing streams of the Pennine foothills, then more crucially by the coal mined in the south of the county around

Bolton and Wigan. Wealth accumulated at a fantastic rate as towns sprung up and people moved in from all over the country to serve King Cotton. By the end of the 1800s, Manchester was Britain's richest city outside London and Lancashire textile workers could earn half as much again as their counterparts further south. Just before the First World War, two-thirds of the world's cotton came out of Lancashire. Just think about that. Two-thirds. Don't you think that's amazing?

The reverse of the coin is, of course, well documented. The appalling living conditions endured by the early cotton workers, miners and so on; the almost irreversible pollution of land, air and water that took place, and then the misery of the Depression when the inevitable decline set in. Even now, many of the Lancashire mill towns are struggling to free themselves from the grip of the bad times. Most, if not all, of the dark, satanic mills have closed down although many of the buildings remain, some put to other uses, some decaying and many still with the trademark slender chimneys.

Witches and Waterfalls –
Pendle and Ingleborough to Kendal

Packhorse bridge near Downham

So, goodbye to the traditional Lancashire of mill towns and chimneys and hello to the not-so-well-known Lancashire of pretty villages and rolling hills. Past the solidly impressive Shuttleworth Hall, still a working farm, I walked down to the village of Altham, much of which has been swamped by new industrial units. Whatever you might think about the old mills, they had a certain style that is sadly lacking in these prefabricated cuboids. More farms with more deranged dogs threatening to throttle themselves in their apparent endeavours to tear me limb from limb, before a thoroughly pleasant stretch of riverside walking took me past Whalley Banks where the dry stone walls and whitewashed cottages reminded me that I was getting closer to the Lakes all the time.

Whalley is an atmospheric large village on the banks of the Calder, well known for its fourteenth century Abbey, its even older parish church and a brick-built forty-eight arched railway viaduct. It was over a week since I had approached Greater Manchester along the rural banks of the Bridgewater Canal but even this far north the buses still had the word 'Mancunian' written on them. Shaking myself free from Manchester was proving more difficult than I thought.

Steady rain accompanied me as I left Whalley via yet another golf course. Somewhere here I met a jolly-looking fellow walker who had an encyclopaedic knowledge of the various Ways and Trails of East Lancashire and seemed intent on sharing it with me. Was I doing the Witches' Way? No. He was. Had I done the Dales Way? No. He had. What was I doing? Would I be doing the Ribble Way? When I said I would be walking the bit between Sawley and the Yorkshire border he said, 'I don't want to put you off, but it's a right mucky mess, is t' Ribble Way. Witches' Way is what I'm doing.'

I'd been through plenty of right mucky messes on my journey so far, so wasn't too perturbed by this helpful advice as I continued through some quietly attractive scenery. Of the industry and modern lines of communication that I'd been walking through for days, there was not a sign. There were some route finding difficulties at a horse-riding place where a very strident lady pointed me in the right direction and sent me off feeling like a ten year old who'd been caught scrumping apples and then, after passing through the village of Sabden, I started the ascent of the wonderful Pendle Hill. A long, gradual climb by the side of the rather dreary Ogden Clough took me up into the mist-shrouded world of the summit plateau where a very strong wind gave added wetting power to the rain. At just over 1,800 feet, Pendle Hill is not particularly high but is a major landmark for miles around, its great prow overlooking and dominating the Ribble valley. The views from the top are said to be stupendous but I'll have to take their word for it – I did, at least, see the Beacon, a great pile of stones reputed to be a bronze-age burial mound.

Although an ancient royal hunting ground and a very attractive area in its own right, the Forest of Pendle has, over the years, come to be best known perhaps for the Pendle witches. There are conflicting versions of the story. Depending on whose side you're on, these people with the splendid names Demdike, Chattox and Nutter (not Blackburn Rovers' half-back line, though they should have been) were misunderstood old ladies who dabbled in herbal remedies, or malevolent old crones using witchcraft to further their own ambitions. What is beyond dispute, however, is the fact that they were tried at Lancaster in 1612, found guilty and hung.

A steep descent from the top of the hill took me through the hidden olde worlde villages of Barley and Downham and it was interesting to see the daffodils still flowering, just as they had been at Land's End nearly two months previously. Downham is one of those villages that still has a squire, Lord Clitheroe of Downham – wouldn't it be great if he was a descendant of Jimmy? – and he apparently refuses to allow the village skyline to be cluttered with TV aerials and satellite dishes. The place smacks so much of rural perfection that *Whistle Down the Wind* was filmed here back in the days when I thought I might still stand a romantic chance with its star, the flawless Hayley Mills.

It was only a couple of easy miles from here to Sawley as I crossed the embankment — or 'agger' — of the old Roman road from York to Ribchester and then the most perfect stone packhorse bridge across Smithies Brook. Sawley is a tiny place dominated by and famous for what's left of the Cistercian Abbey dating from 1147.

Of more significance to me, though, Sawley is where I parted company with the Red Rose Walk — well done, Tom. I certainly couldn't have fashioned such an interesting and intricate route to take me out of one of Britain's biggest industrial areas. I joined the 'mucky mess' of the Ribble Way and the two or three miles alongside the river bank to Gisburn were entirely delightful. This was most definitely the best river scenery since the Wye near Hay and even the murky weather could not disguise the colours and patterns of this stretch of walking.

In the rain, I passed through Gisburn, once in Yorkshire and now in Lancashire — another casualty of the 1974 boundary changes — and passed by the Norman motte and bailey of Castle Haugh on the way to the neat village of Paythorne. It was surprising, given the relatively sylvan aspect of these Ribblesdale villages and the fact that we were nearly into May, just how wintry the scene still was. There appeared to be no sign of spring in the trees which were still showing as spidery black silhouettes against the grey sky, and the walk across the cheerless tundra of Paythorne Moor was made still more dismal by another barmy dog chained to a farm building. Somewhere in this reedy, rushy wilderness I crossed out of Lancashire into North Yorkshire but, rather surprisingly, there were no big signs, checkpoints or customs posts and militiamen with machine guns.

Saying my farewells to the Ribble Way somewhere near Rathmell, I had a frustrating time trying to locate public footpaths but eventually reached Lawkland by way of lanes running past the excellently named farms of Sheepwash and Wham. This was clearly Yorkshire Dales country now – pale limestone walls edging the fields and great whalebacked fells looming out of the wet, grey air across the valley – and I passed the National Park sign with its distinctive Swaledale sheep logo before reaching the day's end at Austwick, another unspoiled village, haphazardly arranged around a triangular green.

Approaching from the east, Austwick is the first of several settlements crouching in the shadow of Ingleborough, the 'big, blue hill'. From most angles, Ingleborough's shape makes it unmistakable and it can be easily picked out from surprising distances. Resembling a pyramid that has been sliced across at mid-height Ingleborough makes its brooding presence felt for a distance far exceeding that which you would expect for its relatively modest height. At 2,372 feet it is tall enough to be recognised as a mountain but is hardly a giant. And yet ... in the eighteenth century, Thomas Pennant, traveller extraordinaire, reckoned it was the highest ground in Britain and calculated its height at over 4,000 feet. Wrong as Pennant was, there can be little doubt that for sheer variety of scenery it has few equals – dazzling limestone pavements, waterfalls, woods, pretty villages, rough moorland, a few cliffs, gorges and the greatest and most famous pothole in the country: Gaping Gill. All in all, Ingleborough was too good to be avoided. I thought my route ought to include a bit of Yorkshire, and what better bit is there than this corner of Craven?

An excellent walk from Austwick across fields took me to Clapham, one of those places where you think, 'I could live here, no problem.' There's a pub, a café and a couple of shops, a tree-lined beck runs through the village in between two parallel lanes of grey cottages and there's another fine packhorse bridge. Mr Wainwright calls the ascent of Ingleborough from Clapham a classic, and there's no arguing with that. It is — even if you do have to pay to gain access to the Reginald Farrer Nature Trail just above the village. The Farrers used to own the Ingleborough Estate and have been benefactors to Clapham for generations. Reginald, who died in 1920 aged only 40, was a botanist of world renown specialising in Himalayan plants which he managed to cultivate in the warmer conditions of Yorkshire. So keen was he to establish his plants on an inaccessible limestone cliff rising sheer from the waters of Clapham Tarn that he rowed across the lake and fired seeds at the precipice from a shotgun. Many of them germinated and flourished. Presumably he took plants which were common in their natural habitat, for he had no time for those people who picked rare wild flowers. As he so delicately put it, 'Accursed for ever more, into the lowest of Eight Hot Hells, be all reckless uprooters of rarities'. And his father generated electricity for his saw mill and gave Clapham electric street lights long before most other places in Britain were used to such luxury.

The walk was pleasant through the grounds of the Estate and past the entrance to Ingleborough Cave which was opened up in 1837. It was always suspected that the water disappearing at

Gaping Gill a mile or so away found its way into Ingleborough Cave but the link was not finally proved until 1983.

The way then enters Trow Gill a long limestone canyon below Clapdale Hall, reputedly the home of the witch of Clapham. The way out of the Gill, up a narrowing limestone staircase reminiscent of Ebbor Gorge back in the Mendips, took me up to the shelf of land on which there are many potholes. Most of them have small, insignificant entrances, the only clue to their existence being the little paths leading to them but walking across this moorland in the dark would be a hazardous undertaking indeed. I'm sure they're big enough to swallow an unsuspecting walker. Gaping Gill though is something else – it could swallow an army of walkers in one gulp. Unlike the other holes round here, the entrance is unmissable: a fearful round hole twenty feet across and 365 feet deep. Attempts have been made to fence off the steep grass slope immediately above the abyss but there have been fatalities here. If ever you visit this place – and you should – keep a close eye on yourself and your companions. The drop to the bottom is vertical and the first successful descent was not made until 1895, more than fifty years after explorations started. Visitors can now descend this chasm (for a small fee which goes to charity) in the relative safety of a bosun's chair on certain days in the summer and see for themselves the huge cathedral-like chamber measuring 460 feet long and 100 feet high, and a very worthwhile trip it is. The Gill entrance is particularly awe-inspiring after heavy rain when a raging brown cataract thunders over the limestone lip. On one memorable visit in such conditions my companion, a chap not given to hyperbole, said it was the scariest thing he'd ever seen.

The day which had started so sunny and warm at Austwick had by now turned cold and grey and it was a slimy slog through black slutch to reach the ridge of Little Ingleborough. I have been up Ingleborough five or six times, I have seen the summit from below, but on every occasion I've been up there the weather has varied from bad to awful and I've never seen any view at all. Today was no exception. I impressed and amazed myself with my navigational skills by locating the trig point and through the thick, grey soup I could make out some strange orange objects. On closer inspection these turned out to be tents and the inhabitants told me they were marshals and first aiders for the Three Peaks Fell Race. What magnificent timing – of all the days to choose to be on Ingleborough! I feared that this would be like the Rossendale Bike Race all over again. However, the runners were approaching Ingleborough from another direction so I would not be trampled in the rush. My efforts to impress my new acquaintances by pretending I was the leading competitor failed completely.

By the time I'd walked a mile or so off the top towards Ingleton the weather improved again so that the summit was bathed in golden sunshine. If only I'd been half an hour later. Still, there's always the next time…

Ingleton came as a bit of a shock. By lunchtime the day had turned warm and sunny again and there were plenty of people about. I'd arranged to meet five friends at the entrance to the

Ingleton Waterfalls Walk and we all looked and felt a bit overdressed as, with our boots and rucksacks and paraphernalia, we mingled with trippers in sandals and shorts and tee-shirts.

There may be a few people who are unfamiliar with this famous walk up the valley of the River Doe. If you are, go and do it. OK, you have to pay to get in but it's not fantastically expensive and you get some superbly well maintained footpaths and bridges for your money. You also get a hut selling ice cream and the best waterfall scenery I saw on the whole trip. There may be more impressive individual falls than you see here but, taken as a whole, the succession of cascades rounded off by the mini-Niagara of Thornton Force is unsurpassed. To the twin Pecca Falls I gave the Waterfall of the Walk Award and I'm sure they're very grateful.

As our journey was to take us ever higher and ever westwards we did not do the 'return journey' down the Greta valley but this too is thoroughly recommended. The steep and rough slopes leading up towards the ridge of Gragareth reminded us why we were wearing boots and not flip-flops and it was good to reach the long, almost level summit ridge. This was my second 2,000 footer of the day; Gragareth had, in fact, once been regarded as the highest point in Lancashire. There is a very substantial stone wall along this ridge and I regret to say we climbed it, having been unable to find any other way across. (We didn't do any damage though, honest.) This wall is the county boundary between Yorkshire and Lancashire and more than compensates for the complete lack of visible borders on Paythorne Moor by the Ribble.

The summit of Gragareth is undistinguished apart from being the only place on my walk from where I could see all of the Three Peaks, Ingleborough, Whernside and Penyghent, at once. The highlight of the fell is a feature half a mile west of the top known as the Three Men of Gragareth, a trio of stone columns standing watch over the lonely country of Leck Fell. A little more sheltered from what had become a cold wind, they offered an obvious resting place and we sat and tried to discern the Lakes hills through an increasingly thick haze. A long descent past the solitary farmstead of Leck Fell House took us to the day's end at Cowan Bridge, an unremarkable village famous for being the place where the Bronte sisters went to school. The building is now a privately owned cottage and there is, thank goodness, no Bronte museum or heritage centre here.

The short return to Lancashire ended as, alone again, I entered Cumbria near Kirkby Lonsdale. Almost inevitably, the heavens opened just as I crossed the county boundary and I must have cut a bedraggled figure as I approached Kirkby by way of the Devil's Bridge. This graceful three-arched structure over the Lune dates from the fifteenth century; there was a bridge here before that and it was the earlier one which owed its name to Lucifer. Apparently an old woman had arrived at the river bank one day to retrieve her cow which had wandered across the stream to chomp at the sweeter grass on the other side. However, heavy rain during the day had caused the waters to rise to such an extent that neither party could cross. Just as things were beginning to look very bleak, Old Nick arrived – like he does – and offered to build a bridge for the old woman provided that he could take the soul of the first living thing to cross. The old woman agreed — well, what choice did she have? — and the Devil worked all night to build his bridge. In the morning, just as she was about to cross, the Devil reminded her of what she had promised. But she wasn't as daft as all that and threw a bun over the bridge and told her dog to go and fetch it, which of course it did. So the Devil was thwarted and another poor dog was condemned to eternal damnation. The present bridge is only a single carriageway wide and, in case you're worried about it, I ought to tell you that it has not been open to traffic since 1932, when a much more functional one was built to carry the main road from Kendal to Skipton.

Kirkby Lonsdale is, by any standards, an exceptionally interesting small town. At least one writer has likened it to a French or German town with its collection of tall buildings and narrow streets but to me it looks typically Cumbrian — or, to be more accurate, Westmerian. Modern Cumbria is a mongrel, conceived in the Local Government boundary changes of 1974, and is made up of the ancient counties of Westmorland and Cumberland, along with 'Lancashire north of the Sands' (Furness and Coniston) and a bit of Yorkshire. I don't think the residents of any of these counties were too happy about the change and their reasons are based not just on sentimentality for the old days. The geographical structure of the core of the county is such that the valleys radiate outwards from a central dome, so the traditional gathering points and market towns tend to be on the periphery — places like Kendal and Barrow and Whitehaven. The modern 'capital' of Cumbria, Carlisle, has as much to do with

Barrow historically as it has with Timbuktu. The Yorkshire folk were particularly upset about the changes. One old resident of Sedbergh commented that she was against the proposed move from Yorkshire to Cumbria simply because it 'rained too much over there'. This is the kind of irrefutable logic that Whitehall hadn't reckoned with when they started mucking things about.

Where was I? Oh yes, Kirkby Lonsdale. Nice place with narrow streets and old buildings. Don't visit it at the weekend though, if you can help it. It gets very busy and the Devil's Bridge in particular is crowded with ice cream vans, burger bars, and day trippers. It is also a popular haunt of bikers and they, at least, give the place a colourful, almost exotic flavour. Unlike most towns built on a river, Kirkby is all to one side of it. To the east there are a few cottages and a caravan site but the town is entirely on the western bank, high above the river. The older buildings are of grey limestone, there is a Market Square and Cross, some old pubs with projecting upper floors supported on stone pillars, a very old and very beautiful church, the oldest parts of which date back to 1115 and, like every town should, it has a fine collection of unusual street names: Jingling Lane, Cocking Yard, Radical Steps and Fisherty Brow to name just a few. There is also an elevated walkway above a bend in the river and Ruskin, arbiter on all matters scenic, declared the view to be one of the loveliest in England. Well, it's pleasant certainly, but I don't think modern tastes would admit it to the Top 50.

Knowing that I was less than a day's walk from home, I allowed myself the luxury of an hour or so wandering round Kirkby – the churchyard, Ruskin's View and the shops – and wondered if, in my list of 'Things That I'd Seen on the Walk Which Would Be in the UK Entry For the World's Best Scenery', Kirkby Lonsdale would edge out Llanidloes as the best small town

There are several ways of getting from Kirkby to Kendal on foot and I am sorry to say that, given the inclement weather, I opted for the soft option of using tarmac lanes for the first part of the journey – very quiet ones, admittedly, but tarmac nonetheless. But what splendid places they go past! In a distance of less than a couple of miles I passed places called Hot Ridding and Pant End – wow! – and, in between these two breathless sounding spots, I saw the sign pointing to the operatically monickered farm of Tosca. Then, tucked away in a little fold in the hills, a small, attractive reservoir by the name of Tarnhouse Tarn. Now this name bears some thinking about. Presumably there used to be a tarn and somebody built a house nearby. Not unnaturally, this would be called Tarn House. So why is the tarn now called Tarnhouse Tarn? If another house is built, will it be called Tarnhouse Tarn House? It should be. You can go on playing this game for ever. It's what happens when you've been on your own too long. My favourite example of this sort of compound place name occurs in the western Lake District where there is a farm called Low High Snab. And if that's not just splendid, I'll eat hay with a donkey.

The summit of the climb to cross the low hills separating the valleys of the Lune and the Kent revealed a view as evocative as any I saw on the entire journey. After nearly two months seeing new and unfamiliar sights unfold, here was a whole bunch of old friends: the great bulk of Farleton Knott overlooking the entrance to Cumbria from the south; tree-covered Arnside Knott with the silvery waters of Morecambe Bay behind it; the limestone scar of Whitbarrow; the upland of Scout Scar beyond Kendal, and to the right the eastern Lakes fells around Kentmere and Longsleddale. The exciting, serrated skyline of the bigger Lakes hills, which is often such a well-known feature of the views from the higher ground east of Kendal, was invisible in the gathering gloom and murk of a deteriorating April day.

By the time I had found my way via various footpaths and bridle ways to the summit of The Helm, a long, low hill lying just outside Kendal's boundaries, the weather had become vile. The summit of The Helm is all of 600 feet above the sea and the gentle promenade along this ridge is usually a favourite with people of all shapes and sizes. On this day, though, it was spectacularly wild with a wind reminiscent of the worst that the Cornish coast and the Arans had thrown at me. This, added to the by now heavy rain, made for an invigorating walk along the hill and down into Kendal. Although it clearly wasn't, it felt like journey's end as I walked through my front door, cleverly remembering to open it first.

And, wouldn't you just know it – the sun shone the moment I arrived.

CHAPTER FIVE – THE LAKES TO THE CLYDE

ZIG-ZAG WANDERER

Some More Useless Things You Didn't Want to Know – Kendal to Langdale

Garden at Bowston, near Kendal

It has often been said by academics, scholars and sundry other ne'er-do-wells that more words have been written about the Lake District than about any other part of Britain. Every nook and cranny of the area must have been examined, dissected, delved into and chronicled. How is it possible, you wonder, for so many different guidebooks to appear? There are guides to individual fells, walks for motorists (whatever that may mean – we'll be having 'Drives for Pedestrians' soon), walks on the level, walks to pubs, walks from pubs, walks based on tea shops, walks along the ridges, various rounds and circuits and horseshoes and ways and trails, walks for acrobats, walks for basket-weavers, computer programmers, astrologers and even Leeds United supporters.

In amongst this plethora of verbiage there are, of course, some classics. Wordsworth's *Guide to the Lakes* is meant to be one such but I've not read it. (I'm surprised he had time to write it, given that he spent so much time wandering around with Coleridge.) There are Harry Griffin's evocative books, anything by the gifted Norman Nicholson, who brought a poet's eye and a poet's turn of phrase to his prose works, and, of course, the unique, unrepeatable, irreplaceable Wainwright Guides – all seven of them. Every page of these lovingly crafted works of art is hand-drawn. The original versions, published by our very own *Westmorland Gazette*, contained not a single line of printer's type. Written over a period of a dozen or so years in the fifties and sixties, Wainwright's guides are, just as he predicted, becoming increasingly unreliable – if judged simply as guidebooks. The level of detail in them is such that the changes over the last thirty or forty years – and, by gum, there have been plenty – conspire to undermine the accuracy of the routes he describes. However, as books to read after you've completed your walk, or to skim through for ideas as to where you might go, or simply to pick up and read from cover to cover like novels, they are perfect. Mr Wainwright's quirky, unique style, his painstaking attention to detail and the sheer artistry of the little books makes them a joy to read. Add to all this his pithy sense of humour, which became increasingly acerbic with age, and you have the ideal palliative for anybody suffering from Lake District withdrawal symptoms, a common and incurable ailment afflicting the many people who fall under the spell of this corner of England.

It was way back before England won the World Cup that, at the age of thirteen, I first came to the Lakes on a school walking holiday. 'Hiking' it was called then and green cotton anoraks with a zipped pouch on the front were the last word in hi-tech gear. With the benefit of hindsight, I suspect that I only volunteered to go on the holiday because I thought it would be a laugh and I'd have loads of opportunity to mess about away from parental control. But, from the instant we arrived at the youth hostel in Borrowdale, I was smitten, bowled over, discumknockerated – completely enthralled. I had never seen anything like it. I mean, Sale and the Cheshire countryside weren't bad – I can't try and claim it was an industrial wasteland – and we visited the Peak District sometimes and even, on rare occasions, Yorkshire, but the scenery and the whole ambience of the Lakes was something way beyond my experience.

Even after all these years, I can still call to mind that ladder stile with its little wooden sign bearing the one word inscription which seemed to me to be pointing the way to a magic kingdom – *Glaramara* it said. I didn't know what or who Glaramara was, but the very word was enough to lift the holiday out of the mundane and into another realm altogether. I suppose I was lucky. If the fell we'd been attempting to walk up that day had been Robinson or Low Pike, would the effect have been so memorable? So we came to live in Kendal as soon as we could, and here we've stayed – despite the weather.

Strictly, Kendal is not in the Lake District – it lies just outside the National Park boundary, but it is most certainly a part of what you might call the Greater Lake District. The Lakes planning authority has its headquarters here, as does South Lakeland District Council, the official body looking after the lives of people in Windermere and Ambleside, Grasmere and Langdale. The town is a major employer of people who live in the Lakes and it's where many of the Lakes folk come to do their shopping and conduct their business. It's also the place where visitors to the area like to congregate on a wet day, when they don't know what else to do with themselves and their children. Why they should want to walk round big shoe shops – that's shoe shops that are big, not shops that stock big shoes – and stand five abreast across the pavement of the main street is beyond me, but each to his own. So, to my mind, Kendal is as much a part of the Lake District as Helvellyn is. So there.

It's known as the Gateway to the Lakes – because it's the Gateway to the Lakes – and the Auld Grey Town, because the older buildings are constructed from the locally quarried grey limestone which blends in so well with the usual colour of the sky. If you stand on one of Kendal's mini-uplands like the Castle Hill or the mighty Benson Knott just to the east of the town on a typical day of hopeless drizzle, you'll be hard pressed to tell where the buildings end and the air begins. But, weather notwithstanding, Kendal is a great town. Squeezed, as Walt Unsworth says, into a gap between two fells, on the banks of the River Kent, Kendal must enjoy one of the finest locations of any British town of similar size. With more than 20,000 inhabitants it is not small, and because it serves such a large surrounding area it has all the trappings of many much bigger places. The town's river, the Kent, winds between the old town and the abrupt little hill on which stand the ruins of Kendal Castle, reputedly the birth place of Katherine Parr, the only one of his several wives to survive good old 'Enery the Eightf.

I'd thought of Kendal as roughly half way on my journey; if that was really the case, though, I reckoned I'd have to speed up or curtail my wanderings a little. It had taken me two months to get this far and I didn't feel I could afford another two months to finish. And it's not as if I'd been loafing about. Over the last couple of weeks I had enjoyed what was probably the best compromise between progress and pleasure that I achieved on the entire walk. I had got over the problems of sore feet and gammy legs and felt that I'd reached a decent level of fitness so that the walking was, on the whole, no serious effort. Significantly, though, I had been walking towards home and I think that this played a big psychological part in the process. From now on I'd be travelling away from home – and, of course, home would get ever more remote as I headed northwards. So even though the walking became easier and easier physically, it got tougher and tougher mentally.

After a couple of days at home catching up on the accrued jumble of life, I left Kendal along the riverside path in brilliant sunshine. It struck me just how quickly the town is left behind and open country reached but, in only a couple of miles, I reached Burneside, a village dominated in just about every way by the huge papermill of James Cropper. Croppers casts a benevolent presence over much of the surrounding area – they even paid to repair the long-disused dam at the reservoir at the head of the Kentmere valley just to improve the visual amenity. Let's hear it for Croppers. There are rows of neat cottages at Burneside – and some more at Bowston, a mile upstream – which I took to be built by the mill owners. They are all of a similar style and are reminiscent of the Cadbury houses at Bourneville, albeit on a much smaller scale. But why are the new mill buildings so out of keeping with the rest of the place? On a scale of one to horrendous, the hideous block that has recently been thrown up would score several million. The fact that it has been built overlooking the rambling fourteenth century ruin of the pele (that's pele as in peel, not as in the Brazilian footballer) tower at Burneside Hall farm just makes it even more up-yours.

The hamlet of Bowston was notable chiefly for the incredible front garden of one of the cottages just by the route. Amidst hand-painted notices exhorting walkers to 'Smile, it won't hurt', was a motley collection of garden figures. Many people have gnomes but this garden also contained plastic Godzillas, stone owls, model dogs and numerous other figurines. I'd put this garden up there along with White Castle and Healey Dell as one of the unexpected highlights of the walk but it is with a touch of regret that I have to report that, although it remains a neat and attractive garden, it no longer contains all those splendid objects.

Lazy riverside walking brought me to Staveley from where, at long last, I caught my first sight of the Lakes hills. The haze of the early morning was slowly lifting and by the time I had reached the crest of the low ridge separating the Kentmere and Troutbeck valleys, conditions had improved so much that the view spread out before me was far more extensive than I had thought possible. From the shimmering waters of Morecambe Bay in the south, round to the much nearer wall of the High Street fells, range upon receding range of purple hills filled the horizon. They had been reluctant to show themselves at all, but this sudden view of the big fells at the head of Langdale and beyond had been well worth the wait.

A steep descent to the Troutbeck valley took me past the long disused Applethwaite Quarry, now a huge natural rock garden and, judging by the tyre tracks and litter, a favourite haunt of youngsters with motorcycles who like the odd illicit beer or three – the youngsters, that is, not the motorcycles. Troutbeck is typical Lakeland: a green, deep trench of a valley, a chortling stream and a village of absurdly attractive white cottages built up on the fellside so as to be out of the wet valley bottom, many of them still displaying the original spinning galleries. Spinning is a traditional industry now virtually defunct, but many of Westmorland's older cottages still possess the rooms, or galleries, where the activity was carried out. The village church, unusually called Jesus Church, is remarkable for its stained glass east window designed by Sir Edward Burne-Jones with the help of Ford Madox Brown and William Morris, who both happened to be fishing nearby when Burne-Jones was working on it.

Troutbeck was also home for the last twenty years of his life to Hugh Hird, the so-called Kentmere Giant. Said to be the illegitimate son of a monk from Furness Abbey in sunny Barrow, Hugh arrived in Kentmere with his disgraced mother some time during the reign of Edward VI. He was of unusually large size and his prodigious feats of strength soon made him famous far beyond the confines of his adopted home. Summoned to the Court of the King, he continued to amaze and impress with his party tricks as well as his huge appetite. As a reward for all this, he was offered whatever gift he wanted, and he settled for a cottage in the Troutbeck valley – who wouldn't? – where he lived the rest of his days. He died with his boots on, single-handedly attempting to uproot a tree near his home.

The way between Troutbeck and Ambleside is fantastically and unfairly blessed with brilliant views over Windermere and across to the Coniston and Langdale fells. For such relatively little effort it is almost inconceivable that you can have such a wealth of perfection as your very own. Half way along the track is a place called Skelghyll and it was somewhere here that a couple of hundred years ago the villainous Monkswell had his hideout. He posed as a 'gentleman' in order to wangle invites to the homes of the local gentry; he would then case the joints and return with his gang to clean out his unsuspecting hosts. Rumbled by a servant at Skelghyll, he fled to pastures new.

Ambleside is reputed to be Westmorland's most central town and, for those of you who have been in solitary confinement on the planet Tharg for the last few years, it is a very busy holiday resort. Dismissed as being of 'no architectural merit whatsoever' and as having an 'air of Victorian dullness', Ambleside is a necessary part of the Lake District scene. Its vast array of outdoor-gear shops (it was once regarded as the Anorak Capital of the World) keeps many would-be walkers off the hills, leaving them that little bit less crowded for the impecunious like me. It's handy for buses and cafes and possesses pubs, eateries and a Tourist Information Centre. It also has the Bridge House, a little cottage built on a tiny hump-backed bridge. It was once inhabited by a woman and her enormous brood of children, and anywhere with such a splendidly ridiculous building can't be all bad. The Romans had a fort here built by Agricola in AD79 which, I was delighted to learn, was liable to flooding. See, the Romans weren't that clever after all. Serves them right for slagging off Lancashire and hurling abuse at me when I was walking through North Wales.

I left Ambleside by walking past St Mary's Church, which was designed by Sir Gilbert Scott. A noble structure it is but, with its tall elegant spire, not very typical of the Lakes. A short climb took me on to Todd Crags, a shoulder of Loughrigg Fell, and another place where the quality of the view outweighs the effort expended in reaching it. This corner of Loughrigg is entirely wonderful: a series of ups and downs, little tarns, rock outcrops and ever-changing views make for fascinating walking.

All too soon I was down in Langdale at Skelwith Force, a waterfall which, although it is only a few feet high, carries a higher volume of water than any other fall in the Lakes. It is all of twenty seconds' walk from the road so is liable to be busy. There was only one group of people there when I arrived but, such was their public-spiritidness, they had chosen to have their picnic on a large flat rock right by the water's edge thereby denying anyone else the chance of viewing the fall to its full effect. Secretly hoping that one of their number would fall in, I sloped off towards Elterwater and Chapel Stile, the latter a hamlet whose cottages seem to spring from the very rock of the steepening valley sides. The old gunpowder works here was started in 1764; there was no shortage of water power and the coppice woods were ideal for producing charcoal, one of the essential ingredients. The place closed down just after the First World War and the site has now been transformed into a timeshare and leisure complex – and a great job they've made of it too. Some of the old buildings have been retained and the whole place is well screened by trees.

By the time I was heading along the slopes of Side Pike towards the road head at Dungeon Ghyll, the day was blisteringly hot but, surprisingly, the views across the valley to the climbing crags of

Middle Fell and Gimmer Crag were sharp and clear. I sat and watched brightly-clad athletes climbing up the apparently vertical walls of grey rock and wondered about the injustice of it all – how I could have been born such a wimp? I've tried rock climbing several times and I love the feel of the rock and the physical movements of balance and upward progress. But I'm always terrified. Every move is completed with muttered thanks to God for getting me up another bit without sending me plunging to my doom. I know you don't have to look down and I know that, as second man, you're on the end of a rope and would have to be a complete cretin to come to any grief but, once you're more than a dozen or so feet off the ground, all rational thought processes are suspended. I think it's something to do with the supply of oxygen to the brain.

A thoroughly pleasant and satisfying day ended at the Old Dungeon Ghyll Hotel and a bus ride back to Kendal which was soon transformed from an idyllic trundle with just me and the driver into complete bedlam when the entire third form from a school invaded the vehicle in the manner of marauding pirates boarding a Spanish galleon. No wonder the school crest is one of skull couchant and crossbones rampant.

Sunshine and Snowstorm – Scafell Pike, Keswick and Carlisle

On the way to Scafell Pike

An early start next morning saw me striding out along the wide, green and enjoyably flat valley bottom of Mickleden, the northern-most of the two branches into which Great Langdale is divided. It's almost impossible to believe that this utterly rural spot was once the heart of Europe's heavy industry – a sort of Neolithic Ruhr Valley – but high up on the vertiginous scree slopes of Pike o' Stickle is the site of a stone axe 'factory'. There are, in fact, several such sites in this area, all about 3,000 years old and none of them discovered until 1921. The evidence that the commercial infrastructure must have been pretty sophisticated is clear because, although many rough axes have been found here, no finished ones have. This indicates that the rough versions must have been shipped somewhere else for refining, and the finished articles have been found as far afield as Bournemouth and Scotland and the Isle of Man. Geologists know that they are Langdale axes because of the particularly hard type of rock they're fashioned from and because they all have 'A Present From Lakeland' chiselled on them.

My way onto the high ground of Scafell Pike was to be up the steep gash of Rossett Gill, a well-known walkers' highway with a lurid reputation for its unremittingly steep and rough path. But the ascent was no trouble and, dare I say it, actually enjoyable. A major factor in Rossett Gill's demotion from the top of the league table of Awful Paths is that it has been 'improved' in the now time-honoured fashion of setting big stones as in a giant staircase (cf. Snowdon) and that many of the Lakes' other paths are now far worse.

Arrival at Esk Hause brought Great Gable into view, always a great moment on any walk in the Lakes, and there were only two other people on the top of Scafell Pike when I got there. They were training for the '4 Peaks Challenge', an annual event clearly devised by a madman with a grudge against humanity. There are teams of four – three walkers / runners and one driver. What these people have to do is ascend the highest peaks in the four countries of the British Isles, Ben Nevis, Scafell Pike, Snowdon and Carrantuohill (yes, in deepest south west Ireland), in forty-eight hours. It's all done for charity apparently and very good luck to them. The two I chatted to seemed oddly cagey when it came to revealing details of how they intended to achieve their aim, but I have no doubt at all that they made it. It always cheers me up to think that whatever you do in life, there's always somebody else doing something so totally hatstand as to make you feel contentedly normal again.

Comfortably the lowest of the three tops of Wales, England and Scotland it might be, but Scafell Pike is also the toughest. It is not a particularly steep or long ascent and the main ways up offer no terrifying cliffs or narrow ridges to balance along, but the entire summit dome is composed of an unstable mass of huge tottering boulders, every one of which is set at an angle designed to cause maximum discomfort to ankles and feet. It is a masterpiece of design. Snowdon is a far more elegant structure and has a much more dramatic and purer mountain form; Ben Nevis is massive and fearsome and possesses some of Britain's most savage cliffs on its North face, but neither mountain can compete with Scafell Pike for sheer bloody-mindedness. I'd thought before I set off from Land's End that I'd be lucky to get one of the three tops clear of cloud. Well, the weather on Snowdon had been stupendous and here I was again in sunshine on Scafell Pike — what had I done to deserve such good fortune?

Overwhelmed with a feeling of well-being, I attempted to fashion my own way off the top. A slithering descent over steep scree and grass did eventually bring me down to the main path — and crowds — of the Corridor Route. This was a Bank Holiday Saturday and the sun was beating down, so seething humanity was inevitable. Sty Head and the shores of its rectangular Tarn were busier than the streets of Ambleside had been two days before. Summer had definitely arrived. People were stretched out on the grass, soaking up the sunshine and obviously intent on walking no further. Some hardy souls were even swimming in the tarn. In an arrangement that had disaster written all over it, I had agreed to meet a friend, Bill at Sty Head. I thought that the chances of our actually meeting were not great but, right on cue — well, all right, only an hour late – Bill wandered up from Borrowdale having left the getaway car parked somewhere down in that valley.

Brilliant to have some company again as we set off downhill, poor old Bill having to retrace his steps almost exactly. We whiled away the hours by testing each other's knowledge of Frank Zappa lyrics; Bill won handsomely, but only because he cheated by asking me ones I didn't know. It was at Seathwaite that I heard a cuckoo – not exactly worth writing to the *Times* about, but it was the first of my journey – and the riverside path down Borrowdale to Grange was just perfect, as Borrowdale always is, despite the thickening cloud and steeply dropping temperature. The view across Derwentwater to Catbells is the stuff of paradise; however many times I see it, it always looks fresh. I suppose the infinite combinations of the weather and the light make for a different view each time. The branches of the fringe of trees on the water's edge give you the means to frame your very own picture of water, fell and sky – like an artist, you can compose a picture to suit your taste and mood. This had been another almost perfect day and the crossing from Langdale to Borrowdale had taken me out of Kendal's 'catchment area' and into Carlisle's, so I felt that progress had been made.

You expect changeable weather in the Lakes but it excelled itself that weekend as the summer sunshine was replaced overnight by high winds, thunder, rain and blizzards. Because, by some sort of miraculous fluke, I was at home, I was able to sit out the worst of the weather – if it had happened a few days earlier or later I'd have been caught up in it – but I was in danger of losing momentum and felt that I needed to move again on the Monday even though conditions were far from ideal. The snow which I later learned had claimed two lives on the Lakes fells had turned to a cold rain, and the high level route over the Caldbeck fells was abandoned in favour of a lower alternative along the flanks of Skiddaw. I had more friends, John, Elaine and Alan, for company as we set off in the rain from Borrowdale along the shore of Derwentwater and past the little rocky outcrop of Friar's Crag, near which is a memorial to Canon Rawnsley, co-founder of the National Trust and all-round good egg.

The rain stopped for our brief wander through Keswick, one of my favourite places in the whole universe. Despite the crowds and its grey, muddly appearance, Keswick has always struck me as a friendly place. Its most interesting-looking building is now a Tourist Information Centre – the Moot Hall, a white painted building plonked on an island in the middle of the main street. Built as recently as 1813, but incorporating materials from a ruined mansion on Lord's Island on Derwentwater, the Moot Hall is now notable mainly for its one-handed clock. Keswick also has a couple of museums – one a pencil museum, celebrating Keswick's fame as a producer of fine pencils, and now boasting the World's Biggest Pencil. Who says the Lakes isn't exciting, huh? The other is more of your standard type of museum but still manages to amaze, mainly by virtue of the unique 'rock and steel band instrument', which consists of a seven octave keyboard made entirely of stones of different sizes, all of which were found on Skiddaw. Apparently, it took Joseph Richardson, the inventor of this wondrous device, thirteen years of searching and chiselling to get the required notes. He then added to his contraption with bells and other steel notes and went on the road with it, even giving three Royal Command performances for Queen Victoria. Not quite as portable as a Stradivarius but just as remarkable. The museum was established in 1779 by one Peter Crosthwaite who, rather splendidly, called himself 'Admiral of the Keswick Regatta, Keeper of the Museum, Guide, Pilot, Geographer and Hydrographer to the Nobility and Gentry'. What a guy.

We can't leave Keswick without at least mentioning the Lake Poets who all hung out here in the early nineteenth century. Coleridge lived here for three years or so, as did Southey and Shelley, and Wordsworth was born in Cockermouth, just up the road. There, I've mentioned them. There is a little-known story about Shelley which deals with his attempted purchase of a nearby convent. The Mother Superior was not keen to sell and Percy Bysshe's boasts in the local pubs that he had bought the place brought the rebuke from his solicitor, now immortalised in the song title 'Wait till the nun signs, Shelley'. And, if you believe that, you'll believe anything.

We set off over the awful A66, which at least takes the traffic out of the town centre but could surely have been more sympathetically 'improved', for the short ascent of Latrigg, one of Lakeland's famed short walks and viewpoints. At barely 1,200 feet high it's hardly a giant but the rain, which had started again just after we left Keswick, was now blowing straight into our faces, carried on a vicious north-easterly which increased in ferocity as we turned the big corner on the track above the Glenderaterra valley. We were now walking more or less due north and the wind was coming straight at us, its strength magnified by the funnelling effect of it being squeezed through the gap in the hills ahead of us.

Our first target was Skiddaw House, once a shepherds' cottage and now refurbished as England's remotest Youth Hostel. We saw nobody on our wildly invigorating trek round the eastern flanks of Skiddaw and, given the vile weather, I'm not surprised. The rain had given way to horizontal sleet and by the time Skiddaw House came into sight, it was snowing. We took refuge in what I would describe as a 'rude shelter' – there, I've always wanted to write that – and, as we stood around, forming as bedraggled a heap of humanity as you are ever likely to see, the hostel warden appeared and offered us a cup of tea. Accepting his offer with an almost embarrassing alacrity, we trudged into his upland abode where he told us of the weather warnings – which, thankfully, we hadn't heard. I didn't need an enforced break right now, especially given the trouble I was having getting going again.

Reluctantly, we prised ourselves away from the dry warmth of the Hostel and set off into the hostile weather. As we descended towards Bassenthwaite, the rain got heavier but at least it was only rain now and the wind had dropped considerably. One of the advantages of being out in such inclement conditions is that you do get to see the waterfalls at their finest and Whitewater Dash, one of the Lakes' longest and least known cascades was breathtakingly savage. A camera could not do justice to the foaming brown torrent hurtling down the rockslides and gullies, but it didn't stop us trying to get the photo of a lifetime.

For the first and only time on my journey, the weather had forced me to make an alteration to my proposed route. I had intended to end the day at Caldbeck but had ended up half a day's walk short of my objective. Having to spend the following day drying out my saturated clothing left me still further behind a schedule that was becoming increasingly improbable. It would be a long day's walk from Bassenthwaite to Carlisle but I felt it was one I had to do to regain some of the lost time.

Arnold accompanied me on the first part of the journey, a pleasant and generally uneventful walk away from the snow topped hills and across the quiet north-western corner of the Lakes. We walked past the seldom-visited Little Tarn and Over Water, and passed by the pink house of Orthwaite Hall. Arnold's knowledge of bird-life made for an interesting morning – warblers, goldfinches, herons and buzzards were apparently spotted by our keen eyes. Getting the hang of this wildlife stuff at last, maybe. We also saw a two-legged lamb on the walk over Uldale Common but, in the context of the journey as a whole, the most significant sight was a first glimpse of the Scottish hills across the Solway Firth.

Arnold was to meet Margaret for a pub lunch and, displaying an iron will, I rejected his invitations to join them and meandered off to find a sheltered place to have my bit of bread and water. The Howk is a little gorge on a stream feeding the River Caldew, where the ruins of a bobbin mill still stand and where, until quite recently, was one of England's biggest water wheels, 42 feet in diameter. There is a dramatic wooded glen with little waterfalls and, on the day I was there, it was completely deserted. The sun shone while I found a perfect place to have my lunch and it was with difficulty that I forced myself to get moving again. I put the Howk high up on the list of Unsuspected Gems.

Caldbeck is famous for its association with John Peel – he of the 'coat so grey' – but this was in the days before he joined Radio One and became a national treasure. In the graveyard of the sixteenth-century church of St Kentigern lie the remains of Mary Robinson, the 'Maid of Buttermere' who, as a young woman in 1802, fell under the spell of a real baddie, a middle-aged con artist by the name of John Hatfield. He had a habit of posing as MPs, lords and other men of substance and had a history of jail sentences behind him. Quite how he persuaded the innocent Mary to become his wife I don't know but, within a year of their marriage, he was found out, brought to trial, convicted and hanged and poor old Mary was left a widow. There is a happier ending though: Mary eventually married a Caldbeck farmer, with whom she had a large family.

I was to follow the Cumbria Way from Caldbeck to Carlisle and, for much of this stretch, the route follows the banks of the Caldew pretty closely. After all the rain we'd had the river was impressive indeed but the tracks had been turned into the worst quagmires I had encountered since that sunken lane in Devon. Slithering and sliding, I passed by the village of Sebergham and then Rose Castle, the red-stone home of the Bishops of Carlisle for over seven centuries. By now the landscape had become Englishly rural: big fields, cattle, posh houses and a river. Gone were the becks and stone walls and hills of the Lakes. It would be a long time before I was to see comparable scenery again. Walking across one meadow near Hawksdale Hall, I had a very bad attack of the Boys – three or four of these psychopathic morons had been tracking me stride for stride across their domain. I could feel myself accelerating in a pointless attempt to shake them off when all of a sudden I was stopped dead in my tracks. For what seemed like an eternity I couldn't work out what had happened. Eventually I realised that one of the buggers had grabbed my rucksack strap in its mouth.

'Oy, gerroff,' I shouted.

Other than giving me a baleful stare, this elicited no response from the barging bully which now held a limpet-like grip over my future progress. I seriously considered freeing myself from the rucksack and running off but realised this would be a complete loss of face – not to mention a complete loss of most of my worldly goods. So I stood my ground and, with a stroke of genius I was later to feel really proud of, said the one word guaranteed to strike terror into any bovine's heart:

'Bovril!'

'Ooh, you bitch,' said the Boy as he let go and flounced off in a very camp way with all his mates looking a bit nonplussed.

'Ooh, suit you, Sir!', I said, marvelling at my handling of the situation.

Smirking with smug complacency, I pressed on through Dalston, an ordinary looking place made to look gloomy first by the steady drizzle that had now developed and second by an unprepossessing food factory. An uneventful walk between the river and the railway was suddenly interrupted by a spectacular reminder of the power of nature. A short stretch of the path had been swept away into the river which looked to be threatening the stability of the railway as well. Dire warnings about trespassing on the permanent way had to be ignored as I climbed what was left of the fence and walked along the trackside for just a few yards. At this late hour, the alternative of walking back to Dalston and finding another route was not even an option.

The city of Carlisle, its skyline having been visible for miles across the flat meadows, was approached past a sad, boarded-up mill building by the weir at Holme Head, and entered unpromisingly along a street lined with gas holders and civic amenity sites. The Caldew had been an excellent companion and it brought back memories of the Wye and the Ribble. The street lights were on by the time I got to Carlisle city centre and a waiting lift home to Kendal. This had been a day tinged with sadness at leaving the Lakes, but hugely successful in getting me back into the rhythm of the journey. Scotland was beckoning now!

Carlisle, the Border City, is the largest place for miles around: northwards you have to go over a hundred miles to Glasgow before you reach anywhere bigger, and southwards it's about the same distance to Preston. Size isn't everything, as they say, and I found Carlisle a surprisingly drab place for one of such geographical significance. It has not been served well by a bizarre piece of town planning which caused the ring road to be shoved right between two of the city's most important buildings, its Castle and its Cathedral. The latter boasts a fantastic fourteenth-century east window reckoned, by those that know about such things, to be the finest in England. To be fair, Carlisle was never meant to be pretty. It was built on 'the highway of war', close to the Scottish border and to Hadrian's Wall. Just about every possible combination of warring factions have had their battles in and around Carlisle — Celts, Romans, Picts, Scots, Saxons, Danes, Royalists, Roundheads and Carlisle United and Workington supporters.

I Can't See the Wood for the Trees – Longtown, Langholm and Moffat

The White Esk at Castle O'er Forest, near Eskdalemuir

Thinking that the next time I left Kendal would be the last until I finished my journey, I spent three whole days engaged in what I termed 'planning'. What this really meant was that I sat for hours gazing into space in a sort of gormless, slack-jawed stupor with, every so often, furious bursts of frenetic activity where I tried to get accommodation sorted out for the first few days in Scotland. I didn't like having to book more than a day or two ahead but the vast area of lonely country between the Scottish border and the industrial region towards Glasgow is not well-endowed with suitable places to stay. One of the very few B&Bs I knew about on my proposed route was booked up so I had to revise my plans accordingly. This was OK. As I said, I had no fixed itinerary – apart from Ben Nevis and John o' Groats – and changing things around was part of the challenge and the pleasure. Wasn't it?

One immediate problem was that I could find nowhere between Carlisle and Langholm, too big a step to do in one day. So, gawping in desperation at my book of Scottish Hill Tracks, I did really useful things like try to devise complex routes through the rough and remote country north of Fort William. A fat lot of use this was in solving my immediate logistical difficulty and I think I'd probably be sat there still if it hadn't been for a phone call from Bill saying he would give me a lift to Carlisle. So we took two cars, left one at Longtown a few miles further north, drove back to Carlisle and walked to Longtown. Simple, eh?

For the morning we were joined by Clive, Bill's brother-in-law, a sixties' music buff and bird-watcher extraordinaire. This was an amazing experience for me. I don't think I'd ever met anyone who was so knowledgeable about any subject as Clive was about birds. His enthusiasm had to be witnessed to be believed. While we were still in the confines of the built up part of Carlisle he had identified ten or twelve different birds, just by their songs. They all sounded alike to me – just a twittering noise. Seen one sparrow, seen 'em all, was my take on it. But Clive was in his element.

We walked along the banks of the Eden, Cumbria's biggest river, as it wound its sedate way down to the Solway. There were more Boys out grazing but, because there were three of us, they left us alone. I could hear them muttering though. I could make out words like 'Revenge' and 'Bastard' and 'Tear you limb from limb' over the sound of chomping.

Hey, now listen to this. I'm going to put on a sort of rustic accent and David Attenborough-like voice, so pay attention. As we tramped along the river bank we were startled by the sight of a pair of red-breasted mergansers flapping away in alarm from some unknown foe. A cormorant made an ungainly landing on the water and we were carefully watched from the opposite bank by a cautious heron. Not bad eh? And we saw a goldeneye – I think. Or is that a James Bond film? Clive and Bill also saw a kingfisher, but Muggins didn't. I felt guilty at not being able to spot it so told a little fib and pretended I had. At Carr Beds, a sort of sandy island in the river, Clive told us of a time when a rare American bird visited here – a yellowlegs, I think he said. Does that sound right to you?

We reached Rockcliffe, a village with a border feel to it, situated as it is near the confluence of the Eden and the Scottish-born Esk and, for the only time on the whole journey I was persuaded to have a lunchtime drink. That's what comes of falling in with bad company. The Crown and Thistle was an excellent place to sit and watch nothing much happen and the very name tells you I was nearly in Scotland.

Clive left us at Rockcliffe and Bill and I continued on very quiet and very straight lanes across the Solway countryside. Whether it's because of the flat land or not, I don't know, but the noise from the A74 trunk road – which is just the M6 with a Scottish name – was appalling. We sneaked under this monster at the prosaically named Metal Bridge and found that the bridge over the Esk we had been told we could use had long since gone. Another detour then, but a good one. For all its flatness this country looks welcoming; there are big houses and the horizon is dotted with stands of trees, relieving what could have been a monotonous hour or two.

The day ended in pouring rain as we walked past a succession of strange corrugated iron sheds, now an industrial estate but goodness knows what they were originally built as, and on past Arthuret Church, a little gem of a place with no village for it to belong to. It is reputed to have been built on or near the site of the Battle of Ardderyd in 573AD and a sign outside says King Arthur may be buried here. It's a long way from Glastonbury and there was no M6 in those days so I'm not convinced.

Longtown is a surprising spot. Nothing special to look at but the streets are unusually wide and there is an air of spaciousness about the place, not felt in many Cumbrian towns. The reason may be to do with the volatile history of this border country – the so-called Debatable Land – where raiders from both sides of the border would create mayhem and havoc in their quest for justice and peace. I can understand the Longtown village elders reasoning that if a place is going to be ridden and marched through by armies, let's make the streets wide enough for them. No point making them cross by having everywhere twisting and narrow. The grid-iron pattern of the wide streets, the pollarded trees and the painted sandstone edgings around the windows on the house fronts all combine to make Longtown unique. One thing puzzled me mightily though – why is the gents' WC so well defended? I hadn't seen such a fearsome array of barbed wire since the military camps I'd passed on the Cornwall and Devon coasts. Longtown is England's last – or first, depending on your point of view – settlement and there is a fine bridge over the Esk here. Bizarrely echoing the Dee near Chirk, the Esk does not form the border and both banks are English at Longtown.

As I left Kendal next morning I knew this would be it. I'd be heading away from home into an increasingly distant and unknown land. 'It's only Scotland,' you might say and you'd be right, of course. But to me it might as well have been the Amazon basin. I had just two nights' accommodation sorted out and still no real idea which direction I'd take once I got to Fort William. I hadn't even given too much thought to getting through Glasgow yet. The word 'Scotland' conjured up visions of terrifying mountains and huge tracts of hostile countryside with nowhere to stay, and I had an irrational fear of bumping into the Krankies. On top of all this, I had come to realise that my walk was just messing about. Other people had lives to lead and things to do and here I was ... playing. Still, if this really was the chance of a lifetime, get on with it and make the most of it.

It was back to the full pack, of course, so I had to tread a little gingerly at first. The exit from Longtown did not make for a promising start. A gloomy little track crept between an ugly industrial building and a messy hedge cum fence. A forlorn looking waymark arrow, erected courtesy of the East Cumbria Countryside Project, did at least encourage me to go on and, just to add to the joys of the morning, I then had to walk the whole length of a muddy field accompanied by the most playful(?) gang of Boys I had yet encountered. Their cousins in the Caldew valley had clearly been in touch because they were very plainly intent on having a go.

One in particular kept putting his head down and running at me. When I tell people about this, they say things like, 'They're just curious.' Well, I was curious to see Wells Cathedral, but I didn't run at it like a rhinoceros on heat charging at a Land-Rover.

The stile out of the field had been uprooted and chucked over the fence but, once I had escaped, the going was completely delightful through riverside woodland where there were deer grazing, quite unconcerned by my presence. Just a small thing, maybe, but moments like this reminded me why I had set off in the first place. Out of the wood, I arrived at the eerie-looking Kirkandrews Church, whose churchyard contains some very ancient, tilting gravestones. The building itself is a squat affair with a strange sundial type of clock on the tower, the whole thing topped by a circular Italian style tower, all columns and domes. Just outside the gate is a dodgy-looking suspension bridge over the Esk and I was pleased to see that crossing the river here would be of no benefit to me.

Instead I had a mile or so of the A7 to deal with and it was on this stretch of road at Scotsdike that I entered Scotland. Jolly good and hurrah, I thought. A big sign says, quite simply 'Scotland Welcomes You'. A brief burst of sunshine was not the good omen I thought, because by the time I'd reached Canonbie it was bucketing down. There is a disused railway running from here to Langholm but the bridges appeared to have disappeared and I wasn't sure whether the private farmland which had now absorbed the railway was fair game for walkers or not. I never did get to grips with this

Freedom to Roam thing. There are accounts by Scottish walkers of crossing from Scotland to England where they bemoan the sudden lack of Freedom to Roam and dislike the restrictions imposed by following a network of public rights of way. It's a point of view, but at least you know where you are with a public footpath – well, sometimes you do. Anyway, I stuck with quiet tarmac lanes almost all the way to Langholm, with the views ahead becoming increasingly dominated by the whaleback of Whita Hill. A detour along Jenny Noble's walk revealed a sudden, dramatic view of Langholm stretched out along the narrowing valley.

Whether anybody actually falls in love with Langholm I don't know but I found it a rather cheerless place. Its tall, dark mill buildings give it an almost Pennine appearance and fitted in somehow with the bleak, inhospitable weather. A keen wind had sprung up to send the clouds scudding across a damp sky and I had to hurry my evening walk round the town just to keep warm. For all that, there were small knots of brave youngsters who seemed grimly determined to have fun on a travelling fair which had arrived in the town and I do have to admit that the area around the confluence of the Esk and the valley of the Ewes Water is very attractive.

Nervous about finding myself on the wrong side of the river with no means of getting across if I had to, in the morning I asked whether it was possible to get along the north bank of the Esk towards Westerkirk. I was obviously asking the wrong people because nobody seemed to know. A couple of ladies I met on the

'Duchess's Walk' in the parkland of the Duke of Buccleuch's estate thought maybe I could, but it would be a long way round. Their earnest advice was to stick to the road on the south side, so that's what I did. One of them walked with me for a while and, as we crossed the single span of the rainbow-arched Duchess's Bridge, she remarked, 'The water's big today,' a picturesque and, I thought, accurate description. The Esk is a sizeable river and by the following afternoon I would have followed it almost from sea to source. As I followed the valley into the hills I was reminded of the mid-Wales countryside around Rhayader. There were more trees here but there was a similar sense of spaciousness, remoteness and adventure.

I visited the tiny settlement of Bentpath, an appropriately named place to pass through on a meandering journey such as this, and the birthplace of Thomas Telford, one of whose masterpieces I had crossed weeks before near Llangollen. Regrettably, I forgot to look for his memorial there – a bad oversight. The countryside around the confluence of the Black and White Esks is superb. The valley has climbed about 300 feet since Langholm and the scenery is a lot less pastoral and considerably wilder and more open. And there was nobody about at all: not a soul, not a car. Just great, it was. I found one or two diversions along forest tracks in Castle O'er Forest which enabled me to escape the tarmac for a while and where the stillness was almost shattering. Apart from the wind in the trees and the sound of the river, I could hear – nothing at all.

Is the Esk better than the Wye, I asked myself? I know these comparisons are futile and meaningless and one cannot be 'better' than the other, but I can't help doing this when I'm walking on my own. What do other people think about? For some odd reason which I still can't come to terms with, I found myself almost obsessed with how many Gene Pitney hits I could name. I never owned a Gene Pitney record and, with the notable exception of the magnificent *24 Hours From Tulsa*, wasn't even sure I liked them that much. But for days this bugged me.

A chap repairing a fence asked me if I was 'getting there' and I watched a lapwing chase off a seagull and a buzzard. Mostly though, when I could shake off the Gene Pitney thing, I was left alone to think deep thoughts. Like is Castle O'er Forest a forest named after Castle O'er, or is it a castle 'O'er the Forest'? I suppose it's the former, because my map says there is a place called Castle O'er. All I saw there though was a collection of ordinary looking houses, no castle – o'er or otherwise.

My day's walking was to end at Eskdalemuir which, according to the weather records it keeps, is one of Scotland's coldest and wettest places. Rather spectacularly, three and a half inches of rain fell in an hour here in 1953 – in June would you believe? No cricket that day, I'll wager. I had no such problems although I was woken at four thirty in the morning by a noisy bunch of Belgians who had come here for the stalking; apparently this business requires an insanely early start to give the humans a chance of taking their prey by surprise. Something like that anyway.

Even though Carlisle was still the main town serving this region, I really felt that I'd arrived in Scotland proper now. The big river in its big valley and the big fields with the big cattle all fitted my notion of what Scottish countryside would look like and through the fading light of the previous evening I had caught a glimpse of some high hills with what looked like snow streaking their upper slopes. The fact that part of the next day's walk was to be through completely unknown territory with no roads and no guidebook added to the feeling that I was treading a daring route and the hubbub of the stalkers setting off in the pre-dawn gloom was the final piece in the jigsaw. Pity they weren't Scots, but my breakfast companion told me that only overseas visitors or those paid for by corporate hospitality can afford the 'sport' now.

It came as a surprise then to find the first item of note as I pressed on towards the metropolis that is Moffat, was a Tibetan Buddhist Monastery. Astonishing! There it is in amongst the conifers complete with prayer wheels, colourful walls, golden roof and dozens of flags on poles. It was set up in 1967 by a group of Tibetan monks who had to flee their country when the Chinese invaded – and I thought it was just grand.

Only the almost incessant roar of jets thundering above me disturbed my cretinous thought processes as I trudged on through seemingly endless miles of forest. The little cluster of cottages at Kiddamhill struck me as the loneliest settlement I had seen on the whole journey and I gave up counting the trees at 3,428,607 because I suddenly thought of another Gene Pitney song – *Backstage*, I think it was – and lost my place.

As I sat and ate the biggest packed lunch I had ever seen, there wasn't a lot to look at – unless you're really into conifers in a big way – so I read the map and was intrigued to see so many 'Antiquities' marked on it, especially in the Eskdalemuir area. Mostly 'Settlements', but also a place mysteriously called Dell's Jingle and some things called Loupin' Stanes. Must go back to have a proper look one day. I also noticed that there's a hill near Eskdalemuir called Ewe Knowe. Must be the cause of much confusion between walkers swapping tales at the end of the day. 'Where've you been today?' 'Ewe Knowe'. And so on, and so on, until one of them cracks.

A brief oasis of open hill country inspired me to tackle the steep upper slopes of Loch Fell which, at 2,257 feet, is the highest ground I'd been on since Scafell Pike and, because it has a trig point on the top, must be a proper hill. Not an overly attractive spot in its own right, with a collection of post and wire fences, but as a viewpoint Loch Fell was staggering. Hills everywhere. I could see back to the Solway and the Lakes and in every other direction, the rows of purple hills gave me some idea of the scale of the country I was travelling through.

It would have been a simple descent northwards to pick up the Southern Upland Way, but in an attempt to cut a corner and save five minutes I was lured down a promising looking gap between two dark blocks of conifers. Firebreak, I thought, jolly good. A very steep descent on slippery grass sped me on my way and at first there was no problem. Even when the gap narrowed to just a few feet I wasn't unduly alarmed. I was still going the right way and it was very much downhill. Gradually though, things became distinctly uncomfortable as first I had to push the branches away with my hands, then crouch, then crawl. Eventually I was reduced to a whimpering, slithering thing as I wriggled along the ground forcing my way through tangled, and increasingly spiky, vegetation. Immediate visibility was down to about two feet – only the steep gradient acted as a reliable guide. Fallen tree trunks obstructed my way. It was sometimes easier to crawl under than clamber over them.

Stifling my rising panic and an urge to use naughty language, I persevered. Nothing goes on for ever and after what felt like several hours, I suddenly popped out like a cork from a bottle onto the track my map promised I'd find. Battered, bruised and bloody, and with my hair full of pine needles, I had sufficient presence of mind to take a photograph of what, from this side, was just a black wall of trees – just for old times' sake, you understand. I also took the opportunity to withdraw some f-words from my swear-bank account. All this time on my own had put me well in credit and you can't take them with you, can you?

Thinking that things were now bound to improve, I discovered, after about half an hour's easy walking along the forest road, that I had lost my wallet. This contained just about everything I needed. I wouldn't be able to book any accommodation, buy food, get money from the bank, or arrange transport home; in short, I was stuffed. Panic stations.

'Calm down Jacko. Think. Where did you last have it? You definitely had it when you left Eskdalemuir. Did you have it when you stopped for your lunch?'

'Yes, I think so.'

'Well, there you are. You don't have to go any further back than just the other side of Loch Fell.'

'But that's miles and it's about a thousand feet of ascent and I'll have to go through all those trees again. I CAN'T!!'

'You know you'll have to don't you? So just do it.'

So I set off back, hoping against hope I would see it lying on the forest road. But I didn't. I located the exit point from my Conifer Hell and, leaving my rucksack at the bottom, squirmed into the blackness. Miraculously, at the second of the fallen tree trunks, I found it, just lying there on the ground waiting to be picked up. You beauty! Oh, thank you, thank you, thank you. Etc.

It seemed a very long way down to Moffat but, unsurprisingly, I was content with my lot. The sun started to shine as I arrived and I was lucky to find a bed for the night in the first B&B I tried. Lucky, not just because it was first class with a friendly landlady, but also because when I caught sight of myself in the mirror I realised how horrific I looked. How the poor woman managed to avoid fainting at the sight of me I don't know. I resembled the sole survivor of some doomsday nightmare which, I suppose, in a way, I was.

Gold, Coal and a Great Big Hole – The Lowther Hills to Coatbridge

The summit of Lowther Hill

Founded on the strength of its wool trade, as proclaimed by the amusing giant ram statue in the main square, Moffat became a fashionable spa town when mineral springs were discovered here a couple of hundred years ago. It's a bit more up-market than some fading resorts and has an air of comfortable gentility despite the coach loads of trippers and the wool shops. After the rigours of the day and the slightly austere pleasures of Langholm and Eskdalemuir, Moffat felt a good place to be.

Over breakfast I chatted to the only other guest, an excellent old boy by the name of Ernie. He was well into his seventies and told me that he likes to get up to the north of Scotland as often as he can, even though he lives in far-off Portsmouth. He always stays in Moffat on his way up and he has to stay in the same B&Bs every year because he can barely read or write and, since his wife died, he finds it difficult to book anywhere in advance. He spent all his working life as a farmer and told me that, as a young man, he saw no need to learn his Three R's. Full of regret now, of course, but he's still leading the sort of retirement that would make many a more learned pensioner green with envy.

I walked through the green and pleasant land of the valley of the River Annan with its patchwork of stone-walled fields, before rejoining the Southern Upland Way. Still trembling at the memory of my battle with nature on the slopes of Loch Fell, it was reassuring to be following a recognised route with its welcoming waymark posts. Where the English and Welsh long distance trails are marked with the acorn logo, Scotland's have a thistle inside a hexagon, and I very quickly got used to looking for the next marker to guide me through the huge forest above Beattock. But then, at an idyllic looking spot by a little tree-girt tarn, I was aurally molested by two large dogs, barking and howling in what had become a tiresomely familiar way. Their owners then appeared, totally unconcerned of course, and said rather accusingly that their dogs weren't used to seeing people up here. Obviously my fault then.

For hours you just plod on up gentle slopes and across streams through millions of trees – it's like I imagine Canada to be, only more Scottish. Exit from the forest on to the top of Beld Knowe and Hods Hill revealed views of yet more mountains, in particular my next day's objective, the tortured summit of Lowther Hill with its giant golf balls and other accoutrements. Down to the unwelcoming Daer Reservoir, and past a forlorn school building – closed six or seven years previously – to my farmhouse accommodation where I spent a very pleasant evening chatting to three ladies, Janie, Jeannie and Joanie, who were all from south-west Scotland and were walking the Southern Upland Way from west to east, in stages of a few days at a time. These were splendid people – proper walkers. Forget your hard men with iron legs and your wiry athletic women built like whippets. Janie, Jeannie and Joanie had it sorted. The Southern Upland Way is not a stroll. It's a switchback of considerable ups and downs, mostly across rough tussocky grass – much tougher than its more celebrated cousin, the West Highland Way – and these women were covering fair distances each day. But they were having a laugh as well.

'We're vairy civilised,' Janie told me. 'We stop quite often for sherry and nuts and a blether.' They warned me about all the big hills I'd be crossing the next day, and I warned them about the dogs they might encounter. They were obviously not as stupid as me, so I did not feel it necessary to reveal to them the shocking details of my near-death experience on Loch Fell.

Lambing was still in progress here and primroses were blooming on the grassy banks by the roadside. Spring is indeed late in these parts. One of the lambs, christened Belinda by Janie or Jeannie or Joanie, was not thriving and had been brought into the house to be fed by hand; her mother couldn't cope seemingly. I often wonder what became of Belinda.

I was away early on a morning of brilliant blue sky in order to allow plenty of time for the fearsome crossing of the Lowther

Hills which, as it turned out, wasn't too bad. There were a couple of steep ups and downs, a little like the headlands and coves in north Cornwall only bigger, and I was fairly soon on the top of Lowther Hill, by which time a cold wind had blown up and the sun had disappeared. Just over 2,500 feet high, Lowther Hill was the summit of my walk through southern Scotland but it is a top to flee from: ugly fences; grim concrete block-houses; a big mast and two giant golf ball affairs which at least had the merit of a certain geometric perfection.

An easy descent, crossing the summit building access road with its red and yellow snow posts, leads to Wanlockhead, Scotland's highest village. Its buildings, from this lofty vantage point, look to have been scattered any old how as if by a giant hand. Even on closer inspection there appears to be little sense of order to the layout of this most interesting of places. On the outskirts of the village is the most dilapidated collection of buildings you could imagine – four or five huts with corrugated iron roofs, boarded-up windows and an oddly intact, but horrifically ugly, thirty-foot high chimney. A poster nailed to an SUW waymark proclaimed in unmissable primary colours 'STOP – Lager Ales Good Food'. Well, it seemed to have stopped here all right, for a little lower still stands yer actual Pub With No Beer, the even more decrepit Walk-Inn Mountain Lodge.

Just before reaching the village I met a group of half a dozen folk who were engaged on the unenviable task of completing the SUW in one go; twelve days they reckoned it would take them. A daunting prospect, indeed – wild though this country is, I couldn't help feeling that there must be better walks to do in a fortnight than this one.

I have seen Wanlockhead described as a hotchpotch – fair enough I suppose – and the state of the buildings there varies from the immaculate (such as the recently renovated mining museum) to the ramshackle. But what a lot to see! Gold and lead were discovered in this inhospitable place and, just as in Dylife in mid-Wales – remember? – a village sprang up. This one is bigger though and has survived. It even held the World Gold Panning Championships in 1992 (yes, the World Championships) and you can still spend your fiver and have a go now, if you want. I resisted the temptation but such was the Wild West ambience, I was unable to stop myself saying 'Yee-hah' in a very silly voice. The post office declares itself to be Britain's highest and I think it's great that Scotland's highest village should be in what is officially part of the Lowlands. Makes you proud to be British doesn't it?

A short walk along an old railway track brought me to Leadhills – guess what they used to mine here – which possesses Britain's oldest subscription library, founded in 1741. A little narrow gauge railway was a temptation but I was not surprised to find it closed – open weekends only – so, stifling my disappointment, I set off across more open country by means of an almost level track which contoured a hill known as Hunt Law; that's numbers 8 and 10 taken care of in your Great Britain football team to take on the Rest of the World. Well, it would have been, forty-odd years ago. It was easy going if a little bleak as far as the indescribably lonely building at Snarhead, but then the path disappeared and it was an ankle-jarring few miles down the valley of Snar Water to the road.

Friends of mine, Darryl and Madeline, live not too far away and they had come to my rescue by putting me up for three nights and ferrying me to and fro. This was a great help because the area between the Southern Uplands and Glasgow is not holiday country and accommodation is scarce. Darryl had arranged to meet me where Snar Water runs into Duneaton Water, a fearsomely lonely stretch of road indeed. You could see the very few cars there were coming for miles along the flat valley road and I began to feel like Cary Grant in *North by North West*. Certainly if any crop-dusting aeroplanes had appeared over the horizon, I'd have legged it.

After the stop-start nature of the walking through Cumbria, it had been grand to get back into the rhythm and mood of the bigger journey but, after five longish days, I was anxious not to repeat the mistakes I made earlier and treated myself to a Saturday off. Sunday dawned cold and grey as I tramped along the road which would take me out of the Duneaton Water valley and into the parallel one of the Douglas Water. Both rivers are tributaries of the Clyde so it was plain that I must be getting closer to Glasgow. Not that there was much sign of it here in this wilderness where the only splash of colour was provided by the strikingly red tarmac of the road surface. An appalling mess of rubbish bags just dumped by the roadside somehow seemed to fit in with the general air of hopelessness. I had been told that massive open-cast coal workings were to be started in the valley very soon, so perhaps there was not a lot of incentive to keep the place spick and span.

The easy climb out of Douglas through well-maintained pastureland heralded a change from the rather cheerless uplands of the last couple of days to a more gentle landscape – or so it seemed. My map promised two or three miles of what looked like clear track and then lanes would lead me through farmland to Strathaven, my intended destination. But the next two miles were to prove the most difficult of the whole venture.

Even at this modest height, I was beginning to be enveloped by a spooky white mist and the sinister squatting outline of concrete coal conveyors could be discerned through the gloom to my right. I checked the map. Yup, there's the disused railway I've just crossed and there's the forest on the skyline and there's the path heading towards it. No mention of a coal mine on the map. Perhaps it was an optical illusion. Whatever, it didn't appear to be on the line of my walk so, undaunted, I pressed on. I began to feel a little less confident, however, as the black wall of the coal tips increased in height and appeared to be getting closer to my route. Still, the track went on and entered the forest as the map had predicted. There was a fence across the track though, which had to be climbed at a locked gate, and that didn't feel right. Vague doubts were becoming more substantial and were confirmed when the path into the forest disappeared, completely engulfed in new conifer growth. I battled on for a few minutes through the dripping green spikiness until, mindful of the episode on Loch Fell, I realised that it was useless and retreated to the forest edge.

Now what? Easy, just follow the forest boundary and pick up the path again where it emerges on the other side. So that's what I'd do. After all, this was Scotland, where people are expected to find their own routes without being molly-coddled by public footpaths and the like. The narrowing gap between fence and forest was the only channel for forward progress and my worst fears were confirmed as I found that the track exiting from the trees was again blocked by the same fence. In order to regain the track, I climbed the fence again, trying to kid myself that by crossing it twice, I had put myself back on the 'legal' side, if you get my drift. Two negatives make a positive, and all that stuff. And, just fleetingly – very fleetingly – there were signs that all would be well again. The path was clear and crossed a stream at a little bridge but then it disappeared, swallowed up by the encroaching wall of earth and whatever else thrown up by the coal site.

Other than turning round and retracing my steps to Douglas – then where would I go? – I had no choice but to continue somehow. I was being diverted further and further west by the embankment and being pushed back into the conifer plantation so I broke free by clambering to the top of the bank. Nothing in my data file of life experiences had prepared me for the sight that greeted me as I crested the rise. I'd obviously died and gone to hell. A hideous black hole a hundred feet deep and stretching ahead to the horizon offered no hope of getting any further. Unable to take in the awful prospect in one go, I concentrated on the immediate surroundings. Right beneath my feet was a steep-sided pit containing pools of orange water, and long flexible pipes looking like the tentacles of some creature from the underworld were asthmatically discharging yet more slime into the hole. Obviously no way down there, so I walked along the embankment until I found what looked like a road of sorts and took that.

To say that this landscape was like you imagine the world would look in a nuclear winter makes it sound prettier than it was. The track I was on was composed of coal-dust, rain and diesel and formed an energy-sapping sludge as tiring to walk through as it was uninspiring to gaze upon. After half a lifetime floundering through this post-apocalyptic nightmare, I reached a big yellow machine of unknown purpose but obvious menace. There were two tiny specks on the top of this giant contraption and, on closer inspection, I could see they were humanoid. Hastening down from their perch, they enquired as to my well-being and, after exchanging a few bon-mots, suggested I take the right fork in the road. At least, it sounded something like that.

I hurried on until eventually, after slithering down more greasy black slopes, I reached a public road at Coalburn. By this time it was pouring with rain. Thank goodness it had held off long enough for me to cross the worst of the ooze and thank goodness it was a Sunday. At least the place was quiet. Apart from those two guys on the yellow machine, there had been nobody else about. It may have been more difficult if the place had been swarming with people.

Coalburn is plain, with severe looking houses lining both sides of the main street, one or two functional shops and a miners' centre. You immediately notice the wire mesh at the windows, a sign, surely, that the big city approaches. One thing I must say, though, is that any people I met in this area were unfailingly cheerful and friendly. They all had some comment to make, even it was only about the weather.

After all that excitement, it was an uneventful and increasingly bucolic walk along lanes to Strathaven. Trying to seek shelter under a bridge over a stream, I disturbed a heron which flapped away effortlessly into the sodden sky and caused me to think that that wouldn't have had too much trouble crossing the open cast site. Strathaven – which I'm told is pronounced Strayven – is the biggest place I'd seen since Carlisle and offered shops and cafes, a ruined castle tower and some grim-looking houses.

Still two more days before I reckoned I'd be away from the built-up area of Glasgow, so loins had to be girded up as I said my farewells to Darryl and Madeline for the last time in the weak early morning sunshine. When things got difficult, as they certainly had yesterday, it was comforting to know that friends would be there at the end of the day to offer a sympathetic ear – as well as food, accommodation and transport, of course. I thought that this would be the last time I'd see any familiar faces on the journey so it was a particularly poignant parting.

Quiet, surprisingly rural lanes hastened me to Millheugh, where I entered Chatelherault, one of Glasgow's country parks. My path ran along the edge of the deep gorge of the River Avon with spectacular views to the right down through deciduous woodland to the water below. Much footpath restoration work has been going on, and the signs announcing the 'greening of our conurbation' stood in stark contrast to the unfeasible amounts of rubbish that had been left lying about along the lanes to my left. Crisp bags, hooch cans, a typewriter and even a burnt-out car all added their own *je ne sais quoi* to the scene.

Chatelherault is a surprise. As country parks go, much of it is unspoilt and untamed and all of it is grand, with cliffs and a deep valley and a rushing river. There's also the enormously impressive house, designed by William Adam and built as a hunting lodge for the Duke of Hamilton in 1744. The whole place — parkland and house — fell into dereliction and was restored and opened as recently as 1986. You wonder how the same species responsible for dumping all that rubbish can also be capable of the huge civic pride involved in restoring a place like Chatelherault for us all to enjoy.

Sneaking between Hamilton and Motherwell and walking briefly along the banks of the Clyde, I passed from one grassy oasis to another, the massive Strathclyde Country Park where the Strathclyde Loch offers opportunities for water sports. A network of paths provides miles of walking and there are facilities also for football, hockey, rugby, cricket, golf, putting, tennis, bowling, jogging, orienteering, cross-country running, fishing and horse-riding. And, of course, walking to John o' Groats. Lunch in the sunshine at the remains of a Roman bath-house was almost perfect but I couldn't tarry long and headed uphill along the dramatic South Calder valley, with its dark sandstone cliffs and massive railway viaduct. I left the park and had to trudge through a very uninspiring landscape of cubic houses and heavy traffic, the only relief coming from the thought that somewhere around here is where Matt Busby was born. Passing near the birthplace of Thomas Telford was special enough, but Matt Busby! I mean.

The 'clearly defined and easy to follow path' that my guidebook promised, had been obliterated by an enormous building project called Eurocentral. I don't know what it is, but it was very inconvenient as I had to make a lengthy detour along main roads until I found my way on to the Monkland Canal near Calderbank. From here to Coatbridge it was just a matter of following the canal through some astonishingly quiet countryside – all cattle and songbirds and sunshine. Coatbridge, unfortunately, was not so pleasant as I struggled along crowded streets in my efforts to secure a bed for the night. There were plenty of shops and banks and offices but Coatbridge was not the hotel-festooned wonderland I'd expected and so, after more and more desperate telephone calls to increasingly distant and expensive alternatives, I found my way to the Hotel of the Squat Hairy Types.

Never mind! The West Highland Way was on the horizon, Glasgow was nearly behind me and I was about to embark on another exciting stage of my journey!

CHAPTER SIX - THE HIGHLANDS

I CAN SEE FOR MILES

Romans and Lomond – Coatbridge to Crianlarich

Loch Lomond

Phantasmagoria! Sorry, but the word was just bursting to be written and I couldn't work it in anywhere sensible, so I thought I'd start a chapter with it. And why not? It's as good a word as most, and better than some; 'distended', for instance, is not a fit word to start a chapter with. Neither are 'benchmarking' or 'teflon'.

They'd been telling me in the Hotel of the Squat Hairy Types, with what I regarded as unseemly glee, that I needn't think that I'd nearly finished my walk yet. 'Oh, no,' they'd said. 'You've got a long way to go yet, you're not even close.' Well, I knew all this but nevertheless I could not shake the feeling that now Glasgow was as good as behind me, I was well on the way. No more big cities to worry about, not even any big towns. The West Highland Way appeared to offer a pretty quick route across the first chunk of the Scottish Highlands by threading a way through the hills as far as Fort William at the foot of the Great Glen. Then there was Ben Nevis and then…? I still hadn't decided on a route from Fort William to the end, but no need to rush into anything hasty. These things need thinking about carefully, I reasoned.

For all the theoretical optimism though, I was struggling to overcome a very real sense of gloom which I could only partly ascribe to the pouring rain and difficult exit from Coatbridge. I felt useless, as if as I were wasting my time, piddling around with this nonsensical and futile project, while friends and family were struggling on with the daily grind. This kind of thought was never, I think, very far from the surface but was generally kept in check by the excitement and effort of my journey. But, after a couple of rather dreary and difficult days, the weeping skies were the catalyst needed to let the genie out of the bottle.

They've done their best with Coatbridge, they really have. The entrance into the town along the Monkland Canal had been perfectly pleasant in the previous afternoon's sunshine, and new building work reveals that the place is at least being cared for. The people are fiercely proud of their industrial history. This area was once known as the Workshop of the World and since the loss of the great coal and steel industries, museums and heritage centres have been opened up to commemorate past glories. Unlike many places, Coatbridge has been planned with pedestrians in mind; there are underpasses and walkways to help the walker negotiate a way through the traffic of the town centre. But I have never seen litter like Coatbridge litter. Who are the morons responsible for this accumulation of trash? Every bridge I walked under, and every concrete corner I came to, was full of broken glass, flattened cans and the ubiquitous fag and crisp packets. Unprepossessing streets led to better walking along disused railway tracks to yet another spectacular mess of old rubbish fires and tips. 'Another bit of spare ground, lads. Let's have a bonfire and smash some bottles.'

Still, everyone I met along the way was friendly. One chap remarked that the rain was 'good for the sken' and another thought I'd be better off with an umbrella than with the waterproofs I had. He was probably right. At Bridgend, near Moodiesburn, I passed the site of a tragic coal mine fire in 1957 in which 47 miners lost their lives. The pit had to be flooded and was never worked again. Somewhere near here, I had to take evasive action from a bunch of fierce looking Boys who had strayed on to the path, and arrival at Kirkintilloch in time for lunch coincided with the heaviest downpour of a very wet day. Shelter was obtained under another bridge, this one mercifully free of jagged glass fragments and the smell of wee.

My map says that the Antonine Wall (Course Of) runs through Kirkintilloch and I'm sorry that I saw no evidence of it. The Wall was put up in about 140AD when the Romans still had ambitions of conquering the whole of Britain. They'd already advanced as far north as Stirling before being withdrawn by their bosses back home in Italy and then, for some reason, decided to have another go. Antonine was not really a military man and made the embarrassing and rather elementary error of putting up his coast to coast wall without realising that he was shutting in hordes of very cross Scots right behind him at Ibrox and Parkhead. 'They're behind you,' his legionnaires would mutter in Latin as he carried on with his doomed enterprise. Nevertheless, it was a good thing for history teachers and setters of pub quizzes.

Travelling north from Kirkintilloch I entered the ancient province of Lennox, named after a powerful bunch of Eurythmic earls who ran this area for five centuries from about 1150 onwards. I was more impressed, however, with the fact that I had passed into East Dunbartonshire, a name that to me sounded magically Scottish. I don't mean to be flippant, but I think one of the joys of travelling through Scotland is the way the place names shout 'Football Coupon' at you. Just the previous day near Coatbridge, for example, I had walked past Albion Rovers' ground.

Straight ahead the Campsie Fells reared up with such ferocity that it seemed they would be insurmountable. The south-facing slopes are very steep and rugged, seamed with gullies and waterfalls, and the swirling cloud being chased up the hillside by a freshening wind added an almost Arthurian aspect to an already dramatic picture. A view of hills was just what I needed, though, to refresh my tired head and this, combined with the gratifyingly easy walking along a disused railway line from Milton of Campsie, pulled me out of the decline that had set in. Over to the west I could make out the magical skyline of the Highlands, my sense of excitement intensified by the fact that I didn't have a clue what any of the seemingly gigantic hills were called. I supposed Ben Lomond was one of them but I couldn't be sure.

It was early evening when I arrived at Strathblane but I had been unable to find an affordable bed for the night there so had to press on a few more weary miles to Killearn. A lady in the village store recommended that I use the 'Water Track', a waterworks road up above the valley and as level as the hilly terrain would allow. It certainly offered great views ahead to the hills and kept me away from main roads and cattle and the other menaces of lowland walking.

It was a very tired Jacko who arrived late at Killearn for the most over-priced accommodation of the whole trip. For the first and only time, I had to pay extra for breakfast – and it was only a so-called continental breakfast at that. For those of you who don't already know, when you see the expression 'Continental Breakfast' in this country, it means, 'We can't be bothered cooking. Here's a bowl of cornflakes and a glass of orange juice.' Also, for the first and only time, there was no hot water so I had to wait for a bath.

It was goodbye to commuter land the following day as I headed towards the hills, leaving the West Highland Way wanderers to tackle Conic Hill as I chose the easy route along lanes and byways. I had a last look back at the flat-topped clenched fist of the Campsies with the strange, aggressive outlier of Dumgoyne like an upraised thumb wishing me good luck, and reached the village of Drymen – pronounced to rhyme with swimmin' and women – an almost English looking place with its village green, and one of great significance. It was the biggest settlement I'd be passing through for some days so I had to stock up with the essentials of life before I set off into what I feared may be Really Wild Country.

The sun shone through the cloud cover as I reached the shores of Loch Lomond at Balmaha and I had lunch near the top of the little hill of Craigie Fort. What a fantastic viewpoint! The wide lower end of the loch was studded with wooded islands and there were dozens of little boats at rest in the still water. To the north, though, the loch narrows and the eye is drawn to the apparently endless hills. Loch Lomond is Britain's largest inland sheet of water and I would have plenty of chance to get an appreciation of what this really means, as I had to walk nearly all of its 23 mile length.

A friendly West Highland Way footpath warden came and spoke to me while I ate, and offered all manner of up to date information on modern path management. Having persuaded me to sign up for a year's subscription to 'Footpath Monthly – the Magazine for Men Who Know Where They're Going' (April's centrefold was Scottish Path of the Year, a scantily-clad track in Glencoe, draped seductively over a heather-covered hillside) he departed, leaving me with some dog-eared back numbers which he didn't want his wife to catch him with.

From here to Rowardennan Youth Hostel, the walking was along a twisting switchback through the marvellous oak woods of the Queen Elizabeth Forest Park which extends eastwards from here to the Trossachs and covers an area of 42,000 acres. I don't know about you but I don't know what 42,000 acres means, except it's probably quite big. There are certainly lots of trees. Lots and lots and lots, in fact. I know John Hillaby said the Forest of Dean was the finest woodland in Britain, but this must run it pretty close. The leaves were a vivid green and the forest floor was a mass of bluebells. The distant views were of hills and the gently lapping waters of the loch were never more than a few yards away, but the path was far too unruly to be called a lakeside one as it wound in and out of bays and up and over rocky headlands. I started to catch glimpses of Ben Lomond towering over everything else and, in my recently rediscovered optimistic mode, I seriously considered trying to fashion a route over it which would take in the summit and return me to the West Highland Way safely and without too much deviation from the little furrow I was ploughing.

But at Rowardennan Youth Hostel I met two chaps, Angus and Hamish, who were walking the WHW for the umpteenth time and they warned me about the rigours of the next day's trek. Very rough, they said it was, and long, too, especially as I had failed to find accommodation before Crianlarich, a good twenty miles away. (I hadn't managed to find any at Crianlarich either but that's another story.) The footpath warden I'd met earlier had also spoken darkly about the difficulty of the Way alongside the Loch north of Rowardennan, so all in all I decided to leave Ben Lomond alone for another day. The youth hostel was just great; the wardens hailed from Blackpool and told me they wanted to retire to Kendal, which is odd in a way because I suspect there are more than a few people in Kendal who would be quite happy retiring to Blackpool, and a few – a different bunch I should think – who would like to retire to Loch Lomondside. Just goes to show. As the great Petula Clark sang, 'The Other Man's Grass is Always Greener'.

I got talking to a very nice lady called Louise who worked on a farm in the grounds of a stately home in the north of England and was on her way to take part in 'Operation Osprey' at Loch Garten. I think this consists of volunteering to give up your time to watch the nests containing the very precious osprey eggs so that they don't get stolen by greedy bastards who can make a few quid out of them. Actually, just a few days before I met Louise there had been just such a theft so even having these unpaid watchers and guardians is not foolproof. I'm not condoning it but I can understand people nicking the eggs if they can make money from doing so. But I don't understand who buys them. I'm told that rare birds' eggs are stolen to order – but by whom? What do they do with them? They surely don't fry them to have with Cumberland sausage, do they? Life's such a mystery sometimes. Before going to Loch Garten, Louise was going to visit the Black Isle to see the dolphins. She was also hoping to catch sight of the grebes – Slovenian ones at that. Unfortunately she was driving north and not walking. She would have made an excellent companion for a day or two and I could have honed my ornithological expertise to hitherto unimagined heights.

Blue sky and that cool, crystal clear air unique to northern uplands greeted me the next morning as I prepared for what promised to be a tough day. A very easy start along a forest road was followed by some much rougher up and down stuff in amongst the trees and boulders by the lake shore. The views across the water to the Arrochar hills were stunning but it was remarkable how, in amongst this jumble of mountain and crag, just one hill holds centre stage for such a long time. This is Ben Arthur, better known as The Cobbler, not 3,000 feet high but with a jagged crest and noble shape that many a bigger mountain would be proud of. Well, I doubt that this is strictly true – it's unlikely that mountains feel pride – or anything else for that matter, but what the heck.

At Cailness there is a memorial to a teacher called Bill Lobban who committed what must be the ultimate sacrifice: he gave up his life to save that of another. In November 1975, the stream flooded and a student on an Outdoor Pursuits course slipped into the swollen waters. It was Bill who managed to rescue the student but in doing so was swept into the loch. Just thinking about this act of incredible selflessness and bravery brought a tear to my eye but before I could start to wax too lyrical about humankind in general I came across more piles of litter. Anybody coming to this place has almost certainly done it by dint of their own efforts, which makes the propensity to throw junk around all the more surprising.

I hurried past the incongruously placed and extraordinarily huge hotel at Inversnaid, built at the end of a road coming from the east and not, thank goodness, running along the lake shore. There is no doubting the taste of the nineteenth century tourists who flocked to this spot, for the situation and views are simply outstanding. Amongst those who were entranced by this place are our old friends Wordsworth and Coleridge who came here in 1803. Another visitor was the Jesuit poet Gerard Manley Hopkins whose famous words are inscribed on a stone near here:

'What would the world be, once bereft

Of wet and wildness? Let them be left,

O let them be left, wildness and wet;

Long live the weeds and the wilderness yet.'

I don't know how good this is as poetry but I'm sure we can all applaud the sentiments and it might be a good idea if every council and planning authority had the words writ large on the walls of all their offices.

The couple of miles immediately beyond Inversnaid are very rough as they wind up, over, through, between, across and down boulders and craglets and tree roots. Every yard of progress has to be really earned here but, for anyone used to the rougher kind of fell-walking, there are no difficulties or frights. I'm no dare-devil but I didn't regard this as oo-er walking at all. Slow yes, but scary no. As the way threads its intricate and tortuous passage along the thickly wooded and improbably steep slopes, the sense of isolation is profound. But this feeling is in some respects an illusion – less than a mile away across the water is the A82, one of western Scotland's busiest roads, and the massive pipelines of the Loch Sloy hydro-electric scheme dominate the view. At the end of the seventeenth century, however, the remoteness would have been very real and it was here that Rob Roy MacGregor had his hideout. Whatever the legends and stories about this bloke it appears that the truth, as usual, is a little more prosaic. He had a cattle droving business and, until the age of forty, lived a relatively placid life, his only real excitement coming from the occasional raid into the Scottish Lowlands. His fortunes took a distinctly dodgy turn when his head drover ran off with all the money that had been put by to acquire that year's cattle. The charming Duke of Montrose had our hero bankrupted, outlawed, evicted and, as a final gesture of kinship and goodwill, burnt his house down. Unsurprisingly Rob Roy took umbrage and, following the advice of the local Job Centre, chose a career in General Outlaw-ology. He settled down in later life and lived in to his seventies, eventually dying of a broken heart because of the continued refusal of the authorities to admit Loch Lomond Rovers to the Scottish Football League. Amongst all the teetering boulders and stones by the lakeside is a crevice reputed to be the cave where Roy of the Rovers himself hid from his pursuers. It will come as no surprise to you to learn that the dynamic duo of Wordsworth and Coleridge visited this spot.

As if all the spectacular scenery and the story of Rob Roy were not enough for one day, there are also the feral goats. My guidebook gave the impression that these animals are shy and not easily seen but, as I crested a little rise on the path, I came across a group of seven or eight goats who appeared totally unconcerned by my arrival. They even posed for a few photos and the head Billy refused to let me past until I'd given him a fiver and promised to send a copy of the best pictures to him.

Eventually I reached the head of Loch Lomond and climbed up to the low pass leading to Glen Falloch from where there was a satisfying view back down the length of the lake with the graceful cone of Ben Lomond dominating the middle distance. Ahead were the snow-smeared slopes of three giant hills which I later learned were Beinn Oss, Beinn Dubhchraig and Beinn Lui. After the rigours of the morning's walk through the jumble of rocks and trees by the lake shore, the path up Glen Falloch marked a return to easier going. The river makes a convivial companion as it sweeps down the glen over a series of small but noisy waterfalls. Unfortunately, although it is inaccessible because of the intervening stream, the A82 is so close as to be intrusively loud and even the sound of the cataracts could not drown out the traffic thundering along the strip of tarmac away to my left.

It was late afternoon by the time I hauled myself up the hillside to join the old military road that would lead me without further excitement to Crianlarich. This path appeared to climb constantly without actually gaining height, a frustrating and unwelcome trick at this time of day. There was recompense, however, in the views across to the knobbly ridges forming the western slopes of the hugely impressive Cruach Ardrain range, which I really must go back and visit one day. I was back in sheep country again which meant (a) dry stone walls which are profoundly quiet and still as they fulfil their purpose, and (b) dogs which are neither of those things. It seemed that the further north I progressed on my journey the more unhinged the dogs became. The animals at the farm just below me were the loudest and most berserk I had yet encountered — I was just grateful that I had no need to enter the farmyard.

Just above Crianlarich the way passes through a gate in a deer fence which marks the boundary between Glen Falloch and Strath Fillan, the latter valley being part of the drainage system of the River Tay which empties into the North Sea. For the first time on my journey I had crossed the main east-west watershed of Great Britain, albeit briefly. Diddle de dee.

Southey and Telford Have a Laugh – Over Rannoch Moor to Fort William

Above Tyndrum

The search for accommodation was now becoming problematic. Even as early in the year as May it seemed that the popularity of the West Highland Way was going to cause difficulties. The Youth Hostel at Crianlarich just managed to find me a bed for the night but I was having no luck booking ahead for the following day. Everywhere appeared to be full and it was only thanks to the timely intervention of a group of West Highland Wayfarers from the Gillespie Memorial Church in Dunfermline that I was able to get a place at the end of the next day's walk. They had been wise virgins and had arranged their stopovers well in advance. Fortunately for me, one of their party had cried off so they had a spare place, which I took with alacrity. I had suddenly discovered one of the big disadvantages of walking the planned and waymarked trails. When they are busy – as the West Highland Way was – they will be busy all the way because the same number of people are competing for limited accommodation which, in this case, is available only at infrequent but well-known places en route. Many people seemed to be hitch-hiking to places far removed from the Way, and some walkers I talked to found it quite normal to catch buses or trains to find a bed for the night and then use transport back to the start point the following morning. The proximity of the road and railway has its advantages after all.

Crianlarich is splendidly situated right amongst the big hills of the Southern Highlands but its ease of access has given it the feel of a place which would sooner do business with car- and coach-borne visitors than with walkers. A surly couple in a shop in the village did little to dispel this feeling as they ran through a limited but eloquent repertoire of grunts and irritable finger-jabbings in response to my requests for provisions for the day.

From Crianlarich (Settlement of the Hostile Shopkeepers) to Bridge of Orchy (Crossing Place of the Expensive Beer), the West Highland Way pretty closely follows the old military road, the not so old A82 and the even less old railway line as all four routes wend their way along Strath Fillan to Tyndrum and then over the pass into Argyll. Quite early in the day, after a brief foray onto the wooded lower slopes of Fiarach to the south west of the valley, I crossed the River Fillan at Kirkton Farm from where there is an exciting retrospective view of the massive, yet shapely, Crianlarich hills – Ben More, Stob Binnein and Cruach Ardrain. The last named is still standing despite the Freewheelin' Bob Dylan's assertion that Ardrain's A-Gonna Fall; even he couldn't be right all the time, it seems.

Just beyond the farm is another of the magical places I came across quite unexpectedly. The ruined St Fillan's Chapel has historical associations with Robert the Bruce and the battle of Bannockburn, St Fillan having been an Irish monk who came over to these parts in the eighth century. The bell of the chapel also has a history. It was supposedly used as part of a bizarre treatment for insanity whereby the patients were dipped in the river and tied to a tombstone all night with the bell hanging over them. And if they weren't barmy before the proceedings, they almost certainly would be afterwards.

Although the going from here to Tyndrum – pronounced Tyne-drum, not Tin-drum, I was reliably informed – was easy and uneventful, there were fantastic views leftwards to the craggy north-east face of Ben Lui, another splendid hill which I added to my burgeoning list of Places To Go Back And Visit Another Time. The gleaming snow decorating the summit and lining the black gullies pointing down to the hugely impressive hollow of Choire Gaothach just added to the slight misgivings I was having about passing these places in such an unseemly rush. As I kept saying, 'I might never pass this way again.' Still, I couldn't dally and I couldn't visit them all. At least the weather was perfect and this enabled me to see the hills. It would have been a cheerless slog through the mist and rain.

Tyndrum is a straggling, unprepossessing sort of a place, now dominated by a hotel so huge that I wondered whether I was looking at it through a giant telescope. There are two separate railway lines at Tyndrum, one heading off west to Oban, the other aiming for Fort William, and each has its own station. It seems bizarre that a tiny settlement like this should be able to boast such a large slice of Britain's railway infrastructure when many much bigger places — the marvellous Llanidloes and Kirkby Lonsdale, to name but two — are devoid of any kind of rail access at all.

A short climb from Tyndrum is the pass leading to Glen Orchy and, as I did at the head of Loch Lomond, I got the feeling I was moving into a different phase of the journey. Ahead lies a long straight valley with the unmistakable outline of Beinn Dorain on its right hand side. The closer I got to this huge pyramid of a mountain, the more overwhelming it became, with its incredibly regular, steep grassy slopes soaring skywards. This is what I imagined the Highlands to be all about, the blue sky and fluffy white clouds notwithstanding, and there were even some of those great shaggy Highland cattle standing in the river. With unpleasant memories of the Cumbrian Boys still fresh in my mind, I had to fight back an urge to make a long detour round them, but these ferocious looking beasts were as gentle as lambs and gave me no trouble at all.

Arrival at the Bridge of Orchy Hotel produced one of the Unforgettable Moments of the Walk: the price of a pint of bitter reached record levels. The shock of being charged an astronomical price came very soon after a smart-arse man in a sort of shop had responded with malicious glee to my request for milk that he didn't stock it and that 'any self-respecting hiker would have dried milk with them'. Tosser. Still, the good folk of the Gillespie Church had arranged my accommodation at the bunkhouse and excellent it was, as was the breakfast next morning. I felt that I really did not deserve this good fortune. Making the most of the sunshine I was able to sit outside the pub with my pint and indulge in talking a good class of rubbish to anyone who cared to join in. Amongst other people, I met Clare-Ann, an American lady who had just been up Beinn Dorain, and whose partner, Bill, I had already bumped into between Crianlarich and Tyndrum. And later in the evening Stephen, a friend from Kendal, arrived totally unexpectedly on his way back from a week's walking somewhere in the far north. How about that?

The unseasonal and untypical great weather showed no sign of breaking as I left Bridge of Orchy for what was going to be a long day. The nearest accommodation I'd been able to find was at Kinlochleven, twenty-one tough miles away, but the same applied to other people, including the group from the church (some of whom were not regular walkers) and Angus and Hamish, the chaps I'd met back at Rowardennan. At least this time I had managed to book my own place and had not had to rely on last minute help from others.

Unlike the A82, the WHW does have the decency to cross the old bridge at Bridge of Orchy, and it then climbs to the Mam Carraigh, a deservedly famed viewpoint. The great jumbled hills of the Blackmount line up to your left, while straight ahead beyond Loch Tulla is the vast tract of Rannoch Moor. To the right, and slightly behind, is Beinn Dorain looking just as impressive but a little less shapely from here. Despite the view, I was more affected by the sight of a long railway train leaving Bridge of Orchy station before its lonely traverse of Rannoch Moor. The locomotive and the coaches it was pulling were completely dwarfed by the massive hillside behind, which made even more surprising the loudness of the 'farp' sound the engine made as it set off. In these majestic surroundings, the noise seemed to possess an almost romantic inevitability as it echoed round the hillsides — like the last, desperate howl of a doomed beast.

Fearing that I might be cracking up at last, I marched down the slope to the Inveroran hotel on the edge of some woodland which is supposed to be a remnant of the ancient Wood of Caledon, a huge pine forest that once spread right over the Central Highlands. There has been an inn on this site at Inveroran for a couple of hundred years and the dreaded Wordsworths stayed here in 1803, noting that 'the butter was not eatable and there were only four eggs in the house, which they had boiled as hard as stones'. I mean, what can you say? I can just imagine the proprietor thinking after he'd taken their booking, 'It's them poets from the English Lakes again. They'll be here in a fortnight — better put the eggs on now.' The thing that intrigues me most about this yarn is how the Wordsworths knew there were only four eggs in the house. Did they undertake a thorough search in the dead of night? Or did they just breeze into the place shouting, 'I wandered lonely as a cloud… How many eggs you got then?' I'm beginning to understand now why de Quincey calculated how many miles Wordsworth walked — the other parts of his lifestyle were obviously too murky to be delved into.

That other Lakes poet and gentleman, Robert Southey, also stayed here and called the place a 'wretched hovel'. And he was with Thomas Telford at the time. That must have been a good night they had at Inveroran. Picture the scene as the umpteenth pint of McEwan's disappears down their throats. Robert says in a poet's voice, which I imagine to be a cross between John Inman's and Leonard Cohen's, 'How about this to put in a poem, Tom? My name is Death: the last best friend am I.'

Thomas, sounding like Kenny Dalglish on speed, replies, 'Brulliant, son. But I've just had a great idea – I'll build a road in Wales and call it the A5. Whadda ye think?'

Robert laughs uncontrollably and then says, 'Oh, the arts babblative and scribblative.'

Thomas meanwhile has constructed some kind of tottering edifice from beer mats and is pouring his drink along a little trench in the masterpiece he has fashioned. 'Ach, Robbie, son. Forget the A5. I've a better notion. A bridge for a canal.'

Consumed by mirth, both men fall in a hysterical heap and declare their undying love for one another. That's why the aqueduct is now known as Pontcysyllte. They couldn't remember the next day what they'd called it and so decided to give it a name that nobody could pronounce.

The crossing of Rannoch Moor, which had been described as the most serious stretch of the West Highland Way, turned out, in these perfect conditions, to be an easy if somewhat long walk across an incredibly grand landscape of towering hills on the left and desolate blanket bog on the right. The track itself is splendidly made and easy to walk on, and the area around Ba Bridge was as near perfect a resting place as you could hope to find. I chatted to a guy here who had stayed at Southey's 'wretched hovel' the previous night and had found it as delightful as it looked from the outside. He told me that his guidebook to walking in these parts warned against the possibility of becoming a 'contemplative malingerer', a marvellously appropriate phrase to any one of the thousands of us who have from time to time dragged our heels a bit because we just couldn't be bothered to go any faster or further. Certainly, the variety and grandeur of the scenery was just stunning, but I had a long way to go and had to leave my new acquaintance malingering in a contemplative fashion against the parapet of the bridge.

I met Angus and Hamish – or was it Hamish and Angus? – again on the descent to Blackrock Cottage and they pointed out various landmarks to me. 'There are more Munros than you can shake a stick at,' said Angus – or was it Hamish?

Crossing the A82 on this bank holiday Saturday was not easy. Southbound: not a thing. Northbound: a seemingly endless procession of cars, coaches and caravans hurtling along the narrow tarmac into the portals of Glencoe. I'd be glad to see the back of this road for a little while – the constant roar of traffic was getting to be a nuisance – but even so I had to admit that the cars and the concrete bridge gave scale to the massive hills around the head of Glen Etive. Buachaille Etive Mor, that great grey cone of rock is even more impressive and photogenic than I had anticipated.

Just as I had on that first evening at Land's End, I felt lucky to be amongst such unbelievable country. The only real difference is that here I had to share it with several hundred others – still, more than enough to go round, eh?

Everything here was on a grand scale. Landmarks that looked to my Lakes-trained eye to be reachable in a few minutes took an hour to get to. The hills were enormous, as were the crowds milling around the Kingshouse, another of the famous Scottish hotels. Guess who stayed there once upon a time? Yup, the W's and Mr S. Dorothy Wordsworth, not mincing her words, said 'Never did I see such a miserable, such a wretched place.' And Southey reckoned that the innkeeper made a fortune from salt smuggling. Salt smuggling? I ask you. The world must have been a fun place back then. Salt smuggling in pubs was carried on until quite recently, of course, by the clever ploy of putting it in those little blue bags in your packet of crisps. Quite how landlords made a fortune from it is beyond me – I'll think about it and, if I solve this conundrum before the end of the book, I'll let you know.

Beyond Glencoe is Loch Leven and until recently travellers were faced with a choice of either waiting for the ferry or making a long diversion inland to the head of the loch at Kinlochleven. The Ballachulish Bridge, built in the 1970s, has changed all that but when the military road was constructed in the 1740s Majors Wade and Caulfield – little-known forerunners of Millican and Nesbitt and Cannon and Ball – had no such option. As they usually did when faced with a choice of the long, easy way or the short, difficult way, they went for the latter – in this case a reputedly fearsome ascent, rearing out of the depths of Glencoe, a track known as the Devil's Staircase. It turned out to be a well-engineered series of zig-zags leading fairly painlessly to the highest point on the West Highland Way. It was certainly nothing like as tiring an ascent as certain parts of the Southern Upland Way.

The summit of the Staircase rewarded me with views of the Mamores and behind them the huge, shambling bulk of Ben Nevis which looked, even from this distance, considerably higher than any of its neighbours. To get my first real sighting of the highest land in the Kingdom and to know that I would soon be tackling its slopes was a highlight indeed.

Plonking myself down on an accommodating boulder, I reckoned I'd done all the hard work for the day. Just down into Kinlochleven and then find the accommodation I'd booked. Will I never learn? First, the descent seemed endless. Down a bit, level, up a bit, down a bit, level, up a bit. As the corollary of the ever-rising path leading out of Glen Falloch, this one appeared to involve descent without actually losing height. Dropping down a hillside can be pretty hard work for a tired walker; the knees groan and complain, 'What are you doing to us, Daddy?' And all the aches and pains in the universe travel through your boot soles and up your legs, body and neck until they are dissipated by passing through your brain and out of the top of your head.

After several hours of this trudge, I caught sight of the village of Kinlochleven nestling almost Alpine fashion at the foot of the slopes about 10,000 feet below me. Soul destroying, or what? The monotony of the descent was broken by arrival at the line of the six enormous pipes carrying water down from the Blackwater Reservoir to the aluminium works in the village. The construction of the dam, the pipeline and the works was a massive undertaking and was one of the last major civil engineering projects to use the traditional navvy method of working: hard manual labour, lawlessness, riotous drinking and wild sex. Kinlochleven almost owes its very existence to the coming of the aluminium works but, despite the prosperity that came with it, there were problems. The River Leven formed the old county boundary between Argyll and Inverness and, as luck would have it, the town grew on both sides of the river. So the little place of barely 2,000 souls had two different sets of local government bye-laws to contend with, and there were even two police stations. This is the stuff of those oh-so whimsical TV comedies – except it was real. Great, isn't it? Unfortunately, reorganisation in 1975 'rationalised' the situation and the place has returned to a relatively peaceful normality.

Some people have said that the effect of an industrial town, artificially created and plonked in the midst of such outstanding scenery, is jarring to the senses. I found no such problem with Kinlochleven. It is dwarfed by the scale of the surroundings and, in any case, it made a change to see some real houses and real people going about their daily lives. Apart from the length of the descent from the top of the Devil's Staircase, the other thing I hadn't reckoned with was the fact that I had unwittingly booked ahead into a place half way up the opposite hill side. So an already long day was extended even further as I stumbled along the rapidly darkening woodland track leading to the Mamore Lodge.

A former hunting lodge on the Mamore estate, the place was built round the time of the First World War by British Aluminium as part of the price for obtaining the land they needed for their works. After the expensive and dismal accommodation near Glasgow and the crowded, communal living of the hostels of the last three nights, this place was luxury. Redolent of turn of the century gentility, yet engagingly eccentric, the building was a maze of hallways and staircases. The bedrooms were named after people. Mine was 'Miss Marie Keppell', whoever she was – not Lulu's real name, is it? The one I was in at least boasted some splendidly robust and suitably noisy plumbing. Proper taps you needed both hands to turn on and off – none of your namby-pamby, turn-of-the-millennium, airy-fairy designer chic here.

The welcome was warm, the meal was good, the beer excellent and the view westward from the dining room window into the fading light at the end of Loch Leven was fantastic. The most fjord-like of all the lakes I'd seen, Loch Leven leads the eye unerringly to the conical hill of Sgorr na Ciche – better known, unfortunately, as the Pap of Glencoe. In *The Lost Continent*, Bill Bryson talks about the mountains known as the Tetons being so named because of their supposed resemblance to the shape of a female breast, and then goes on to surmise that the people responsible must have been away from women-folk for a long time. Well, isn't that what the word 'pap' means? So, the same thought processes must have gone on here. And you can read whatever interpretation you like into The Old Man of Coniston.

The eavesdropping potential was high as I sat and ate my dinner. A group of walkers listened to the loudest amongst them hold forth at length about such fascinating topics as the colour availability of Lowe Alpine shorts – amazingly varied, apparently – and his early boy scout days. I was becoming increasingly desperate to hear these disembodied and mundane snippets from other people's chatter; at first I thought they might offer a way into a discussion with fellow travellers but now I decided it was easier and more interesting to simply listen to unrelated sound bites.

The next day, under a colourless sky, I walked the rest of the West Highland Way to Fort William, an unspectacular journey through the gloomy Lairigmor. This I found to be one of the drabbest sections of the entire walk: a dusty, hard track through uninspiring countryside with a line of electricity poles for relentless company. The melancholy ruins of a couple of cottages near the top of the pass didn't help, but things improved somewhat in the afternoon when Ben Nevis loomed into sight. Not especially attractive from this viewpoint, there was, nevertheless, no denying the impressiveness of the sheer size of Britain's biggest hill.

The WHW is a good walk – no doubt about that – but things are huge and I became, dare I say it, a little jaded with the big views and the wide sweeps. Apart from the stretch near Rob Roy's hideyhole on Loch Lomond, it had been very much WYSIWYG walking

– everything laid out before you and no surprises. But just before the end and as an antidote to the gloom of the Lairigmor, there was the sight of the little lake of Lun da Bhra with its surround of pines and then some surprisingly switchback walking through a marvellous patch of primroses with unexpected views northwards over an almost English landscape of farming country. All too soon, back into an area of forestry working and the inevitable huge valley. This time it was Glen Nevis and I was quickly into Fort William, another of those places whose charms are so severely limited that it is described in much of the tourist blurb merely as 'bustling'.

The Top of My World – Ben Nevis

The top of Ben Nevis

In all truth, Fort William is not much of a place to look at; the little park I walked through on my arrival and the church behind it were the visual highlights of this utilitarian town. But because the next day was set aside for the ascent of Ben Nevis, and the day after that was to be a planned rest day, the Fort would be my home for three nights. I found a decent and relatively inexpensive hotel where my room had the luxury of a bath and where the bar seemed happy to stay open and sell me beer. John Hillaby reckoned the town had the atmosphere of a frontier post where everyone seemed to be on the point of moving on to somewhere else. I think I know what he meant, but the population seemed no more transient to me than it does in any other holiday resort.

What did strike me though was the large number of those people who congregate on benches and drink too much. From a distance they look like teenagers – they gather in flocks like younger people do and make the same sort of sounds – but on closer acquaintance they are clearly much older. For this reason, if no other, their juvenile behaviour takes on a more threatening and unpleasant aspect. They also possess big dogs which, almost without exception, display a dignified solemnity noticeably lacking in their owners. Rather strangely, the female humans look much younger and less raddled than the males. I wondered how such devastated specimens could attract these ladies and flirted with the notion of asking if I could join their gang just so I could find out – purely in the interests of scientific research, you understand. However, when I realised just how warily these frightening-looking men were looking at me, it dawned on me that to most folk I must have appeared even more horrific.

Phil, an old friend from Kendal now exiled in the suburbs of Edinburgh, had said he would join me for the ascent of Ben Nevis and he drove up that evening so that we could plan our assault on Britain's highest summit in the comfort of a warm hotel bar. A computer programmer by profession and an excellent and thoroughly safe rock-climber, Phil displayed none of the qualities required by those two activities by forgetting to bring his walking gear with him. He'd packed it – immaculately, I have little doubt – but failed the Krypton Factor test by omitting to actually put it in the car when he set off. A simple mistake, of course, which has probably dogged many attempts to tame the universe. How many people, I wonder, had actually climbed Mount Everest before Hillary and Tensing, but had forgotten to take the Union Jack with them? Or, had two unknown Russian blokes got to the moon before Neil Armstrong?

'Where is the camera, Boris?'

'I thought you had packed it, Ivan.'

I have never been able to completely shake off the feeling that Phil forgot his gear half on purpose, either so that he wouldn't have to flog 4,500 feet up a big hill and 4,500 feet down again or — and this is my preferred theory — so that he could cock a snook at British walking tradition which demands that one usually dons shiny and conspicuously expensive outdoor gear. Instead, Phil reached the top looking as if he'd stepped straight out of Greenwoods' window: grey slacks, a white shirt, snazzy grey coat and peaked cap set at a jaunty angle. I don't think he was wearing a tie but I wouldn't have been surprised if he had. In the absence of a rucksack, he tried to set off with his butties etc contained in a white plastic bag but I'm afraid to say I drew the line at this appalling lack of taste and offered to carry his stuff in my sack where it was at least hidden from public scrutiny. I mean to say — some standards have to be maintained.

After the days of almost completely uninterrupted sunshine I had enjoyed on the West Highland Way, it came as no surprise to see it dawn cool, grey and drizzly on the morning of the Climb Up the Big Hill. The treetops seemed to be lost in the cheerless mist and the mountain weather forecast gave us little hope of improvement. Displaying stiff upper lip-ness of an extraordinary degree of rigidity and an almost reckless optimism we set off from the car park in Glen Nevis and were soon swallowed up by the gathering gloom. This was a bank holiday Monday so we were not the only souls about and, despite the conditions, the well-trodden path was easy to follow. After a few hundred feet the views were non-existent, and it was somewhat eerie to be able to hear the babble of conversation from other pilgrims so clearly without being able to see anybody.

After the jagged ascents of Snowdon and Scafell Pike, the way up Ben Nevis was relatively easy – but long and unrelenting. The zigzags, which I had read about, appeared to be endless but, eventually, we crossed an exciting snowfield; this was another great moment in the journey. Just briefly, I could pretend I was a real mountaineer. (I decided to be Reinhold Messner.) People like Chris Bonington probably have to go 20,000 feet higher than I was in order to get the same thrill. This is just one of the many advantages to be gained from a life of ineptitude and under-achieving.

Before I set off on this walk I did not really believe in miracles, but I had had enough evidence on the journey to make me think again. The episode of the lost wallet, the glorious weather on Snowdon and Scafell Pike and the fact that I had survived the unspeakable horrors of the opencast coal site were all pointers to the possibility that something was working in my favour. As we neared the summit of Ben Nevis through the swirling cloud I was happy just to be there; after all, it was the highest and potentially the most challenging of the three tops I'd set as targets, and it seemed that nothing could prevent Phil and me getting there safely. I don't think I was at all bothered by the lack of a view – I had expected these conditions on Snowdon and Scafell Pike as well. And I'd read that the summit of the Ben is hidden in cloud for more than 300 days a year so it was hardly surprising that we couldn't see much. But, as the angle eased to a definite plateau-like gradient, we suddenly found ourselves on the edge of something very much steeper and, just as we got there, the mist seemed to dissolve. People talk about it opening like curtains but this mist just melted away and immediately beneath our feet were the tremendous cliffs of the great north face of Ben Nevis. We both quickly took photos as we were convinced the clouds would re-materialise at any moment but they didn't. Much more rapidly than we would have believed possible, a pale blue sky appeared and there we were, bathed in a milky sunshine. The snow-lined gullies and black pinnacles of Tower Ridge were displayed to perfection and the feeling of elation I experienced was like the one I had had all those weeks ago when I set off from Land's End. Never again on this walk would I feel quite so blessed.

It was a simple stroll from our vantage point to the big cairn marking the summit not just of my walk but of Britain as well and, fittingly, the view was thesaurus-defyingly immense. There were mountains in every direction, most of them in areas with evocative and magical names, areas I had never been to and probably never will, places like Ardgour and Knoydart, their rippled skylines stretching away into infinity. And, nearer – and seeming almost like home – the shores of Loch Linnhe and the northern suburbs of Fort William. Fantastic!

The descent – for once I used the same route up and down – was almost bound to be an anticlimax, and so it proved, despite the increasing detail in the nearer views. Looking back up those awful zig-zags we were thankful to have completed the ascent in cloud; the sight of that bouldery staircase climbing remorselessly upwards must be very out-facing in clear weather.

Back at sea level, it had become very warm and I bumped into Clare-Ann and Bill, the American couple I'd first met at Bridge of Orchy. As I'd found in Cornwall, it was a good feeling to meet new acquaintances and be able to chat to them as if they'd been friends for life. Anyway, Phil had to get back to Edinburgh. It had been great to see him and the encouragement he gave me was a real tonic. I thought we'd done pretty well for two clapped-out old buggers and was marginally surprised that we did not get a civic reception.

The problem now exercising my feeble brain was deciding on my route from here. I still hadn't sorted it out and had no clear idea which of many options I'd choose. I had a rest day to think about it but frittered most of it away in a laundry where I met Fort William's answer to Dot Cotton. I also took up the challenge of trying to get a fish dinner with only one fish. Darryl had told me weeks ago that it was impossible but I thought he was pulling my leg. So I went into a splendid fish and chip shop and asked the lady behind the counter whether it was, indeed, possible to buy a fish dinner with only one fish.

'Oh, aye. No problem.'

'Well, can I have fish and chips with just one fish then please?'

'Aye.'

Much wrapping took place and I was charged what seemed like a small fortune. When I unwrapped my meal outside – guess what? A few chips surrounded by two enormous fish, both of them direct descendants of Moby Dick. What can you do?

Still wrestling with the route-selection problem, I sat and munched away at my lunch. My heart told me to stay with the west coast – I wanted to see Torridon and Coigach and Cape Wrath – but my head said to go east up the Great Glen. I had to go east some time and accommodation would, I thought, be a problem if I took the western option. I decided to see what advice the Tourist Information Centre could offer and the answer was simple. None. So I was almost reduced to the level of Luke Rhinehart's Dice Man. Toss a coin, I thought. In the end, though, common sense prevailed. I realised how tired I was getting, I had been away from home for far too long as it was and therefore decided to go for what seemed to be the easier option and head for the Caledonian Canal.

Yes, I was tired and just a little bit dispirited as I left Fort William. Maybe I'd been gearing up for Ben Nevis and now needed a fresh objective. And yet I was still keen enough to look for the start of a definite new stage in the journey. After the mountain miles of the West Highlands I thought the Caledonian Canal would provide just that, rather like the end of the South West Coastal Path, and crossing the Severn Bridge into Wales had done. So, I made the small detour to the very end of the Canal at Corpach simply so that I could say, if only to myself, that I'd started this next phase of the trip right on the coast. Well, it's not much of a coast really; Loch Linnhe is a sea loch, right enough, but here, near its head, is fairly narrow and unimpressive, hemmed in as it is by hilly country. The name Corpach means City of the Dead – it was from here that Scottish kings were taken across the sea to Iona for burial – but the most interesting thing to look at now is the pepperpot lighthouse on the quay.

I had an unhappy few minutes trying to find my way out of Fort William on to the track to Corpach. Once I'd negotiated the frighteningly busy main road, I had to do battle with a supermarket car park – a terrifying experience to a bumpkin like me. My guidebook promised me a path to the right of McDonald's but there was a road here which led to a motel. I did find a path eventually and it was an untidy, scruffy affair with a litter problem almost as acute as Coatbridge's. Still, it took me in the right direction and the views back to Ben Nevis would have been excellent were it not for the low cloud which appeared to have regained its habitual position over the hills.

The Great Glen and Beyond – Fort William to Cannich

The Caledonian Canal

'Welcome to the Caledonian Canal' proclaimed a large sign, and I could not have felt better if it had been erected solely for my benefit. Before we go any further, I ought to share with you some Fantastically Fascinating Facts about this waterway. Originally proposed at the time of the Napoleonic Wars as a sort of YTS scheme to try and staunch the flow of rural emigration – which was having a serious effect on the ability of the area to recruit conscripts – design of the canal was entrusted to the one and only Thomas Telford. The Great Glen is an obvious route for a crossing from the North Sea to the Atlantic, as two-thirds of the distance already consisted of the long, navigable lochs of Ness, Oich and Lochy. To a guy with Telford's track record, nowt of a job, you'd have thought. But, as seems to be the case with all British canals, the venture was beset with problems. It took nearly twenty years to build the thing and Telford's proposal that it should be made twenty feet deep was compromised. In the end the canal was only fourteen feet deep. The upshot of all this bureaucratic footling was that by the time it was finished the canal was not deep enough to take the larger cargo ships and, in any case, bigger, better vessels were being constructed which could laugh at the heavy seas of the Pentland Firth and so avoid the tolls and locks and the rest of the paraphernalia that goes with canal travel. But what a magnificent white elephant it is! Tourists soon latched on to its scenic attractions and by 1847 steamers were ferrying folk from Glasgow to Inverness at a cost of thirty shillings a go.

Scorching along the towpath in improving weather, I soon arrived at the flight of eight locks known as Neptune's Staircase which is undeniably impressive – but not as impressive as it's made to look on photographs taken with the aid of a huge telephoto lens. Very undemanding walking under the fringe of trees lining the towpath rewarded me with grand views of Ben Nevis and Aonach Mor away to my right. I was beginning to feel a lot more relaxed; the fretting about which route to take had gone, the route finding was totally straightforward and the almost complete lack of gradients made for rapid progress. All in all I felt pretty pleased with myself. Even my rucksack, which had been too big and too heavy ever since I'd left Land's End, felt good on my shoulders. Getting to grips with this walking stuff, at last. When I reached Gairlochy, though, I met a chap walking back to Fort William after having spent three days camping in Knoydart. If ever any single event was designed to make me feel inferior, this was it. Without in any way appearing macho or belligerent, this fellow seemed so totally self-reliant and at ease with the world around him that I felt like an impostor, a fraud. He also had on his back a rucksack the size of a Renault Clio – so much for the pathetic specimen I was carrying. I tried to convince myself that his was probably packed full of bubble-wrap and had nothing of any substance in it at all.

Much better for my frame of mind was the sight of an enormous ship passing through the lock gates at Gairlochy. It was a tight squeeze, and no mistake. Whatever they pay the driver, or pilot, or whatever they're called, is not enough. I was sure that we were witnessing the first passage of the QE2 through these waters but it turned out to be a sort of cargo boat from Gothenburg called the Origo.

The country around here saw much of the activity leading up to the Jacobite uprising of 1745 when the biggest of the bigwigs, Donald Cameron, was persuaded by Bonnie Prince Charlie to espouse the Stuart cause and take up arms against the government troops. Much romance, of course, surrounds BPC and his exploits – notably his escape from Skye with Flora MacDonald – but the inevitable and grisly side of the truth is that thousands of soldiers died, most tragically at Culloden where 4,500 highlanders were wiped out in twenty-five minutes. Realising that he was not going to be on the winning side, Charlie's tactical advice to his followers was to 'let every man seek safety in the best way he can', before he legged it to the nearest ship and escaped to France. A spectacularly daring adventure, perhaps, but as usual the ordinary chap paid a dear price for it. Of the five Cameron brothers only one escaped punishment – and that was because he had emigrated to Jamaica and the Foreign Secretary wanted someone to stay with on his Caribbean holidays.

The journey through the trees on the north-west shore of Loch Lochy followed a tarmac road and then forest tracks. The views across the silvery waters of the loch back towards the hazy outline of Ben Nevis were excellent, but a little sad – I knew now that I probably would not be venturing into such hilly terrain again. Past Achnacarry, ancient ancestral home of the Camerons which was used in the Second World War as a training base for commandos and is now lived in by the twenty-sixth Cameron chief, the way crosses the Arkaig, one of Britain's shortest rivers.

At Loch Lochy Youth Hostel I met a couple from Australia, Hans and Rosemary, who were having an extended holiday in Britain walking many of our official Long Distance Footpaths. Quite unexpectedly, I also bumped into Joyce, an acquaintance from Kendal, and another couple at the hostel were from Windermere – still more surprises and coincidences. I spent a happy evening on the Scot II, a former tourist boat now permanently moored as a floating pub and serving excellent food and drink. Alan and Jenny from Oldham told me that they were on holiday sailing along the canal from Inverness and back again. The journey takes about a week at a very relaxed pace, but they said the boat cost about £600 to hire. Sounded like a lot of money to me.

Having become unused to evenings of such high-octane revelry, it was with some difficulty that I ventured out the following morning. The weather had turned distinctly summery now – the blue skies which had been above my head for most of the last week were now accompanied by a rise in temperature – so much so, in fact, that it was becoming important to find shade wherever I could. I had in front of me a long day's trek to Invermoriston on the shores of Loch Ness, so it was good to set off through the trees of the Leitirfearn nature reserve.

The way along the shore of Loch Oich followed the long abandoned route of the Invergarry and Fort Augustus Railway Company's line to Spean Bridge and it was, by a comfortable margin, the best walking I enjoyed in the Great Glen. The story of the railway is a typical one of Victorian engineering flair on the one hand, and big business's desire to stifle the innovator on the other. In the late nineteenth century, while two rail companies, the North British and the Highland, were squabbling about which one of them should build a railway through the Glen, the Invergarry and Fort Augustus came along and nicked the rights from under the noses of the big two. Stung into retaliatory action the Highland Railway, having first offered its own line as a link into Inverness, then closed it leaving the I & FA's passengers stranded in the middle of nowhere. Having spent all its money on viaducts and tunnels and stuff, the I & FA went to the wall and the line died an undignified and agonisingly slow death, not finally expiring until 1946. Modern walkers have every reason to be grateful for this bit of capitalist spite as the not-so-permanent way offers an excellent alternative to the roads and Land-Rover tracks on the opposite shore. The not-quite-straight route carved a mossy green tunnel through the woods and the feel of the springy turf under my feet, the sweet smell of damp undergrowth and the sound of the bird song I can still recall with almost worrying clarity.

All too soon the railway becomes too overgrown to walk along and I had to follow the scarcely less pleasant former military road for the rest of the length of the Loch – this gave views across the water to Glengarry Castle – and then climbed up to the railway again where I enjoyed the mild excitement of crossing a disused – obviously – railway bridge. Was it safe? Would it collapse under the weight of my rucksack?

From Oich Bridge there are tremendous views back along the Loch towards the main east-west watershed which I had recently crossed – for the last time on this trip. I was now heading downhill towards the North Sea and the rest of the journey would be spent on the eastern side of Britain; it would seem strange, after having spent so many weeks on the west. My guidebook promised that the stretch from here to Fort Augustus would be one of the highlights of the Way. I must have missed something because I found it a weary route-march under a hot sun and along an unsympathetically 'improved' towpath, wide enough and hard enough under foot to take motor traffic. 'The sun poured down like honey,' as the great L. Cohen sang and, although I had donned my silly sunhat to stop my brains being fried, the pale grey surface of the path reflected the scorching heat so that the hair in my nostrils caught fire.

Fort Augustus provided shops and the spectacle of watching one of the massive lock gates being opened to allow through a convoy of boats – or is it ships? When does a boat become a ship? Answers on a postcard please. Completed in 1742 under the guidance of the military road-builder General Wade, the Fort was meant to be of major strategic importance but, being isolated in the middle of the Glen, soon became a target for attack by the very people it was meant to quell. It's not dischuffed clansmen who invade now but coach loads of tourists, and I was glad to be away from the crowds as I climbed through the trees above the town to get a sudden and dramatic view of Loch Ness.

Impressive and grand it certainly is but, after a few minutes, I began to find the scenery a touch monotonous – the Loch is a long, straight trench and the hills on the opposite side show a rare uniformity of slope. Not much in the way of surprises or peeps round corners, so I had to content myself with being amazed at the statistics of Loch Ness. It's not Britain's longest lake but the volume of water it holds is more than all the lakes and reservoirs of England and Wales put together. Don't you think that's quite something?

The descent to Invermoriston was frustratingly reminiscent of the one down to Kinlochleven: a long time coming and then much longer than I had anticipated. My evening at the local pub was notable for a big group of holidaymakers who had seemingly monopolised the entire catering capability of the Great Glen. I had to wait an unfeasibly long time for my meal, by which time I'd drunk enough beer to make me light-headed. While waiting to trough, I pondered on some of life's vital issues and realised that, in general, single travellers — in the numerical, rather than marital, sense — are discriminated against in Scotland. Very few B&Bs offer single rooms and although the one I was staying at did, the official tourist brochure had failed to say so, much to the chagrin of my landlady who told me how much they have to pay to be included in the Guide.

I was told that pine martens frequent the wooded slopes hereabouts but it goes almost without saying that they evaded my eyes pretty comprehensively. I did, however, see some red deer, a great coup for someone as unobservant and unlearned as I am. The scenic highlight of Invermoriston was the double arch of Telford's stone bridge, gracefully spanning the river with a little help from a conveniently placed rocky island.

Not all decisions made late at night and under the influence of too much beer are bad ones. After seeking local advice, I decided to quit the Great Glen and head over the hills to Cannich at the foot of Glen Affric. At first I was not convinced I had chosen wisely because there was a walk of over a mile along a busy main road. I had to dodge a lot of fast moving traffic, including a convoy of sand and gravel lorries, all depositing part of their gritty load in my eyes. Still, it would prove to be useful training for the rigours of the horrendous A9, a pleasure still awaiting me.

My route followed a sinuous Land-Rover track through the trees to Bhlaraidh Reservoir, a mess of black concrete, steel stairways and a huge water pipe. In a few more minutes, though, the trees had been left behind and I was in a moorland wilderness of pale tussocky grass and peaty drainage ditches. More Pennine in appearance and wilder than anywhere I had seen since the Southern Uplands, I suddenly felt just a little isolated. The waymarked and guide-booked trails had been just the job but I had tired a little of the feeling – self-inflicted, admittedly – of being herded along with others of my kind. Up here, between the forests of Invermoriston and Balmacaan, I felt completely alone and, although I was walking along a made path, it seemed nobody had been here for centuries.

Arrival at Loch Liath brought into view some big hills away to the north-west – I didn't know what they were but their upper slopes were covered in snow so they must have been pretty large. Looking later at the map I deduced they were Carn Eige, Britain's eleventh highest peak, and the other 3,500 footers around Loch Affric. Whatever they were, they served to remind me that there was a lot more mountainous country for me to get round or over before my goal would be in sight.

Loch ma Stac, where the track petered out, is a delight. Walking around its bouldery, seaside-like shore, I saw a hare and various types of bird – unknown to me I'm afraid. Perhaps they were grebes. On an isthmus (isn't that a great word?) which in wet weather would, I suppose, be turned into an island, stood a semi-ruinous house. It still had chimney pots and a serviceable roof but its sightless windows and crumbling masonry told a tale of rural depopulation. It could have been Private Fraser's original wild and lonely place. It's certainly a long way from the nearest Asda.

A rocky promontory overlooking the lake cried out to be used as a lunch spot so I obliged and, in the baking heat, was glad of the opportunity to do nothing very much. This was as near perfection as anywhere I'd been on the journey and I just lay there and marvelled at how quiet it was. Some bird song and the gentle sighing of a little waterfall were all that I could hear. What a change from the Great Glen where my senses had been assaulted by the almost constant roar of military jets which presumably use the Glen as an aid to navigation and a place to practice low flying. They had been noticeable in mid-Wales and on the West Highland Way but the number and volume reached new and frightening levels along the Great Glen. One suddenly bursting into earshot over Loch Oich the day before had actually made my ears hurt.

I followed a fascinatingly twisty path down by the infant River Enrick. Perfectly simple to follow at its rocky start, it had the amusing trick of being able to disappear completely as soon as it reached any marshy ground. At a stream junction I could see what looked like a newly-made wide track stretching away over the horizon. It looked quite unappealing so I made another late and contrary decision and chose instead to walk uphill in a westerly direction towards Tomich. It was an easy walk through forest to the reedy shores of Loch na Beinne Moire, another ridiculously attractive little lake, this one complete with men fishing from a rowing boat.

Tomich must be the Neatest Place in the Universe and appears to consist entirely of a hotel and a few cottages. The road walk past Fasnakyle Power Station to Cannich, although pleasant and relatively traffic-free, seemed longer than it really is and I was glad to finally arrive at Cannich Youth Hostel, another top class place, robbed of five-star rating only because they did not sell food or provide meals. The village shop had closed by the time I arrived and although I was able to get a good meal of fish and chips in the Slaters' Arms, I was spared morning starvation only by the intervention of Hugh, a walker from Brechin who spoke uncannily like Sean Connery in the early James Bond films. He had been walking in the nearby hills for some days and, learning of my slight deficiency in the breakfast food department (i.e. I had nothing at all), he generously provided me with tea, biscuits and cereal. You're a good chap, Hugh. It also gave added interest to my cornflakes thinking that Rosa Klebb or Pussy Galore could enter the room at any moment.

We'd got chatting to a group of lads from Workington the previous evening who'd been camping at Mullardoch for three days and were now off to Skye. Their talk of heading westwards into the hills set me thinking that the rest of my journey would mostly be along the eastern seaboard. Talking to Hugh, it dawned on me that if I got a move on and finished the walk in just over a week, the total journey time would be exactly one hundred days. This had a neat ring to it and, although route details still had to be worked out, it almost certainly meant that the highland days were over.

CHAPTER SEVEN – THE FAR NORTH

IT'S ALL OVER NOW

A Couple of Unusual Memorials – Cannich to Dingwall and Tain

Strathpeffer

Over the three months since I'd set off on this pointless adventure, my horrible, neglected body had been transformed into an efficient walking machine. Apart from the weight of the rucksack digging into my shoulders I was comfortable, and it seemed that I had to put relatively little effort into the mechanics of getting from A to

B. The journey had, in some respects, taken on the routine and familiarity of a job – up at seven thirty, on the road by nine, stop for lunch, finish at five, have a meal, fart about, go to bed. Next day – same again. And I wanted to be home – the last of the great adventurers, I'm not. I don't want to give the impression that the walk had become boring, or that I wasn't enjoying it; I think it was just that the novelty had worn off and the inevitable anticlimax of finishing was now not far away. And, although I didn't realise it then, I was just tired out. My rounded belly had disappeared – which was good – but I was losing weight everywhere else as well. I began to resemble a hairy stick and was having trouble recognising the hollow-cheeked individual who peered back at me from the mirror each morning.

Refuelling the body had become embarrassing. I was starting to eat mammoth evening meals in two minutes flat, and I think people were beginning to comment. I became a calorie junkie; chips, steaks, beer by the gallon all disappeared down my throat into what I feared was becoming a bottomless pit. My mind went back to an account I'd read of a group of four nineteenth-century travellers ascending Fairfield in the English Lakes. When I first read it I marvelled at what they had taken to feed the inner man, but now I simply envied them their foresight. Just listen to this: thirty six bottles of beer; two bottles of gin; two bottles of sherry; a gallon of water; four loaves of bread; one leg of lamb; one leg of mutton; two fowls, and one tongue. OK there were four of them – but it was only little old Fairfield, for heaven's sake. I still had over a hundred miles to go and wouldn't have minded some of those goodies being carried along beside me. The upshot of all this nonsense is that I made a decision to put my foot down a bit and cut short some of the meanderings so that I could finish the journey while I was still three-dimensional.

So, on yet another brilliantly bright-blue morning – but one with a welcome cooler edge to it – I left Cannich to stride purposefully out towards the North Sea coast. Cannich is neat and pleasant and makes the most of its situation at the junction of Glen Cannich and Glen Affric. To the west and still in view are some of Britain's biggest hills, while the village itself is situated in a wide fertile valley with a flat floor well-suited to bovine agriculture and tourism of the caravan / chalet variety.

It was a satisfying walk along the banks of the River Glass – satisfying because it was easy, the immediate scenery of riverside, hoary old lichen-covered trees and red deer grazing on the opposite bank was a feast for the eyes, and the notices indicating I was now in Scotland's hunting and shooting area told me I had entered a new phase of the journey. The words 'Beat 4 Access' written on a large noticeboard meant not very much to me, although they sounded vaguely country-sportish. I certainly understood the next sign though: 'Caution – hunters using high powered rifles'. I wish I'd seen one reading: 'Watch Out – pheasants using heavy artillery', but I never did.

For several miles nearly every enclosure appeared to contain nothing but boulders and twisted trees, so it came as a surprise to see in the middle of one field a headstone bearing in large letters the word 'BAMBI'. The rest of the inscription read:

'BORN 8–6–1963. DIED 20–1–1995. WORLD'S OLDEST RED DEER.'

I'm not making this up, honest. I wanted to know how they knew Bambi was the world's oldest – I suppose I'll never find out.

Increasingly suburban lanes led through Hughton and Fanellan to a nasty main road which took me to Beauly and Muir of Ord. The roadside sign welcoming visitors to Beauly spells the place in a Gaelic way, 'Bealaidh-Achadh', but the name is reputed to come from the French beau-lieu – something to do with Mary, Queen of Scots who visited the priory here.

With its long straight railway track and tall grain-silo-type building, Muir of Ord would not have looked out of place in Kansas but the road past the distillery and beyond marked a return to better things. Surprisingly knobbly hills reared up to the west and the dappled sunshine of the woodland I was walking through gave the area an almost Lakeland feel. One of the highlights of this stretch was the ludicrously violent bonfire that two guys had lit by the roadside and which they appeared to be struggling to keep under control. The crackling sound of burning wood could be heard for miles and I felt very brave as I battled through the intense heat which was melting the tarmac on the road. Still, the pyromaniacs seemed happy enough and gave me a cheery wave as I sped past.

A very straight main road took me over the impressively huge River Conon where there were signs warning 'Pedestrians –

sudden rise in water level'. Can anyone explain to me the purpose of such a notice? What evasive action are you meant to take? Almost a candidate for the Most Pointless Notice of the Trip Award. I just wish I'd actually seen the all-time Champion Useless Notice, which reads, 'It Is An Offence To Throw Stones At This Notice'. Anyway, keeping a fearful eye out for sudden cloudbursts, I raced across the bridge and, I am pleased, to say survived.

Strathpeffer was a surprise; like Builth Wells, it is a village which owes its prominence to the discovery of its mineralised spring waters two centuries ago but, unlike Builth Wells, is genteel in a 1950s twin-set and pearls sort of way. The ornate Spa Pavilion is in a state of some decay but it was good to see that it had been acquired for the community by the Council and the Scottish Historic Buildings Trust. The pump room was irresistible – the smell of the sulphurated waters was astonishingly foul. You could drink it if you wanted but, although I hung around for a few minutes, I didn't see anybody brave enough to try.

Between Strathpeffer and Dingwall is a low spiky ridge called Knock Farrel, which made an excellent walk and a welcome change from the tarmac I'd been tramping along. The summit is marked by one of northern Scotland's best examples of a vitrified fort. Built of stone, the fort had a timber 'casing' which, when burnt, caused such massive heat that the stone walls fused together. I think there is still some debate as to whether this was done deliberately or as a result of enemy attack, but it might explain the bizarre behaviour of the Bonfire Men near Muir of Ord.

I've never seen so many rabbits as I did up on Knock Farrel. From a distance they looked like the rats in pictures of the Pied Piper story as they swarmed over the grassy hillside. Close up though, it was a very different picture. Some of them were clearly not well and one particularly pathetic specimen cowered twitching in what I took to be its death throes. I didn't know what to do and felt ashamed at my inability to deal it a swift blow to put it out of its misery.

It was a very unpleasant walk along a main road into Dingwall, not helped by my feelings of self-reproach, but I have to be honest and say I quickly put the rabbit episode out of my mind as I tucked into a big meal in the finest Indian restaurant Dingwall could provide. An ancient Viking meeting place and allegedly the birthplace of Macbeth, Dingwall has a long and fascinating history but I was far too intent on feeding my face and moving on to see much of the place other than the pedestrianised shopping street and a couple of uninteresting main roads.

Between Dingwall and Tain is a countryside of lush farmland, reminiscent in its well-fed comfort of parts of Somerset and Cheshire. Footpaths through this puzzling emerald patchwork appeared to be few and, in any case, given my new resolve to speed along, I was no longer seeking out the wiggly ways. 'Straight ahead, young man,' I thought. Nevertheless I had no wish to resort to using the A roads so it was good to find an agreeably quiet lane running along a sort of balcony overlooking the Cromarty Firth. Not a lot to laugh at, although the colours of gorse and broom and pasture were strikingly vivid.

Evanton came and went in a nondescript blur but up on a hill to my left was a bizarre structure which, to my uncultured eye, looked like the pillar thingies they used to have at the beginning of the Pearl and Dean advertisement breaks at the cinema of my youth. It turns out that the building on the hill is called the Fyrish monument and was built by Sir Hector Munro as a replica of the Gates of Negapatam, an Indian city he captured in 1781. Well, he didn't build it with his own hands of course – he had it constructed as a job creation enterprise, and jolly good it is too.

Allness was remarkable only for having a Gents' toilet which the council wanted me to pay 20p for the privilege of using. For that kind of money I would have wanted a pizza and a cinema seat as well. Gritting my teeth and walking with a peculiarly cross-legged gait, I bid an undignified adieu to Allness, which I was later informed by my landlady at Tain is a 'crime capital'. What sort of crime, I'm not sure, but maybe it's as well I didn't attempt to use the facilities.

Better scenery and more pleasant walking took me to Scotsburn where an old lady told me sadly about how, back in the thirties, this was just a sandy track and she knew everybody who lived along it. Now, though, newcomers are buying up the land, having bungalows built and only appearing occasionally. The result is that she now knows nobody and has only her little dog and her memories for company. She assured me I would be in Sutherland the following day. This sounded mightily impressive and perked me up, as did the eagerly awaited first sight of the North Sea which

I got as I approached Tain. So far, all I had seen were various Firths – Cromarty, Beauly and Colin – stretching away to the horizon, but the sea itself had eluded me until now.

Tain is a splendid place, nicely situated and nice to look at. While Harold was busy getting an eyeful of William's arrows down in Hastings, Tain was becoming Scotland's oldest Royal Burgh. I'm afraid I can't reveal to you the significance of this – if indeed there is any – but thought you might like to know. There is a statue to a nineteenth-century Provost, whose name I have failed to remember, but who has been commemorated in this way because of his 'estimable character and general public usefulness'. I thought this was rather good at the time but now, in the cold light of day, I reckon it makes him sound like a prize bull or a Derby winner. Nearly every motor car I saw in Tain appeared to have been supplied by Ken's Garage; whoever Ken is, he seems to have cornered the used car market in north-eastern Scotland. I noticed the entrance to the Glen Morangie distillery which, like the ones at Glen Goyne and Muir of Ord earlier, I walked past without breaking stride. Iron self-control or incurable stupidity?

Just before crossing the new, incredibly long, bridge over the Dornoch Firth into Sutherland, I passed a big flat stone bearing the inscription 'The Immortal Walter Scott OB. 1832'. On the other side of the bridge is an extraordinarily unhelpful road sign bearing the legend 'Meikle Ferry North (No Ferry)'.

I Do Battle With White Vans and Lapwings – Dornoch to the Pentland Firth

Dunrobin

Having crossed the Dornoch Firth, I was not amazed to find the next town I visited was Dornoch. Well, to tell you the truth, I'd looked at the map and with my now keenly honed navigational skills, I had seen the place was called Dornoch. Suitably satisfied that I had, in fact, arrived at the place I had predicted, I visited the Cathedral and the burial ground where there is a long flat stone called the Plaiden Ell. This is where cloth was measured at the fairs and markets held. Like Tain, Dornoch was a pleasant place to be, doubtless helped by the clear blue sky and welcome sea breeze. (You'd have to put these towns right up there with Wells and Llanidloes and Kirkby Lonsdale.) It wasn't so pleasant for poor old Janet Horne though. A resident of Dornoch, she was the last witch to be burnt in Scotland – and all she did was turn her daughter into a pony.

I had lunch overlooking the golf links which slope right down to the water's edge and enjoyed watching golfers of varying degrees of competence struggle with the frustrations of that mystifying game. Following an old railway seemed to offer straightforward route-finding but I hadn't reckoned with the speed with which prickly gorse can colonise abandoned ground such as this. Emerging onto the road again I felt like a mobile cactus as I marched along removing thorns and other spiny things from various parts of my anatomy.

My wanderings out to the coast had caused me to make a long detour round the inlet of Loch Fleet, whose muddy shore was home to zillions of oystercatchers, gulls, lapwings (hooray) and curlews. Then came a really bad hour or so as I had to do battle with the A9, a foul and bad tempered brute of a road which I hope never to have to walk along again. The road was straight and fast but narrow, with no footway, so I was repeatedly forced to take evasive action as lorries, buses and cars sped along with the sole aim, it seemed, of wiping me off the face of the earth. Almost inevitably the worst offenders were the White Vans. After many close encounters in which I was able to see the occupants of these harbingers of death and destruction at very close quarters, I realised that it appeared almost compulsory for the front seat to contain three males of approximately human origin. One would wear a woolly hat, one a sleeveless vest and one a vacuous grin and baseball cap comically placed reverse-wise on the head. Just occasionally there would be a black-cloaked figure carrying a scythe in there as well.

Seeking refuge from this battering, I turned off at the first available opportunity onto an exceedingly pleasant lane which had the slight drawback of heading south. But not for long, as two left turns led to yet another stroll past golf links and on to Golspie, a rather anonymous looking place which yet manages to be the administrative centre of Sutherland.

After the unremarkable scenery of the last couple of days and the mental bashing I'd just had from the A9, it was like opening a page in a book of fairy stories to be suddenly confronted by the sight of the fantastic towers and turrets of Dunrobin Castle peeping over the trees. Even more impressive from close up, the place could have been the inspiration for Mervyn Peake's Gormenghast. Very like a Loire chateau, narrow circular towers are placed at the corners of the three-faced facade, each topped by a slender, tapering conical roof. The place is the ancestral home of the Dukes of Sutherland who were the nice people responsible for clearing 15,000 souls from their crofting homes in the nineteenth century. Up on the hill above the shore hereabouts is a thirty-foot high statue to the first Duke. The inscription at the foot of this memorial refers to '...a mourning and grateful tenantry...', which could be a sick joke or a very early attempt at post-modernist irony. Unless, of course, they were grateful he'd popped his clogs. I wondered whether the name Dunrobin' has the same kind of origin as Dunroamin' but came to no sensible conclusion.

An almost unbelievably beautiful walk through a field full of bluebells led me back to the shore where a succession of rough, shaggy beaches made for interesting progress to Brora, a small town with a famous football team and a kids' golf course ambitiously called Gleneagles. Unlike most of the settlements north of the Clyde, Brora owes its growth to traditional heavy industry: coal. The deposits were first mined as long ago as 1598 but serious development of the mine started in 1812 – dum-diddy-dum-diddy-dar-dar-dar. The population of the town increased as the evicted tenants of you-know-who settled here and the mine continued to thrive until the 1970s. There are other industries too which have survived – a woollen mill and a distillery and some fishing. And my landlady told me that there's always work at Invergordon when the rigs are being built.

The highlight of my evening in Brora was witnessing an altercation between a peevish American tourist and a splendidly obdurate waitress. Apparently he'd asked for water and had been given a bottle of fizzy mineral water which naturally he was then charged for. I don't know what the American for gobsmacked is, but that's what this guy was. In all his years of travelling he'd never been charged for water before, and what's more he didn't even like the sparkly stuff he'd been offered. The waitress displayed a stoical indifference to his protests and Mr American had to pay up. I don't know how much he left by way of a tip, though. Deeming it wise to steer clear of water, I had a drink of the only other liquid available – Budweiser – so the Americans got their revenge after all.

The way out of Brora was across the golf course and I marvelled at how early the aficionados of this game start their exertions. It was barely eight thirty and yet many folk were about enjoying the fine weather. 'Hello,' they shouted, and 'Enjoy your walk.' It was good to be among such friendly people.

By the time I'd crossed the golf course to rejoin the nightmarish A9, I was suffering from a recurrence of the leg pains I hadn't had since Cheddar. Surely I'd be OK? End in sight and all that. If anyone was driving along the A9 that morning and saw a miserable looking specimen hobbling along, that was me that was. Changes of footwear didn't help but not long after I turned off the main road onto a tiny tarmac track which led up into the incredibly lonely Glen Loth, the ache disappeared as quickly as it had arrived. And good riddance too. Just before the turning off the A9 is a stone marking the 'Place near which (According to Scrope's 'Art of Deerstalking') the last wolf in Sutherland was killed by the hunter Polson in or about the year 1700'. Scrope's 'Art of Deerstalking', huh?

Glen Loth was just grand. Heather-clad hills reared up steeply on my left, while on the right was a stream running through gorse-spattered meadowland. There were also lots of things marked on the map in Olde English lettering – most notably a broch. Brochs are almost exclusively restricted to the north of Scotland and were thought to have been built about 2,000 years ago for defensive purposes. They appear to be roughly circular structures of stone which tapered towards the top and were probably roofed with animal skins. Right next to this broch is a big untidy heap of stones marked on the map as Carn Bran. The head of the Glen is dominated by the dramatic east faces of Ben Dhorain and Ben

Uarie. If ever I come this way again, I'll have to walk over, rather than round, these hills.

There is also a massive view across the wilds of Strath Kildonan from the top of the Glen Loth road and, further east, the rough upland country dominated by the volcanic shape of Morven, a hill which, more than most, just cries out to be climbed. One day, Morven likely, I'll go back…

On the descent to Kildonan, I walked past huge herds of red deer. There they were – just lying around, dozens of them. I took photo after photo. Couldn't believe it. After a while though I realised that they are so numerous in this valley that they barely merited a second glance but the thrill of that first sight of them – complete with antlers and all that – will stay with me for a very long time.

It's difficult to find the words to do justice to the loneliness of this stretch of country. There are a few farmsteads but of people living in them, I saw not a sign. In the early 1800s, in the area near where the present Kildonan station now stands, there was a confrontation between local tenants and the Duke's men who had come to inspect the land as part of the resettlement process. Fifty years later a local man, recently returned from exile in Australia, discovered gold in the gravel bed of the River Helmsdale, and so began the great Kildonan gold rush. Some lucky people struck it rich, none more so of course than our old friend the Duke of You-know-where who sold the plots and then, twirling his waxed moustaches, withdrew permission when he found the wild behaviour of the hoi polloi was disturbing his salmon fishing. Every book has to have a baddie and it looks like I've found mine at last.

The road up the valley carried virtually no traffic and it was a surprise when a car coming along behind me slowed down and stopped. It was an even bigger surprise when the people in the car appeared to know who I was. 'Mr Jackson, is it?' they asked. Briefly alarmed that bounty hunters had been despatched to bring me to justice for having an overdue library book or something, I considered fleeing into the distance but quickly realised this would have been foolish. It turned out to be the people from the B&B at Kinbrace a few long miles further on. Since this is the only accommodation anywhere near here, I'd booked ahead and these good people clearly made an accurate deduction as to my identity. Ellafitzgerald, my dear Watson.

The rest of the way to Kinbrace was remarkable for the lack of traffic; a train, dwarfed by the immensity of the surroundings, trundled along its lonely track, and that was about the only other sign of humanity I had. Most of all, though, I will remember doing battle with the most fearsome of God's creatures I'd ever come across – no, not more Boys, not even a bull or a ram or a dog, but a flock of lapwings. Go on, snigger. Have a laugh at my expense. But I'm telling you, these things just knew no fear. Despite my waxing lyrical about them earlier on, my feelings clearly were not reciprocated. They didn't like me one little bit. The first time I was dive-bombed by one of these little fellows, I assumed it was an accident. Maybe the bird which swooped right at me had got his bearings wrong or something. But it happened again. And again. And again. Lower each time, so that I was having to duck and weave to avoid being struck on the bonce. Like Hitchcock's *The Birds*, it was. I could make comfortable progress only by waving my arms around as I walked. What an impressive sight I must have made. I'm not sure what a whirling dervish is, but that's the phrase that sprang to mind. I suppose the lapwings had their nests in the grass near the road and were alarmed at my presence. But I couldn't believe the fury of their attacks. And just for good measure their mates, the oystercatchers, saw me off the premises with another show of aggressive aeronautics. And then, as I disappeared from their sight, I heard them laughing.

There was bloodshed too, I'm afraid. There must be some traffic on this road at some time because there was an astonishing number of squashed rabbits lying on the tarmac. The long dry spell and the heat had combined to make these carcasses give off the pungent smell of rotting flesh so the rest of my day's walk was not an olfactory delight.

No matter! The B&B at Kinbrace, Tigh-Achen-Echan, was top class and, true to my new found ability to eat whatever was put in front of me, I made short work of the biggest and best evening meal of the whole trip. I wrote in my notes that I felt thin so I suppose that made my gluttony acceptable. At least there was no-one else in the room to witness it.

Kinbrace is truly remote. I found the immediate surroundings a little desolate — flat topped, grey-brown hills stretched away into the distance in all directions away from the wide flat valley bottom. The snow posts lining the road side and the lonely silver thread of the single-track railway line snaking away across the moor reinforced the feeling of isolation. And there's not much there. My B&B, a school, a shop and a railway platform and very little else. But the hospitality made up for it.

Mr Mackenzie told me about the hard winters they used to get up here. One year he remembers particularly clearly. He said it must have been in the late forties when he was a schoolboy; drifting snow caused the road to be closed and the railway, usually the lifeline in such conditions, was also blocked, so much so that the snowplough attached to the front of the rescue locomotive became a victim of the weather too. An aeroplane sent to take photographs crashed when it struck trees and the school was closed seemingly for weeks.

Marlene told me about her childhood back down the valley at Kildonan and how the Strath, as she called it, is now divided into six estates, each owned by some member of the aristocracy. Lord Leverhulme – he of soap powder fame – owns one of them apparently. I could have spent ages just listening to these tales – the accent is the softest thing. Almost Scandinavian in its lilting gentleness, hearing it is a little like being wrapped in a warm, furry blanket.

Ever since my walk through the Great Glen, people had been telling me about another pedestrian who was attempting to reach John o' Groats. 'He's not carrying anything like as much stuff as you,' they'd said, as if I were some kind of idiot, adding that he was a Methodist minister. They all said the same thing. They told me his name but, for the purposes of this account, we'll call him Stanley. Well, I was walking at a fair old lick by now and was getting no nearer to him. If anything, he was drawing further away from me. For days now I'd hoped to make Stanley's acquaintance, but this bionic vicar was not going to be caught and I spent a good part of my time imagining a sort of caped superman speeding effortlessly along as I floundered in his wake. Well, thank goodness for Marlene. She mentioned him as well but said he'd arrived at Kinbrace by train! 'Well', she said, 'he never intended walking the whole way – just the bits that interested him particularly.' No wonder I couldn't keep up. But now I knew why, I stopped worrying.

The morning brought a sudden change in the weather. Low scudding clouds and an all-enveloping drizzle pushed through by a cold easterly wind, made for an unpleasant start to the day's walking. The sky began to brighten by the time I'd reached the big roadside loch at Achentoul, and the outlines of the twin peaks of Ben Griam Mor and Ben Griam Beg loomed out of the murk like sleeping dinosaurs. Although less than 2,000 feet high, these hills looked huge, rising as they do so abruptly from the surrounding blanket bog which lies like a big wet flannel over the Sutherland rock. This is the so-called Flow Country, the biggest area of peat bog in Europe. From the security of the tarmac along which I was walking, the place has a haunting beauty quite unlike anywhere else I'd seen. The last few days had been spent in pleasant but generally unremarkable surroundings but, by any standards, the country at the head of the Strath of Kildonan is remarkably remarkable.

Just beyond the point where the road crosses into the northward running Strath Halladale, the disused railway station buildings at

Forsinard have been converted into a visitor centre with the emphasis very much on wildlife, in particular birds. There are books for people to log sightings of rarities and they made interesting, if puzzling, reading. Rather personal information about a pair of hen harriers, for example, but I didn't think the sort of people interested in the sex lives of hen harriers would have been bothered about my altercation with the lapwings, so I resisted the temptation to write about it.

Straight as an arrow, Strath Halladale heads for the mainland's north coast with gratifying directness. Just as well really, because I found it a gloomy and unattractive place, especially towards its top end where a long line of giant electricity pylons marched along the skyline, seeming to mock my slow progress. The quantity and quality of ramshackle buildings had reached heretofore unseen levels and it was difficult to tell whether some of these corrugated iron places were inhabited or not. One stone-built cottage with broken windows and dirty net curtains flapping in the breeze looked as if it had been standing guard over the valley for centuries, but the date stone above the door read 1932. Spectacular heaps of wrecked motor cars adorned most of the properties along here, and the road went on and on with very little to keep me amused. The harshness of the climate these people must battle through was brought home to me when I noticed that the primroses were no further on here than they had been in Cornwall twelve or thirteen weeks previously.

When I reached Melvich, which I'd taken to be a coastal settlement, there was no real sign of the sea, so I went to bed having to talk myself into believing that I'd reached the Pentland Firth at last.

Me Against the Caithness Wind – Melvich, Thurso and John o' Groats

Nearly there!

Sunshine again for what would be my last full day's walking before the finish, but accompanied by a strong south-easterly breeze. I don't know why I should have been surprised at just how wild the country was as I set out along the road eastwards towards Thurso, but I was. After all, Cornwall had been just as rugged – but that was in the wet and wild weather of March, not this mini heatwave in early June. It was a great moment when I passed the sign telling me I was entering Caithness, mainland Britain's most north-easterly county. It seemed a very, very long time ago since I'd set off full of hope and vigour from the opposite end of the country and Caithness had seemed no nearer than Cirrus Minor.

Despite the screaming of gulls there was no visible sign of the sea until the wide view over Sandside Bay, with the village of Reay and the glistening white spheres of the nuclear reactor station. The fast breeder reactor at Dounreay was apparently the world's first to produce electricity for general use, but in all the years since production started the plant has generated almost as much ill-feeling and criticism as it has electricity. In a forlorn echo of the situation at Trawsfynydd, the reactor is now being decommissioned, a task however which itself appears to be creating employment.

By now the hills had gone over the horizons west and south, and the level country had the effect of magnifying the verticals so that the plain white church at Reay took on the imposing appearance of a Gothic cathedral. Just before I entered the village I passed a sign which had, in its heyday, read 'Danger, stalking and shooting in progress' but which, under the hand of some wag, had now had its initial letter 's' and 's' removed. 'Danger, talking and hooting in progress' conjured up marvellously surreal images to cheer me on my way.

In the local shop, I came face to face with Mac, the local 'character' who was being dealt with by a painstakingly polite proprietor. Mac had with him a bag containing two bottles of whisky and several cans of lager, spoke an enormous amount of high-quality rubbish and made sure that everyone within range received maximum benefit from the alcohol fumes he was exhaling. When I left the shop, Mac was outside offering one of his cronies a 'wee nip' while a third member of the gang was waiting to drive them away.

On the road hereabouts I met a lady who described the wind as a 'nice breeze'. Well, I don't know what she's used to, but it felt like half a gale to me. I was struggling to walk against it and had come to realise just why the buildings here were built so low and squat against the ferocious elements. Alexander Sutherland's description of it as 'the blighting wind that almost perpetually devastates Caithness' seemed to me to be a more accurate description than a 'nice breeze'.

Although permitting relatively fast progress, which was now my main priority, the straight roads offered little in the way of surprises. I was overtaken by an ageing cyclist and a jogger, which brought home to me in graphic style just how painfully slowly the miles sometimes seem to crawl by when you're on foot. Still, there are things of interest to see: the stone walls were immaculately maintained and the layers of horizontally placed flat stones were reminiscent in style, if not in colour, of those in the limestone country of the Yorkshire Dales. More unusually, some of the field boundaries were made up of lines of thin, upright stones – Caithness flags, a particularly hard wearing sandstone which has been used to make paving slabs for cities all over the globe. Presumably expensive to quarry and maintain, many of the flag 'hedges' were falling into disrepair and were gradually being replaced by the ubiquitous post and wire fences.

One other thing that, as a walker, you cannot fail to notice is the litter strewn along the roadside. Presumably, most of this bounty comes courtesy of passing motorists and their passengers and one of the striking things about it is the depressing sameness of it all – fag and crisp packets, lager cans (bitter drinkers, I was pleased to note, don't tend to throw their rubbish around as freely) and vodka and whisky bottles. The only thing that changed much as I travelled north was the colour of the cans as the brands changed, and a noticeable increase in the quantity of spirits bottles. As old rivals in sporting events, I reckoned an international Throw a Beer Can Out of Your Car competition could be organised between England and Scotland; the Scots, I think, would just about have the edge, but it would be close.

Thurso, a Viking town – the very name may have something to do with Thor – was grey and gritty and didn't inspire me to stop, but then I knew I'd be back here the following night so maybe that affected my decision to speed through the place on my way to my B&B at Castletown. I made a big mistake by opting to stick with the main road out of Thurso and almost instantly regretted my error of judgement. It's very straight, very fast and not wide enough. Incipient paranoia was taking hold of me and I seriously began to believe that many of the cars were actually aiming for me. After all, how many weary travellers must they see on these roads? They must be sick of the sight of them and perhaps one or two being pinged over the fence would not be missed.

Managing to survive this game of human pinball, I arrived at Castletown a nervous wreck but managed to have a look round the place. My knowledge of the Royal family is not exactly encyclopaedic, so it came as something of a surprise to find the local grocer's shop adorned with a crest reading 'By Appointment to HM The Queen Mother'. Well, there's a thing. Nowhere on my end to end journey could compete with this.

For some days now I'd been wondering about how I would feel as I set off on the last morning. With only a dozen or so miles to go, the answer is that I felt no different than I had on all the other mornings in the last couple of weeks. As I said, it was almost like a job now and it was just another day. More sunshine and more of the blighting wind as I trundled along almost deserted lanes through the Scandinavian sounding Inkstack and Barrock. This far corner of the country is like nowhere else I'd seen. The Somerset levels are flatter, but this area must be Britain's Big Sky Country. There are few field boundaries to divide up the enormous tracts of land and the endless views stretching away to where the sky meets the sea in a thin grey line are apparently unchanging. There were some new friends to gaze out on today though – the now uninhabited island of Stroma just off the coast and, much further away, the cliffs of Hoy soaring out of the deep blue sea.

The boomerang-shaped Loch Heilen looks on the map as if it is preparing to launch itself into the air but, on closer acquaintance, appeared as desolate a stretch of water as you could imagine. What buildings there were seemed to be crouching in a vain effort to get out of the perpetual wind. Just as the thrashing ocean had dominated life in Cornwall, here it was that wind. Almost like a physical presence, it battered into me constantly. It was never strong enough to be a gale but it was unceasing, with no let up. It was just there.

Not far now. Peat stacked up in neat piles made a change of scene and there were more tumbledown places by the roadside near Canisbay. I had a little trouble persuading a couple of kind motorists that I really did not want to be picked up. Odd that in over a thousand miles I had only one offer of a lift before I reached north-east Scotland, and now three in a couple of days. They really are the friendliest of folk up here. I'd thought that now, less than three miles from John o' Groats, I'd see all sorts of walkers, cyclists, runners, acrobats and motorists all aiming for the same place as me. But not a soul. Nobody. And the drivers of the cars that stopped seemed perplexed and bewildered by my insistence on continuing in perambulatory mode.

At Huna, a lady came out of her house and spoke to me about the weather in a strangely detached manner, as if I were speaking to her on the phone from another country.

'It's a lovely day, but it's very windy,' she said.

There's no answer to that – she was right on both counts – so all I could do was agree.

The sight of the ornate pointy roof and the dazzling white walls of the famous hotel at John o' Groats were sufficient to spur me on as I tilted for one final time at the A9. It's a shadow of its former self here though – no big lorries, no white vans, just tourists bumbling along – so it caused me no great worries. Closer now. Two hundred yards to go. What will I feel when I've finished? One hundred yards. Will I be able to get something to eat? Fifty yards. What a lot of cars and people. Ten yards. How will I know when I'm there? Is there a finishing line? Failing to find such a landmark, I lurched into the café, feeling strangely devoid of any kind of emotion whatsoever and got a cup of tea and a plate of fish and chips. I was a little bit alarmed that I felt no sense of satisfaction, no inner peace, not even relief. Nothing, except a vague regret.

I had always intended continuing to the real end of the country at Duncansby Head a mile or so further on but, mysteriously, all ambition had deserted me. It would be nice to pretend that, in a spiritual sort of way, I had decided that a journey such as this deserved a grand throwaway gesture – rather like the Sherpas refuse to climb the last few feet of the Himalayan giants because they are the places of the gods. But the reality is that I was simply knackered and now had as much intention of going on as I had of flying to the moon. For a few minutes I watched the continuing coastline stare reproachfully back at me but I finally overcame any finer feelings by discovering there was beer to be had in the bar and the famous book was waiting there to be signed.

The vast majority of the entries in this book were made by cyclists, some by motorists and surprisingly few by walkers. Over a pint I met a chap from Blackburn who had cycled up from Cornwall – it had taken him just two weeks. He said there was a finishing line outside – somehow I'd missed it – and we went and, rather self-consciously, had the obligatory photos taken.

Still unable to find a focus for the jumble of thoughts spinning round in my head, I went for a desultory wander round the knick-knack shops and stood for a while gazing out across the Pentland Firth. Several people have commented on the strong resemblance between John o' Groats and Land's End but, to my eye, they could hardly have been more different. Where Land's End had been wild and elemental and exciting, John o' Groats was just ordinary. The sunny weather and the crowds, of course, had a big part to play in this assessment and I really ought to have gone on to Duncansby where I understand there are bigger cliffs and sea stacks and things.

I'd always thought that it was on journeys such as this that people discover their inner selves and come up with the answer to Life, the Universe and Everything. Well, nothing doing, I'm afraid, but I was at least able to reflect on how lucky I was.

Lucky that the weather had been kinder than I'd dared to hope. I'd only had three or four real drenchings but there had been days of constant sunshine. Almost incredibly, the walk north of Glasgow had given me only three dodgy days. For days on end, the sun shone and shone.

Lucky that I'd avoided any serious injuries or illnesses. Sure, I'd had the gammy leg and the self-inflicted problem with the feet early on, but that's all.

And lucky that I'd been given more support, encouragement and help by friends and family than I deserved and could realistically have expected.

Funny, then that I still had a vague feeling of dissatisfaction – a type of unease that I couldn't shake off. Partly this was down to the loss of focus that completing this project was inevitably going to bring. But there was something more deep-rooted than that, something more fundamental, and I was struggling to identify exactly what it was. After much soul-searching I found two reasons:

the first, and most easily explained, is that I knew in my heart of hearts that I had cheated by avoiding the rugged and remote parts of north west Scotland that I'd promised to myself I'd visit – Coigach and Torridon and Cape Wrath and all those wonderful-sounding places I may yet never see.

The second reason, I think, is that I'd become a different person. I was still Peter Jackson, of course – I hadn't become Baroness Warsi or Sir Tom Jones – but there was a new driving force in there somewhere, something that was going to demand the replacement of this obsession with something else. And I'm still searching.

After 1,300 miles and one hundred days, I had had plenty of opportunity to refine my already considerable talent for moaning and seeing the worst in people, but it had been a truly great experience. And, as Elvis himself said, 'You gotta follow that dream.' My journey had required no special skill, only a determination not to give in when things got a bit tricky. Would I do anything like it again?

You bet I would!

I wish I was doing it now.